States Against Migrants

Deportation in Germany and the United ̣̣̣̣

In this comparative study of the contemporary politics of deportation in
Germany and the United States, Antje Ellermann analyzes the capacity of
the liberal democratic state to control individuals within its borders.
The book grapples with the question of why, in the 1990s, Germany
responded to vociferous public demands for stricter immigration control
by passing and implementing far-reaching policy reforms, whereas the
United States failed to respond effectively to a comparable public mandate. Drawing on extensive field interviews, Ellermann finds that these
cross-national differences reflect institutionally determined variation in
socially coercive state capacity. By tracing the politics of deportation
across the evolution of the policy cycle, beginning with anti-immigrant
populist backlash and ending in the expulsion of migrants by street-level
bureaucrats, Ellermann is also able to show that the conditions underlying
state capacity systematically vary across policy stages. Whereas the ability
to make socially coercive law is contingent on strong institutional linkages
between the public and legislators, implementation depends on the political insulation of bureaucrats.

Antje Ellermann is Assistant Professor of Political Science at the Univer-
sity of British Columbia. Her work has been published in *Comparative
Political Studies*, *West European Politics*, and *Government and Oppos-
ition*. She has been the recipient of research grants from the Social Science
Research Council in the United States and, in Canada, from the Social
Sciences and Humanities Research Council and the Department of Foreign
Affairs and International Trade.

States Against Migrants

Deportation in Germany and the United States

ANTJE ELLERMANN
University of British Columbia

CAMBRIDGE
UNIVERSITY PRESS

CAMBRIDGE UNIVERSITY PRESS
Cambridge, New York, Melbourne, Madrid, Cape Town, Singapore, São Paulo, Delhi

Cambridge University Press
32 Avenue of the Americas, New York, NY 10013-2473, USA

www.cambridge.org
Information on this title: www.cambridge.org/9780521092906

First published 2009

Printed in the United States of America

A catalog record for this publication is available from the British Library.

Library of Congress Cataloging in Publication Data

Ellermann, Antje, 1971–
States against migrants : deportation in Germany and
the United States / Antje Ellermann.
  p. cm.
Includes bibliographical references and index.
ISBN 978-0-521-51568-9 (hardback) – ISBN 978-0-521-09290-6 (pbk.)
1. United States–Emigration and immigration. 2. Deportation–United States.
3. Germany–Emigration and immigration. 4. Deportation–Germany.
I. Title.

JV6483.E54 2009
325.43–dc22   2008042416

ISBN 978-0-521-51568-9 hardback
ISBN 978-0-521-09290-6 paperback

In memory of my mother, Ruthild Ellermann, and for Ruby Skye, whose journey has just begun

Contents

List of Figures

Acknowledgments

One of the greatest challenges of studying the politics of migration control is gaining access to the agencies charged with policing state borders. I am deeply indebted to those individuals who opened doors for me to the tightly guarded world of immigration enforcement. In Germany, I want to particularly thank Lothar Kaden in Beeskow for providing me with unlimited access to his agency and staff. In the United States, I extend special thanks to Mike Magee at the district office in San Diego, who engaged me in many thoughtful discussions about the internal workings of the Immigration and Naturalization Service. Understanding immigration enforcement equally required me to spend time on the other side of the barbed wire, studying the activities of civil society groups that seek to limit the state's reach into migrants' lives. Among the many advocates who gave generously of their time to this project, I want especially to express my appreciation to Marleine Bastien of Fanm Ayisyen Nan Miyami (Haitian Women of Miami) and the members of the Tübingen church sanctuary.

This book grew out of a dissertation at Brandeis University, and I wish to acknowledge and thank the members of my dissertation committee for their guidance along the way: George Ross, Steven Teles, Jeffrey Prottas, and Jytte Klausen. When in the weeks after September 11, 2001, German immigration agencies closed their doors on me, George Ross reassured me that it would all work out in the end (it did). His steady confidence helped propel me through the rough patches that are an inevitable part of any research project. I am particularly indebted to Steven Teles, who patiently and enthusiastically read draft after draft of the thesis and provided me with feedback as thoughtful as any student could ever hope for. His provocative comments and critical insights have shaped this project from beginning to end.

This research could not have happened without the financial and logistical support of many individuals and organizations. The fieldwork for this study was funded by the Social Science Research Council's International Migration Program. While in the field, I received generous institutional support from Thomas Cusack at the Wissenschaftszentrum Berlin für Sozialforschung. Reference staff members at numerous institutions have freely shared their time and knowledge with me. In Germany, this included staff at the Presse- und Informationsamt der Bundesregierung in Berlin, the Landespresseamt in Potsdam, the Dokumentationsstelle Bürgerrechte & Innere Sicherheit at the Freie Universität Berlin, and the Bundesarchiv in Koblenz. In the United States, I thank the staff at the (then) Immigration and Naturalization Service's reference library in Washington, D.C., the press archives of *The Miami Herald*, and the San Diego public library. After my return from the field, a Dissertation Year Fellowship at Brandeis University afforded me the luxury of full-time writing. And in the final writing stage, Sima Godfrey at the University of British Columbia's Institute for European Studies provided me with a beautiful office and a warm and collegial environment that enlivened the solitude of writing.

This research benefited from the constructive feedback and support of many scholars to whom I shall remain indebted for many years to come. I especially want to thank Larry Fuchs for first introducing me to the study of immigration and Jim Hollifield for taking me under his wing and introducing me to a larger community of migration scholars. Virginie Guiraudon read extensive parts of this work, and I have benefited immensely from her insights and constructive critiques. Thomas Faist and Steven Legomsky provided helpful comments at the project's early stages and Alexander Aleinikoff toward the end. Among other fellow scholars who provided valued feedback on this work are Fiona Barker, Tim Büthe, Mignon Duffy, Macartan Humphreys, Christian Joppke, Orit Kedar, Daniel Kryder, Gallya Lahav, John Michael Parrish, Diane Purvin, Benjamin Read, Peter Skerry, and Eiko Thielemann. At Brandeis, the Feminist Social Science Research Group provided an invaluable sounding board. At Harvard, the members of the Comparative Politics Workshop offered crucial input, as did discussants, fellow panelists, and audiences at numerous conferences and seminar presentations, in both Europe and North America.

Frank Hangler and Catherine Hecht provided valuable research assistance. I owe a debt of gratitude to Clare McGovern, who came to the rescue at the very end and with exceptional skill and determination applied the finishing copyediting touches to this work. Anonymous reviewers of the book manuscript provided numerous constructive suggestions that made for a much improved end product. At Cambridge University Press, Eric Crahan and Rakesh Siva Kumar have been helpful guides through the editorial and production process.

An earlier version of Chapter 4 originally appeared in *Comparative Political Studies*, 38(10), 2005, 1219–1244, and parts of the book's overall argument were first published in *West European Politics*, 29(2), 2006, 287–303. I thank the editors for their permission to reuse these materials.

In many of the locations to which my graduate work carried me I had the good fortune of being surrounded by family and friends. One of the joys of studying in Boston was being close to Amy and Steven Lippmann. Judy and Stanley Jacobs and Kathryn Linehan and David Siu provided homes away from home during research visits in Miami and Washington, D.C. In Germany, carefree playtime with the Purrucker family provided welcome respite from the intensity of fieldwork. My father, Manfred Ellermann, has never tired of assuring me of his faith in me. And my grandparents, Johanna and Martin Gruhler, have been part of this journey all along. As a 100-year-old German, my grandfather has lived through more political regimes than most, and the stories he has told me over the years have helped to put the vicissitudes of everyday politics into perspective. My time in Germany also offered me the opportunity to reconnect with one of my earliest mentors, Friedrich Klotter-Bucher, who motivated and shaped my academic career probably more than he knows.

My husband, Alan Jacobs, knows this project nearly as well as I. My toughest critic and greatest source of support, his insights have provoked countless revisions without which this book would be a much inferior product. After many months of pursuing our research on separate continents, I was fortunate that he decided to pack up his office and join me on my travels. Traversing the deserts of the American Southwest in the heat of summer, in a car without air-conditioning and crammed to the roof with archival boxes and desktop computers, was an adventure I would not have missed for anything. His generosity and love have sustained me throughout this endeavor.

The final years of this research coincided with a sad period in my life, when my mother, Ruthild Ellermann, lost her heroic struggle with cancer. During this time, one of my greatest sources of sustenance has been time spent kayaking in British Columbia's wilderness. I am fortunate to be living in a place where these journeys are possible. Not long after my mother left this world, Ruby arrived and lit up my days with her radiant smile. My mother lived to see neither the completion of this book nor the beginning of her granddaughter's life, but I know she would have been absolutely thrilled with both. It is to her memory and to my beautiful daughter that I dedicate this book.

Introduction: Deportation and the State

> The connection between the state and its population has been particularly complex, if for no other reason ... than the modern state in its rules and laws has demanded so much from people. ... Of course, coercion and the threat of coercion, by most definitions, lie at the center of the meaning of the state and its demands for compliance by its population. ... But it is simply impossible for a state to achieve tractability by relying exclusively on its judges and jailers. No matter how vaunted the bureaucracy ... state leaders could easily find their institutions quickly overwhelmed by the enormity of the task of enforcement, even with vast bureaucracies.
>
> (Migdal, 2001, p. 251)

The final decades of the twentieth century have been marked by the progressive expansion of the socially coercive state in the advanced industrialized world. Beginning in the 1980s and extending into the new millennium, liberal democracies faced public demands for hard-edged social regulation in areas such as migration control, criminal justice, and homeland security. In response, elected legislatures enacted far-reaching measures of social control across a range of policy fields and funded the rapid growth of coercive bureaucracies.

To illustrate this point, from 1991 to 2001 the budgets of both the German Federal Border Police[1] and the Canadian immigration service[2] more

---

[1] Federal Border Police, "2002 Annual Report" (*Bundesgrenzschutz Jahresbericht*), Section III.2.1, http://www.bmi.bund.de/nn_121564/Internet/Content/Broschueren/2003/Bundesgrenzschutz-Jahresbericht_2002_Id_90870_de.html (accessed December 14, 2005, site now discontinued).

[2] Statistics Canada, "CANSIM Table 385-0002: Federal, Provincial and Territorial General Government Revenue and Expenditures," http://cansim2.statcan.ca/cgi-win/cnsmcgi.exe?Lang=E&RootDir=CII/&ResultTemplate=CII/CII___&Array_Pick=1&ArrayId=3850002

than doubled, whereas the U.S. Immigration and Naturalization Service's budget nearly quadrupled.[3] Even more dramatically, immigration spending in Britain in the same period underwent a more than sixfold increase.[4] Significantly, these law enforcement initiatives have not been limited to the regulation of migration. In the area of drug control, the budget of the U.S. Drug Enforcement Administration[5] more than tripled between 1985 and 2002. In the field of criminal justice more generally, U.S. government spending on the federal prison system more than quadrupled between 1985 and 2002.[6] Similarly, in Canada, the corrections and rehabilitation services budget doubled from 1989 to 2002.[7]

In North America, governments simultaneously enacted sweeping administrative reforms. The creation of the Department of Homeland Security in March 2003 constituted the most comprehensive case of American bureaucratic reorganization for well over half a century. Just months later, the Canadian government followed suit by announcing the amalgamation of existing agencies into the Department of Public Safety and Emergency Preparedness, including the creation of a new Canada Border Services Agency.

What is striking about these instances of bureaucratic expansion is not only the speed with which these developments have unfolded, nor the emergence of similar patterns across national contexts, but also the timing of public service growth. Across the advanced industrialized world, the growth of coercive administrations has taken place during a period marked by government downsizing. As one scholar remarked, "the growth of law enforcement is the most prominent exception to the general retreat of the state" (Andreas, 2000, pp. 25–6). This trend, although evident across advanced democracies, has been most pronounced in the United States. Whereas from 1985 to 2002 the size of the federal civilian government

---

[3] U.S. Department of Justice, "Immigration and Naturalization Service Budget 1075–2003," www.usdoj.gov/jmd/budgetsummary/btd/1975_2002/2002/pdf/page104-108.pdf

[4] Her Majesty's Treasury, "Public Expenditure Statistical Supplements and Public Expenditure Statistical Analyses." Available from 1999/2000 at http://www.hm-treasury.gov.uk/economic_data_and_tools/finance_spending_statistics/pes_publications/pespub_index.cfm. (accessed December 2005, page now discontinued). Previous PESAs and PESSs available on microfiche.

[5] U.S. Department of Justice, "Drug Enforcement Administration Budget 1975–2003," www.usdoj.gov/jmd/budgetsummary/btd/1975_2002/2002/pdf/page100-103.pdf

[6] U.S. Department of Justice, "Federal Prison System Budget 1975–2003," www.usdoj.gov/jmd/budgetsummary/btd/1975_2002/2002/pdf/page109-112.pdf

[7] Statistics Canada, "CANSIM Table 385-0002: Federal, Provincial and Territorial General Government Revenue and Expenditures," http://cansim2.statcan.ca/cgi-win/cnsmcgi.exe?Lang=E&RootDir=CII/&ResultTemplate=CII/CII___&Array_Pick=1&ArrayId=3850002

workforce contracted by more than 10 percent,[8] positions in the federal Drug Enforcement Administration[9] increased by over 50 percent, and, most staggeringly, employment in both the federal prison system[10] and the immigration service[11] more than tripled. Thus, at the same time as many public agencies have been forced to come to terms with sharp cuts to their operating budgets, bureaucracies such as the U.S. Immigration and Naturalization Service have struggled to manage the rapid inflow of new personnel (Andreas, 1998–99).

While there is unequivocal evidence that the social regulatory state has gained in strength over the past decades, political observers have been profoundly skeptical regarding its capacity to exercise its powers of coercion efficaciously. This pessimism is striking when we consider that Max Weber famously singled out the legitimate exercise of violence as the *sine qua non* of the modern state. Yet, empirically, it appears that the capacity of the state to exercise its coercive powers successfully is far from evident. In the field of migration, for instance, scholars have cast serious doubt on policy-makers' claims that expansive border control policies have been successful at curbing illegal immigration (Cornelius, Martin, & Hollifield, 1994; Andreas, 2000), just as criminal justice scholars have argued that the severity of criminal justice policies hold little relation to levels of crime (Roberts, Stalans, Indermaur et al., 2003; Tonry, 2004). Similarly, few would argue that the drug wars have succeeded in curbing the illicit trafficking of narcotic substances, or that the recently launched "war on terror" has plausibly reduced the terrorist threat.

This book is a study of the politics of coercive social regulation in Germany and the United States. I define coercive social regulation as policies that regulate individual (rather than firm) behavior in highly intrusive ways and, in the process, impose severe personal costs on the regulated. Very often such policies also rely on the routine use of physical force for their enforcement. This study examines one of the most basic, and most heavy-handed tools at the disposal of the state: the deportation of non-citizens.

---

[8] U.S. Census Bureau, "2002 Census of Governments, Volume 3, Public Employment," Table 2, p. 2, www.census.gov/prod/2004pubs/gc023x2.pdf

[9] U.S. Department of Justice website, "Drug Enforcement Administration Authorized Positions 1975–2003," www.usdoj.gov/jmd/budgetsummary/btd/1975_2002/2002/pdf/page100-103.pdf

[10] U.S. Department of Justice, "Federal Prison System Authorized Positions 1975 Thru 2003," www.usdoj.gov/jmd/budgetsummary/btd/1975_2002/2002/pdf/page109-112.pdf

[11] U.S. Department of Justice, "Immigration and Naturalization Service Authorized Positions 1975–2003," www.usdoj.gov/jmd/budgetsummary/btd/1975_2002/2002/pdf/page104-108.pdf, last accessed 14 December 2005.

Deportation is an expression of the basic policing powers of the state: its agents employ this tool to enforce laws that regulate entry across and residence within its borders, and to exclude individuals who may pose a threat to the public order. And yet, the use of deportation as a measure of coercive social regulation is an intensely political and problematic undertaking. Deportation turns out to be an ideal site for exposing the intensity of the conflict that can arise when the exercise of basic public functions runs up against the most fundamental interests of the individual. In consequence, deportation – and, I argue, coercive social regulation more generally – constitutes a type of public policy that, although at the heart of statehood, places extraordinarily high demands on the liberal state.

Germany and the United States are intriguing cases for the study of deportation because they are among the chief deporting states in the advanced industrialized world. In 2000, the U.S. Immigration and Naturalization Service deported close to 86,000 immigrants,[12] whereas German authorities conducted over 35,000 removals (Bundesministerium des Innern, 2003).[13] Remarkably, in both instances, these data reflect a tripling of deportations over less than a decade. Further, in both contexts, the upsurge in deportations occurred during a period of highly politicized immigration politics that culminated in far-reaching policy reform. Despite these commonalities, however, the success of legislative reform initiatives and the implementation of statutory measures have varied considerably between the two countries. As we will see, some legislative and implementation efforts have proven more successful than others. The following examples illustrate the kind of legislative and implementation outcomes that this book seeks to explain.

In the early and mid-1990s, the German parliament and the U.S. Congress undertook sweeping immigration reforms in response to popular perceptions that each state had lost control over its borders. In the United States, most prominently in Southern California, calls for reform targeted the presence of millions of undocumented immigrants, whereas in Germany public fears focused on the arrival of ever-increasing numbers of asylum seekers. When the German Bundestag embarked upon immigration reform there was fierce partisan disagreement over whether the effective control of asylum migration would in fact require the amendment of what many considered to be an excessively liberal constitutional asylum clause. In the

---

[12] This number does not include close to 90,000 "expedited removals" from ports of entry (U.S. Immigration and Naturalization Service, 2003a).

[13] Additional data provided to author by the Federal Ministry of the Interior, Berlin.

end, in 1993 the Bundestag undertook the momentous step of constitutional reform. By contrast, when Congress initiated immigration reform in 1995, Republicans and Democrats concurred that illegal immigration was fundamentally driven by the unquenchable demand of certain economic sectors for cheap labor. The parties agreed that the most effective strategy of immigration control would be to draw up regulatory measures that prevented unauthorized access to the labor market and, in cases of violation, would sanction employers and deport undocumented workers. And yet, when the resulting legislation was passed in 1996, it no longer reflected the goal of curbing illegal immigration by means of worksite enforcement. Instead, Congress targeted its most far-reaching control measures at immigrants convicted of crimes – many of whom held legal residence status – and at immigrants seeking admission at ports of entry. What can account for these divergent outcomes – in Germany, legislation that responded to the substantive concerns of the public; in the United States, a diversion of congressional reform efforts from the public's demand for more effective controls on illegal immigrants to a crackdown on criminal aliens instead?

A similar pattern of cross-national divergence becomes evident when we examine the implementation of deportation laws in the two countries. Just as members of the Bundestag responded to popular calls for immigration reform by regulating the group at the center of political debate – asylum seekers – German bureaucrats have persistently pursued the repatriation of these individuals. Conversely, despite congressional pressure to "crack down" on undocumented immigrants, the Immigration and Naturalization Service has largely neglected the deportation of illegal migrants living within the United States, instead concentrating enforcement efforts on offenders within the United States and migrants at the border.

These examples illustrate the basic questions this book seeks to explain. When faced with the legislation and implementation of a range of coercive policies, state actors in diverse political contexts arrive at different choices regarding whom to target for regulation. What can account for divergent outcomes between national states, and, in some cases, even across jurisdictions within a single country? Importantly, by exploring these questions we gain insight into the scope and the limits of the socially coercive capacity of the liberal democratic state. As the empirical analyses in chapters to come will illustrate, not all migrant groups pose the same degree of challenge to the state's exercise of control. By paying close attention to how legislators and bureaucrats deal with the regulation of groups whose deportation poses particularly high obstacles, we can gauge the coercive strength of a given state.

What factors, then, help us understand why some states are able to exercise their powers of control where others fail? To answer this question we need to specify the basic dynamics that drive the politics of coercive social regulation – forces that distinguish social regulation from other types of public policy, and that present distinct challenges to the state. Before identifying these forces, let us examine why existing works, although providing us with important insights that will be drawn on in the course of this analysis, cannot by themselves answer the questions prompting this study. I will consider two bodies of scholarship whose investigatory lenses closely correspond to the focus of this book: the state-centric works in comparative political science and the immigration literature.

BRINGING SOCIAL REGULATION INTO THE STUDY OF THE STATE

Given its empirical significance, it is surprising to find that the vast literature on state capacity has virtually ignored the study of coercive social regulation. Instead, scholars have focused their analyses on the state's more "benign" interventions, mostly studying capacities in areas of taxation and expenditure and in the sphere of economic regulation. To name but a few examples, the authors of the seminal study of the field *Bringing the State Back In* (Evans, Rueschemeyer, & Skocpol, 1985) confine their case studies of domestic state interventions to the tasks of economic development and social redistribution. Similarly, Theda Skocpol's (1982) study of industrial and agricultural programs in the United States, Hugh Heclo's (1974) comparative analysis of social policy developments in Britain and Sweden, and Daniel Carpenter's (2001) study of the U.S. Postal Service and the Departments of Agriculture and the Interior all hold in common a focus on state capacity in the policy fields of (re)distribution and economic regulation, as does Kent Weaver and Bert Rockman's wide-ranging cross-national study of state capacity (1993). This policy bias, I argue, limits the explanatory leverage of this literature when studying socially coercive state interventions such as deportation. As we will explore in the chapters to come, the politics of coercive social regulation follows a distinct logic that differs from both the regulation of firms and (re)distribution. I will briefly discuss two basic strands within this literature that differ both from each other and from the present study in their basic conception of state capacity.

In an attempt to "bring the state back in,[14]" scholars have conceptualized the state as a distinct, autonomous entity whose preferences and actions are not reducible to societal forces. Eric Nordlinger (1981) defines autonomy as the insulation of the state from the demands of the public and argues that state autonomy is strongest in situations "in which public officials translate their preferences into authoritative actions when state-society preferences are divergent" (1981, p. 118). In a similar vein, Krasner (1978), in his study of U.S. foreign investment policy, attributes strong state capacity to the insulation of the presidency and the Department of State from societal pressures. Underlying this understanding of capacity is, to borrow from Mitchell, an "intellectual vision that sees the state autonomously formulating goals that it then attempts to implement against resistance from international and domestic actors" (1991, p. 10). According to these scholars, we should observe high levels of capacity in cases where state actors operate autonomously from societal forces.

A second strand of the state-centric literature conceives of the relationship between state and society as one of interdependence. In his comparative study of economic development in newly industrializing countries, Peter Evans argues that state autonomy by itself is an insufficient condition for economic development. Instead, state capacity is a function of the "embedded autonomy" of the state – the confluence of the state's "internal coherence" and its "external connectedness" (1995, p. 176). It is only when states are both autonomous and socially embedded, Evans argues, that they will successfully pursue economic development. Similarly, Carpenter (2001), in his remarkable historical study of American bureaucratic development, considers the ability of agency entrepreneurs to establish coalitional networks with societal actors to be a necessary condition for bureaucratic autonomy. "Autonomy," he contends, "does not really consist in the ability of bureaus to take clandestine, undetected actions against the wishes of elected authorities. It exists most powerfully when bureaus have acquired lasting esteem and durable links to social, political, and economic organizations, links that rival or surpass those of politicians" (2001, p. 354). Accordingly, we would expect to observe high levels of bureaucratic capacity in contexts in which administrative agencies have established strong ties with societal constituencies.

The present study both builds upon and departs from these basic assumptions. Although this analysis shares with the literature a central concern with

---

[14] This movement was a reaction to earlier pluralist research, which emphasized societal forces in the study of politics.

the relationship between the state and society, I argue that in the fields of coercive social regulation, the basic conditions underlying state capacity in liberal democracies will vary across stages of the policy process. At the legislative stage, socially coercive capacity hinges upon strong institutional connections between the state and the public. The diffuse benefits and concentrated costs so typical of regulatory policy (Wilson, 1980) create stronger incentives to mobilize for those who stand to lose from regulation – the regulated – than for its potential beneficiaries – the general public. Accordingly, in order to overcome the opposition of the regulated, legislators have to rely on institutionalized channels of public interest articulation that can compensate for the political risks of imposing costs on organized interests.

Once policies of coercive social regulation reach the stage of implementation, however, civil servants face strong incentives to heed the interests of regulated individuals and their advocates as coercive bureaucracies cannot rely upon the support of proregulatory constituencies. This dynamic clearly departs from Carpenter's analysis that identifies the ability of bureaucracies to enter into coalitions with social and economic groups as a crucial condition for capacity-building (2001). Carpenter argues that networks between bureaucratic agencies and societal actors provide bureaucrats with the necessary autonomy from politicians to build institutional capacity. Significantly, this argument hinges on the assumption that bureaucracies have clienteles who are suitable coalition partners. Yet, although this assumption accurately describes the social context in which agencies delivering distributive and redistributive benefits operate, it does not hold for the bureaucracies that operate in fields of coercive social regulation. In this particular policy sphere, groups which oppose regulation are well-organized whereas those who stand to benefit – the potential supporters of coercive agencies – are not. It follows that, because coercive agencies do not have strong constituencies that can provide bureaucrats with much needed political backing, they are vulnerable to the obstructionist interventions of regulated groups.

The dynamics of socially coercive regulation not only differ from those observed in fields of (re)distribution, they also diverge in important ways from the politics of economic regulation. As Raymond Tatalovich and Byron Daynes contend, socially regulatory policies distinguish themselves by the centrality of "moral and normative debates about the place of the individual in the community" (1988, p. 2). The normative nature of political discussion has important implications for the politics of coercive social regulation. Not only is this policy cluster marked by more intense political conflict than the field of economic regulation, but policy losers, when confronted with enforcement, face strong incentives to contest regulation in the

public sphere, rather than, as is common in the relationship between bureaucrats and firms, behind closed doors. Before we pursue these arguments
further, let us first turn to a second body of scholarship of relevance to
the study of socially coercive capacity: the immigration literature.

BRINGING THE STATE INTO THE STUDY OF
MIGRATION CONTROL

Though never applied to the case of deportation, the problem of state
capacity has been at the core of a growing literature studying one of
the most prominent areas of coercive social regulation: migration control.
Without reviewing this vast body of scholarship in its entirety, I will identify
two broad tendencies within these works. First, many immigration scholars
have focused their analyses on the global challenges of migration control,
paying scant attention to concrete state responses. Second, among those
studies that do examine specific institutions, few incorporate immigration
agencies and the stage of implementation into their analysis. In consequence, the migration literature suffers from a set of related explanatory
weaknesses. First, by arguing that liberal states are intrinsically incapable of
controlling their borders, analyses in this mold generally presume a universal
incapacity for immigration control. Because many of these scholars focus
their analyses on the global challenges of migration control, they fail to
consider the responses of individual countries. As a result, they ignore
cross-national variation in state capacity. Second, I shall argue that the
literature's focus on the legislative arena has resulted in scholarly neglect
of the constraints on policy implementation. Legislation, however, is only
the beginning of the story of state capacity. On matters of immigration
control, the gap between the law and its implementation is colossal. By
concluding their analysis with the completion of the legislative process, these
studies tell us little about crucial constraints on state capacity at the stage of
implementation.

Possibly the most distinctive trait of the immigration literature is a profound skepticism about the capacity of democratic states to exert migration
control. These critiques extend across otherwise contrasting modes of
explanation. Arguing that liberal democratic states are intrinsically incapable of immigration control, these analyses generally fail to account for cross-
national variation in control capacity. Rather they distinguish among the
various constraints on states' capacity in this field. Globalization scholars,
for instance, have argued that, because the root causes of international
migration are principally external to the state, any attempt by governments

to regulate it will remain largely ineffectual. Whereas economic arguments (Sassen, 1988; Cornelius, 1998) point to the structural demand for cheap migrant labor as an intractable constraint on the state, legal analyses (Soysal, 1994; Jacobson, 1996) contend that the rise of an international human rights regime has tied the hands of governments intent on the pursuit of migration control. In contrast to globalization approaches, the proponents of the "liberal state thesis" have located constraints largely in the domestic realm. Equally skeptical of the state's capacity in this field, these scholars have argued that the emergence of a "rights-based liberalism" – manifest in a proimmigrant bias in judicial rulings and interest group politics – has obstructed the ability of governments to set and enforce tough migration control policies (Hollifield, 1992; Cornelius, Martin, & Hollifield, 1994; Joppke, 1998; Gibney & Hansen, 2003).

Although these studies have gone a long way to deepen our understanding of the constraints on states' capacity to regulate immigration, they all suffer from what could be described as the "denominator problem." Because these studies set an unrealistically high threshold for effective migration control (Brubaker, 1994), state capacity (or, rather, the lack thereof) is viewed as a constant across the advanced industrialized world.

Not all migration scholars focus their analyses on universal constraints on the state. However, even scholars who have investigated specific institutional responses to immigration have largely ignored the role of the bureaucracy and the politics of implementation in shaping state capacity. For instance, Jeannette Money (1999) examines the electoral conditions under which public preferences for immigration control will translate into legislative reform. Equally focused on the legislative arena, Gary Freeman's interest-based approach (1995, 2002) places the influence of organized interests – agricultural and business lobbies, and ethnic advocacy groups – at the center of the politics of immigration. Whereas Money and Freeman focus on the relationship between elected officials, the electorate, and interest groups, Christian Joppke (1998) studies the role of the courts in shaping states' capacity for regulating immigration. Significantly, Joppke identifies cross-national variation in the power of judicial constraints: these have been considerable in the case of Germany, where migration control is exercised in a context marked by strong constitutional human rights protections and the institution of judicial review. Britain, in contrast, with its long tradition of parliamentary sovereignty and the absence of judicial review, has been much more successful in controlling immigration. These studies have provided us with a nuanced understanding of the political and judicial constraints facing legislators as they design policies of immigration control, and this book will draw on such arguments when discussing the politics of coercive social regulation in the legislative arena. At the same time, however, the explanatory scope of these analyses does not extend into the sphere of implementation – a consequential limitation, as the enforcement of coercive mandates presents the ultimate test of state capacity.

Among the few migration scholars who incorporate implementation into their analysis, most have neglected the study of bureaucrats. Instead, John Torpey (2000), Grete Brochmann and Thomas Hammar (1999), Peter Andreas and Timothy Snyder (2000), and Dita Vogel (2000) examine the development of novel administrative and technological instruments at the disposal of the state, whereas Gallya Lahav and Virginie Guiraudon's recent synopsis of new implementation strategies by European states (2000) largely focuses on nonstate and supranational actors. In a rare departure, Kitty Calavita (1992) investigates the role of the U.S. Immigration and Naturalization Service in the administration of the Bracero program. She argues that, in the 1950s, members of Congress delegated wide powers of administrative discretion to the agency in order to pursue levels of control that would have been too controversial to achieve through legislative means. It is important to bear in mind, however, that Calavita's research draws on a long-gone period of U.S. politics during which immigration policy achieved only intermittent salience at the national level – allowing for relatively unconstrained bureaucratic decision-making. This condition no longer holds today. In a more recent historical study of the INS, Sharon Barrios (1999) paints a picture of the immigration agency as tightly controlled by Congress. These findings will be drawn on in the analyses of subsequent chapters.

DEFINING COERCIVE SOCIAL REGULATION

Although the public policy literature has shed much light on the nature of economic regulation, much less is known about the state's role in the sphere of social regulation. In one of the few existing studies of this field, Tantalovich and Daynes define social regulation as the regulation of social, rather than economic, relationships. By contrast to economic regulatory policies, the authors argue, social regulation is inherently moral in nature: "because they impinge on our private lives and define our social positions, social regulations have at their core a moral and normative debate about the place of the individual in the community" (1988, p. 2). The intrusion of government action into the private lives of individuals, then, renders this policy field highly susceptible to normative conflict. Tantalovich and Daynes' examples of social regulatory policies range from abortion, gun control, and criminal justice to school prayer, affirmative action, and gay rights.

The present analysis examines a distinct subset of social regulatory policies: state interventions that are marked by the coercive regulation of individuals. Although it can be argued that regulation by definition rests on coercion – neither regulated individuals nor firms seek out nor welcome regulation – policies of coercive social regulation distinguish themselves by the state's exercise of its hard coercive powers. The use of physical force against individuals is an integral part of a wide range of law enforcement practices that span the areas of criminal justice, national security, drug control, and migration control.

Socially coercive policies share with Tantalovich and Daynes' larger universe of social regulation an inherent normative component that renders them susceptible to political contestation. However, moral values are not the only source of conflict here. Among the multitude of regulations, socially coercive policies distinguish themselves by the enormity of the stakes for both the state and the individuals subject to regulation. Coercive social regulation routinely imposes severe costs on its targets: once the individual is within the state's reach, regulatory interventions are likely to result in the loss of personal autonomy, including the loss of physical freedom. At the same time, the fact that the government is prepared to use its ultimate weapon of physical force speaks to the importance of this form of state activity.

The significance of coercive social regulation is further reflected in the fact that regulatory enforcement rests in the hands of a specialized public bureaucracy. Unlike the regulation of school prayer, abortion, or affirmative action, fields of coercive social regulation distinguish themselves by vast street-level bureaucracies of law enforcement officers authorized to wield the state's powers of coercion. In the politics of coercive social regulation, then, street-level bureaucrats are key actors in the struggle between the state and the targets of regulation. Significantly, the interaction between state agents and individuals differs decidedly from state–civil society relations in the economic sphere. Because of the economic and political power of regulated firms and industries, regulatory encounters in this area are frequently marked by extensive negotiation and compromise. The relationship between law enforcement officers and individuals, by contrast, is marked by much higher levels of confrontation and a lower likelihood of compromise. We can thus define policies of coercive social regulation as measures that control individual behavior in highly intrusive ways, impose severe personal costs on the regulated, and often rely on the routine use of physical force for their enforcement.

DEFINING STATE CAPACITY

This investigation of state capacity is firmly anchored in democratic theory. According to one prominent framework, we can conceive of the political process as a chain of delegation in which voters entrust the task of legislating to elected representatives, legislators assign the drafting of regulations to executive officials who, in turn, delegate implementation to civil servants (Strøm, Müller, & Bergman, 2003). Correspondingly, this study distinguishes between two basic types of state capacity: first, legislative capacity describes the ability of elected representatives to write into law the broad policy preferences of the general public. Executive capacity, in turn, represents the capacity of the executive arm of the state – both street-level bureaucrats and agency leaders – to implement the ensuing legislative acts. Once we conceive of democratic politics as a process that spans across various policy stages, it follows that challenges to state capacity can arise at each link of the delegation chain. And although, as we will see, political contestation presents a challenge to the state along the entire policy chain, I argue that the conditions underlying socially coercive capacity differ between the stages of legislation and implementation.

These definitions of legislative and executive capacity essentially require us to examine the political capacity of the state. Simply defined as the ability of state actors to pursue a chosen path of action in the face of – actual or potential – opposition, this analytical lens closely corresponds to the ways in which state-centric scholars have approached the study of capacity. Skocpol, for instance, defines state capacity as the ability "to implement official goals, especially over the actual or potential opposition of powerful social groups or in the face of recalcitrant socioeconomic circumstances" (1985, p. 8). By contrast, this approach departs from the immigration literature, which has tended to evaluate state capacity by comparing empirical policy outcomes with the overarching goals of migration control. Not surprisingly, as states have fallen short of putting an end to unauthorized border crossings, or of deporting all undocumented migrants, analyses in this mold consistently have arrived at negative results.

This is not to argue, of course, that political conflict is the only challenge confronting the social regulatory state. In order to exercise control over individuals – many of whom will try to evade regulation – states also require what Michael Mann has called "infrastructural" capacity, which is "the institutional capacity of a central state [. . .] to penetrate its territories and logistically implement decisions" (1993, p. 59). In the case of deportation, for example, states depend upon infrastructural resources to identify, surveil, detain, and physically remove individuals. Moreover, state capacity in the area of migration control requires the exercise of influence in the international arena. Although most states readily readmit citizens returning of their own volition, many governments place high demands upon the return of nationals who have destroyed their identity documents in order to evade repatriation (Ellermann, 2008). Although the question of international influence is beyond the scope of this book, the issue of infrastructural capacity will be addressed in contexts in which it interacts with the state's exercise of political capacity. At the end of the day, the peaceful management of political conflict is one of the principal challenges facing the democratic state.

A PREVIEW OF THE ARGUMENT

My central argument is that deportation, as a case of coercive social regulation, comprises a political endeavor that is distinct from the challenges facing the state in fields of (re)distribution and economic regulation. Two basic characteristics uniquely distinguish the politics of deportation. First, the forced removal of individuals regularly elicits intense political conflict. This conflict arises from the imposition of high, and highly concentrated costs, and – due to deportation's deep intrusion into the private sphere – the normative nature of political debate. As a second distinguishing characteristic, the political salience of deportation's costs and benefits varies across stages of the policy process. I argue that as policy moves from legislation to implementation, public attention changes its focus from the benefits of deportation to its costs, with important consequences. As public attention shifts, so do the incentives of state actors. This shift has important implications as the unstable nature of state actors' incentives threatens to undermine the state's socially coercive capacity. Specifically, as preferences of elected officials change over time, time inconsistency poses a fundamental threat to policy sustainability (Patashnik, 2003). We will now take a closer look at the challenges to state capacity at the various stages of the policy process.

Legislative Capacity

At the early stages of the policy process, legislative reform is typically driven by popular mandates for stricter regulation. Policies of social control target what Arnold has called "politically repellent groups" (1990, p. 80) and proregulatory arguments emphasize the purported public benefits of reform, while denouncing the costs incurred by the status quo. This demonizing[15] discourse provides proregulatory entrepreneurs with a comparative advantage when mobilizing the unorganized public. Once engaged, the public can employ a variety of means of interest articulation to place its demands on the political agenda, ranging from subnational and national elections to grassroots political initiatives. Consequently, legislators face strong incentives to endorse proregulatory policies, as few politicians can afford to be seen as "soft" on issues pertaining to public safety and order.

Once a public backlash has propelled regulatory reform onto the political agenda, those targeted by regulation stand much to gain – and little to lose – from countermobilizing. Public policy analysts have long identified the entrepreneurial mode of regulatory policies – marked by diffuse benefits and concentrated costs – as a key challenge to policy-makers (Wilson, 1980; Freeman, 2002). Although antiregulatory groups – the bearers of concentrated costs – face strong incentives to assert their interests, they are unlikely to do so at the stage of agenda-setting, where punitive policy images dominate political debate. Instead, policy losers are more likely to succeed once negotiations have started to move out of public view, as is the case at the stages of policy formulation and adoption. It is at these later points in the legislative process, when few members of the public follow each twist and turn of legislative bargaining, that organized policy losers enjoy a comparative advantage over society in general. Confronted with the antiregulatory interests of highly attentive and well-prepared constituencies, legislators face strong incentives to pass reforms that, although couched in regulatory terms, at closer sight provide for loopholes that either exempt organized interests from regulation or lessen the costs incurred by these groups.

Under what conditions, then, will legislators possess the capacity to translate popular pressures for regulation into corresponding legislative reform, notwithstanding the opposition of well-organized antiregulatory interests? I argue that legislative capacity essentially depends upon the availability of institutional mechanisms of public interest articulation beyond the agenda-setting stage. Following Andrea Campbell and Kimberley Morgan (2005), I contend that legislators are most likely to pursue regulatory policies where the community can piggyback on well-organized public actors for interest articulation. Among the range of potential public interest actors, subnational governments are particularly well suited to perform this role. Specifically, in the case of immigration, they can overcome the constraints of

---

[15] Daniel Kryder first suggested this term.

spatially concentrated public interest mobilization arising from the geographic concentration of immigrants (Money, 1999) by forming coalitions across spatial jurisdictions. Not all intergovernmental lobbies, however, are equally equipped to fulfill this role. Whether or not these actors can successfully pursue their policy demands will largely depend upon the balance of power between subnational and federal governments, a relationship determined by the institutional structure of intergovernmental relations.

Executive Capacity

Once executive agencies start to enforce social regulatory policies, the public is confronted with the harsh consequences of regulation. In contrast to the generalizing and criminalizing policy discourse that dominates at the stage of legislation, implementation draws attention to the specific individuals affected by coercive interventions. Importantly, many of these individuals will not fit the demonizing policy images so prominent at the legislative stage. Consequently, at this stage, the public will be sympathetic to arguments against regulation, in particular assertions that regulation imposes unduly harsh costs upon well-integrated members of local communities.

Significantly, because the costs of regulation are concentrated on identifiable individuals – and sometimes on ethnic communities or neighborhoods – the likelihood of mobilization is high. Advocates and concerned citizens stage publicity campaigns to draw attention to what they argue is overzealous and inhumane bureaucratic enforcement. At the same time, the proregulatory policy entrepreneurs so dominant at the point of agenda-setting feature less prominently in the politics of implementation. Although they often succeed in rousing initial public support for stricter regulation, these entrepreneurs rarely possess the necessary moral leverage to assert their interests beyond the stage of agenda-setting. As a result, the political momentum of proregulatory campaigns rarely carries over into the sphere of implementation, with the result that the mobilization efforts of antiregulatory advocates meet with little organized opposition.

By contrast, although at the legislative stage antiregulatory interests are forced to operate behind closed doors, once implementation commences they seek out the public arena to provoke opposition to enforcement. As advocates appeal to humanitarian values, public attention shifts from the purported benefits of regulation to its harsh costs, with important political implications. Whereas in earlier stages politicians consider it a liability to withhold their support from socially coercive initiatives, they now fear being perceived as inhumane when confronted with the fate of affected individuals and families. Advocates thus have much to gain by calling upon the constituency services of elected representatives.

Consequently, and contrary to the claims of principal–agent scholars, I argue that, in socially coercive policy fields, elected officials are likely to exert substantial pressure on bureaucrats to refrain from implementation. Where agencies are vulnerable to the interference of their elected overseers, they face strong incentives to concentrate enforcement on groups without constituencies who might protest on their behalf. It follows that executive capacity is contingent on the insulation of bureaucratic agencies from the interference of their constituency-service providing overseers. The degree of bureaucratic insulation, in turn, is determined by the institutions that structure executive–legislative relations.

A final source of political constraint lies in the highly normative nature of coercive social regulation. Where legislators operate in political contexts marked by programmatic parties, representatives from parties with libertarian or socially progressive ideologies will struggle to advocate the adoption of measures of coercive social regulation. Before moving on to the next chapter, where we will further examine the institutional conditions underlying legislative and executive capacity, we will take a closer look at the political and historical context of deportation in Germany and the United States.

A BRIEF POLITICAL HISTORY OF DEPORTATION POLICY

Examining deportation trends in Germany and the United States, we are confronted with strikingly similar developments during the 1990s. In the course of less than a decade, the number of deportations in both countries increased more than threefold, to over 35,000 in Germany (Bundesministerium des Innern, 2003) and close to 92,000 in the United States (U.S. Immigration and Naturalization Service, 2003a). Yet, although both countries experienced a historically unprecedented upsurge in deportations, German and U.S. immigration agencies did not concentrate their removal efforts on the same groups of migrants. In Germany, deportation authorities targeted asylum seekers during a period of intense social backlash against what was widely perceived as economically driven asylum seeking. During the same time period, the American public demanded government action against rising illegal migration. Although immigration authorities stepped up their deportation efforts, they did not focus on illegal immigrants. Instead, they opted to expel convicted criminals and migrants at ports of entry.

What can these differences tell us about the socially coercive capacity of the German and the American states? Do differences in the groups targeted by German and U.S. deportation officers indicate cross-national variation in socially coercive capacity? Or does the upward trend in the total number of deportations reflect a concomitant increase in capacity that is shared by both states? In order to get to the heart of these questions, we will first examine the historical and political contexts that have shaped these developments.

Germany

For much of its postwar history, German immigration politics was based on the premise that the Federal Republic was *kein Einwanderungsland* – not a country of immigration. Although the premise of zero (permanent) immigration constituted a central policy principle, it discounted the reality that the country was in fact undergoing significant levels of de facto immigration: not only had the guestworker program failed to prevent the permanent settlement of migrant workers and their families, but also in the area of asylum policy most applicants ultimately remained and settled in Germany, regardless of the outcome of their claims. Nevertheless, until the late 1970s, matters of immigration did not feature prominently in German political debate. Because policy-making was largely executive-driven, it was sheltered from public and even parliamentary debate.

As Figure 1 shows, between 1977 – the first year for which national data are available – and the late 1980s, the number of deportations conducted by German authorities remained essentially constant, only occasionally surpassing the 10,000 mark. During this period, immigration violations and criminal offenses constituted the most common grounds for deportation.[16] Asylum seekers, by contrast, made up only a small fraction of deportees: data for the late 1970s show that approximately 5 percent of deportations concerned rejected asylum applicants. The numerical insignificance of asylum deportations as a proportion of overall removals can be attributed to the intersection of a number of factors, such as comparatively small numbers of

---

[16] German deportation statistics are disaggregated into asylum and nonasylum grounds. The category of nonasylum deportations lumps together deportations based on illegal entry/overstay with criminal grounds for deportation. Archival materials from this period chronicle the following grounds for deportation: criminal convictions, violations of immigration regulations, illegal entry, and foreigners whose presence was "not in the national interest" (Bayerisches Staatsministerium des Innern, 1963; Bundesministerium des Innern, April 11, 1967; Rheinische Post, February 17, 1960; July 20, 1968; Ausländerreferenten des Bundes und der Länder, October 15–17, 1970; Stuttgarter Zeitung, September 15, 1965).

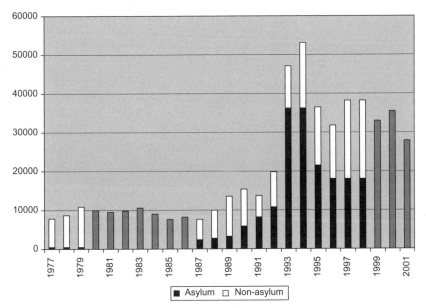

FIGURE 1. Germany, deportations by reason (stacked), 1977–2001.
Source: Bundesministerium des Innern, Bundesgrenzschutzdirektion, Münch 1993.
(Gray colums represent total deportations where no breakdown available)

asylum seekers, their quick absorption into the expanding postwar economy (Arbeitsgemeinschaft der Innenministerien der Bundesländer, March 9, 1964), and the political imperatives of the Cold War. For instance, in a consequential decision, the Federal Conference of Interior Ministers in 1966 decided that refugees from the Eastern Bloc[17] were not to be deported, regardless of the outcome of their asylum hearings (Höfling-Semnar, 1995).[18] This had clear ramifications because until 1973 the vast majority of asylum seekers originated from Eastern Europe.[19]

The late 1970s and early 1980s marked an end to the hitherto consensual and liberal period in German asylum politics as policy-makers became increasingly concerned with the possibility of asylum abuse. With the end

[17] With the exception of Yugoslavia.
[18] In an assessment of this policy two years later, the representatives of the interior ministries reaffirmed this policy decision. The federal representative argued that a more restrictionist policy stance would not only be politically problematic, but it also would be impossible to decide on a case-to-case basis whether or not individuals from Eastern Bloc countries would face political persecution upon their return (Ausländerreferenten des Bundes und der Länder, February 13–15, 1968).
[19] In the 1950s and 1960s, approximately 90 percent of asylum seekers arrived from Eastern Europe. By 1973, this had fallen to 51 percent (Münch, 1993).

of guestworker recruitment in 1973, seeking asylum, for many migrants, had come to constitute the last remaining legal avenue into the country. Aided by Germany's comparatively liberal asylum law, asylum seeking had become an attractive option for those seeking to enter the country for a variety of reasons. By 1980, when in a context of economic stagnation the number of asylum seekers exceeded 100,000 at the same time as the national origins of asylum applicants shifted toward nonwhite countries,[20] the issue of political asylum became construed as a matter of migration control (Höfling-Semnar, 1995). The Bundestag and the Federal Ministry of the Interior passed a series of laws and administrative regulations that aimed to deter asylum seeking and tried to accelerate the clogged-up adjudication process. However, these control measures were largely designed to control the inflow of asylum seekers, rather than to enforce their return (Münch, 1993). Thus, until the late 1980s, the move from liberalism to restrictionism in asylum policy did not have an appreciable impact on deportation figures. It was only in the late 1980s that deportation started to gain prominence as a means of migration control.

With the end of the Cold War, a surge in East–West migration propelled the number of asylum applications to a record high of 438,000 in 1992, up from 37,000 ten years before.[21] Many applicants from Central and Eastern Europe undertook their journey for predominantly economic reasons, bearing greater resemblance to the population of illegal immigrants in the United States than to earlier Cold War cohorts of asylum seekers. This upsurge in applications placed significant demands on local authorities charged with providing public housing and welfare services for applicants waiting for the (progressively lengthy) adjudication of their claims. Calls for a crackdown on asylum seekers mounted, and immigration authorities stepped up their deportation efforts. In 1989, deportation numbers surpassed 10,000, and, by 1994, a record number of over 52,000 migrants were forcibly removed. In the latter half of the decade, deportation numbers settled between 32,000 and 38,000 annually (Figure 1).

The unprecedented increase in deportations in the 1990s can in large measure be attributed to stepped-up asylum removals: the proportion of

---

[20] In the late 1970s, over 50 percent of asylum applicants came from Asian countries, compared to 0.4 percent in 1968. In a similar vein, the proportion of African asylum seekers increased from 2 percent in 1968 to 18.4 percent in 1983 (König, 2000).

[21] Bundesamt für Migration und Flüchtlinge, "Asyl in Zahlen 2006," http://www.bamf.de/cln_006/nn_442496/SharedDocs/Anlagen/DE/DasBAMF/Publikationen/broschuere-asyl-in-zahlen-2006,templateId=raw,property=publicationFile.pdf/broschuere-asyl-in-zahlen-2006.pdf

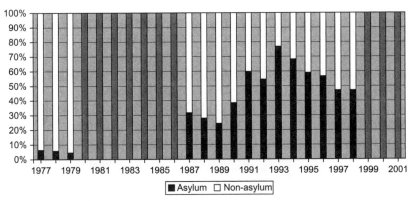

FIGURE 2. Germany, deportations by reason (in percent), 1977–2001.
Source: Bundesministerium des Innern, Bundesgrenzschutzdirektion, Münch 1993.
(Gray colums represent total deportations where no breakdown available)

deportees who had sought asylum increased from 24 percent in 1989 to a staggering 77 percent four years later, before stabilizing at around 50 percent (Figure 2). Significantly, the increase in asylum deportations cannot be solely attributed to a parallel increase in the number of asylum applicants. Whereas in the late 1980s asylum deportations amounted to just under 5 percent of asylum applications, they accounted for 15 to 20 percent of applications in the mid- and late 1990s.[22] In sum, what most distinguishes the 1990s from earlier decades was a sustained, and in large measure successful, effort to target asylum seekers for removal.

United States

In contrast to deportation trends in Germany, which until the late 1980s were marked by stagnation, data from the United States present a long pattern of abrupt peaks followed by substantial drops in removals over the past century. Because of the central significance of immigration in American political development, both support for and backlash against immigration have long been part of political discourse and legislative politics. Historically, deportation waves were often motivated by security concerns. As a wave of anti-Communism swept the country after the end of World War I, for instance, the notorious Palmer raids of 1919/1920 resulted in the deportation of hundreds of alleged Communists and labor unionists to Europe (Panunzio, 1921; Schrecker, 1997). Three decades later, McCarthyism

[22] Author's calculations.

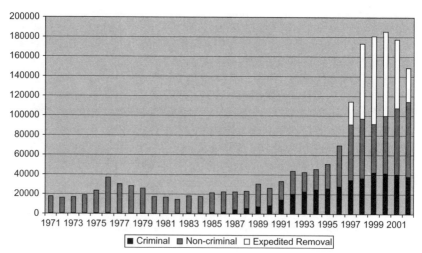

FIGURE 3. United States, removals by reason (stacked), 1971–2002.
Source: INS Statistical Yearbooks.

resulted in yet another wave of politically motivated expulsions (Schrecker, 1997). Other deportation drives were economically driven. In the early 1950s, when the employment of undocumented workers threatened to undercut the dependability of Bracero labor (Calavita, 1992), the INS staged a widely publicized deportation drive. The agency claimed that during "Operation Wetback" some 1,300,000 undocumented immigrants had been apprehended – a figure likely to be vastly exaggerated (Garcia, 1980) but nevertheless significant given the agency's previous (and subsequent) laissez-faire attitude toward undocumented workers in the Southwest.

As Figure 3 shows, this pattern came to an end in the late 1980s, when deportations started to first rise steadily before increasing precipitously to a 2002 high of over 114,200 (nearly 185,000 if expedited removals are included). Once we break down the total number of removals by category, we observe a remarkable divergence in trends across the various groups of deportees (Figure 4). Considering the prominence of illegal immigrants both as the object of American control rhetoric and as the largest group of deportable migrants – a pattern we will observe throughout this book – we would expect this group to account for the steep incline in deportations. However, although variation in the removal of undocumented immigrants largely accounts for ups and downs in overall numbers until the mid-1980s, this is no longer the case after 1985. In fact, as deportations started to increase, the number of deported undocumented migrants (i.e., noncriminal

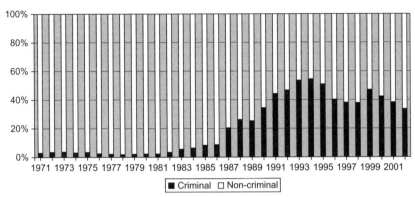

FIGURE 4. United States, deportations by reason (in percent), 1971–2002.
Source: INS Statistical Yearbooks.

deportations) remained constant. Instead, the rise in numbers during this period is solely attributable to the deportation of immigrants convicted of crimes. In a striking development, criminal removals increased fifteen-fold within 10 years and, in 1995, accounted for over 50 percent of total deportations (Figure 4). The prominence of criminal deportations is thus one of the most striking developments in U.S. deportation policy.

Although U.S. deportation data distinguish between criminal and noncriminal grounds, they do not discriminate between asylum and nonasylum cases. Instead, asylum deportations are subsumed under the noncriminal category. How can we explain this lack of administrative and political attention to asylum seekers as a group of deportees? Until the 1980s, only few individuals sought political asylum upon or after arrival in the United States. Instead, most refugees arrived through planned resettlement schemes which gave U.S. immigration authorities full control over the selection of refugee entrants. For many years, the U.S. government successfully checked the spontaneous arrival of asylum seekers from Cuba and Haiti by closely cooperating with the Cuban government and by intercepting boats from Haiti at sea (Gibney, 2004). The number of asylum seekers only started to increase after 1980 when the incorporation of the 1967 UN Protocol into U.S. domestic law rendered the summary exclusion of asylum seekers illegal. Although law enforcement authorities continued to prevent boats from Haiti and Cuba from landing on U.S. shores – thereby barring access to the right to apply for asylum – they could not prevent asylum seekers traveling by air from reaching U.S. soil. In response to rising numbers of asylum applicants and related concerns about asylum abuse, Congress enacted a series of legislative changes in the early and mid-1990s, which were designed to speed up processing and to deter asylum seeking by curtailing the rights of applicants. Numbers subsequently dropped from under 85,000 in 1997 to 55,000 and 41,000 in 1998 and 1999 respectively (Gibney, 2004). Nevertheless, despite the rising significance of asylum in the 1990s, the number of arrivals in the United States was considerably lower than in Germany[23] and mobilization against asylum seekers remained much weaker.[24] Instead, anti-immigrant backlash remained focused on illegal migrants.

The steep deportation wave of the late 1990s that is evident in Figure 3 is in large measure attributable to expedited removals, a new provision instituted by the 1996 Illegal Immigration Reform and Immigrant Responsibility Act. Expedited removal allows for the summary deportation at ports of entry of nonresidents who arrive without valid travel documents or who attempt entry through fraud. Before 1996, these individuals would have been placed in exclusion proceedings and allowed to present their case in a judicial hearing. Although expedited removals can be understood as a subset of noncriminal removals, they distinguish themselves by the ease with which a person can be turned back at a port of entry, in contrast to noncriminal deportees who have to be located and removed from within the country. Because expedited removal provisions pertain to migrants who have not yet entered the United States, it constitutes a form of exclusion rather than deportation, and I will examine this measure only in contexts where it contributes to our understanding of state capacity.

METHOD OF INVESTIGATION

How can we measure a concept as complex as socially coercive state capacity? This is a general problem facing the study of state capacity: how do we measure the obstacles that states are overcoming? Although it is relatively straightforward to examine legislative capacity – much of the legislative process and all statutory output is public record – the measurement of executive capacity, i.e., the degree of congruence between statutory mandate and implementation output, is a much more challenging undertaking. What complicates this picture further is the fact that quantitative

---

[23] Highs of 85,000 in the United States and 438,000 in Germany.

[24] The United States continued its relatively generous refugee resettlement policy after the end of the Cold War and kept its doors open to refugees from the former Soviet Union and Eastern Europe – the same populations that sought entry into Germany via the asylum route.

statistical measures are not necessarily valid indicators of executive capacity because they often do not reflect the degree of difficulty of implementation.

Absolute numbers of deportations are rarely indicative of state capacity because they aggregate factors that determine the degree of difficulty of deportation. These factors include the nationality of the migrant[25] and the degree of social and economic integration.[26] For instance, it requires significantly more capacity to deport a Lebanese national who holds permanent resident status and is married to a U.S. citizen than a Mexican day laborer who only entered the country weeks prior to his apprehension. It follows that a rise in the number of deportations is not necessarily indicative of a concomitant increase in state capacity.

To gauge the difficulty of deportation, then, this study relies upon qualitative data gathered from in-depth interviews with individuals on both sides of the regulatory conflict. The book's empirical chapters draw on over 180 in-person interviews with deportation officers at all four subnational case sites (Baden-Württemberg, Brandenburg, Miami, San Diego), senior civil servants in the two nations' capitals, elected officials at municipal, state, and federal levels of government, legislative staffers, immigrant advocates, and immigration control lobbyists. Interviewing actors engaged in the politics of deportation allowed me to assess the various components of executive capacity: in particular, the extent of opposition to removals and whether bureaucrats felt they had to back down in response to it or could steamroll it. In assessing the degree of political capacity required for deportation, I compared accounts from a variety of actors with different interests. Rather than taking bureaucratic accounts at face value, wherever possible, I triangulated data from diverse interview sources to substantiate claims by public servants concerning, for instance, the efficacy of their efforts to overcome organized opposition to deportation. Likewise, I checked claims by immigrant advocates about the successes of mobilization against bureaucrats' perceptions of the same campaigns.

These interview data are further complemented with statistical data that differentiate between the various administrative grounds for removal. Although data limitations do not allow us to use overall deportation numbers to measure state capacity, interview evidence shows that the various deportation categories differ significantly in the degree of political and

---

[25] Immigration officials often cannot procure travel documents if diplomatic relations between the two governments are highly conflictual or nonexistent.

[26] Integration is shaped by variables such as length of residence and employment and family status. Although deportation data are broken down by nationality, they do not record factors pertaining to integration.

infrastructural effort required for their implementation. They therefore provide us with an additional indicator of executive capacity. For instance, in the United States, the deportation of illegal immigrants from the interior requires immensely more executive capacity than the removal of incarcerated criminal offenders. In Germany, in contrast, the deportation of asylum seekers places much stronger demands on executive capacity than does the repatriation of both illegal immigrants and criminal offenders. It follows that a quantitative comparison of removal categories – both among administrative groups and over time – can serve as a useful proxy for executive capacity. Before further examining these claims, the next chapter will lay out the theoretical framework that will guide the empirical analyses in Chapters 2 to 4.

A Theory of Socially Coercive State Capacity

> The question is: what level of enforcement is the nation comfortable with?
> The closer you get to the ground, the grayer it gets – you can no longer think in
> terms of black and white.
>
> (Personal interview, senior official, INS Headquarters,
> Washington, D.C., August 27, 2002)

This chapter presents a theoretical framework for the study of state capacity in fields of coercive social regulation. Given the pervasive neglect of this policy cluster by the public policy literature and by state-centric scholars, we need to address a basic question before setting out on the path of theory building: what is the distinct nature of coercive social regulation? How do the dynamics of this policy type differ from those driving the politics of economic regulation, and of distribution and redistribution? Once we have identified these forces, we can move on to the larger question of state capacity. Under what conditions, we shall ask, should we expect states to exercise their coercive powers of social regulation successfully?

The theoretical framework developed in this chapter pursues an institutional logic of argument that distinguishes between the factors underlying state capacity at two distinct stages of the policy process. As a first step, we will specify the conditions under which legislators will translate popular demands for social regulation into corresponding statutes. Second, we will examine the conditions under which executive actors will wield the power to implement these legislative mandates. The remainder of this book will empirically test these propositions. The determinants of legislative capacity will be examined in Chapter 2, whereas the proposed conditions underlying executive state capacity will be tested in Chapters 3 and 4. Before further specifying these conditions, this chapter will begin by outlining the basic characteristics of the politics of coercive social regulation.

THE POLITICS OF COERCIVE SOCIAL REGULATION

The modern state, Max Weber has famously argued, can be defined as an institution claiming the monopoly of legitimate coercion within a given territory (1979). It is no coincidence that Weber, in his quest for the ideal-type state, chose its means, rather than substantive ends, as the state's most universal characteristic. Not only do goals vary over time, and across countries, but each state at any given point in time pursues multiple, and often competing, objectives (Anter, 1995). By contrast, all developed states distinguish themselves from nonstate associations by their exclusive authority over the use of physical coercion as the ultimate means for enforcing rules. In order for this definition to apply, then, states have to fulfill two basic conditions. First, the means of violence have to be institutionalized under the centralized control of the state through coercive bureaucracies such as the police and the army. Second, states have to be recognized as the legitimate holders of this monopoly of force (Anter, 1995).

In the domestic sphere, acts of coercive social regulation most closely reflect this understanding of the state. Typically justified in the name of public order and safety, socially coercive policies are marked by the state's routine exercise of its powers of control. Even where law enforcement does not involve the actual use of physical force, compliance regularly rests on the state's threat to employ violence as a measure of last resort. Significantly, as we saw in the introductory chapter, the coercive bureaucracies that implement immigration or criminal justice policies are no mere paper tigers. On the contrary, law enforcement agencies distinguish themselves by the size of their workforces, the large number of field offices, and, perhaps most importantly, the gravity of the implications of bureaucratic intervention for the individuals targeted by the state. In other words, among the many forms of modern state activity, it is in areas of coercive social regulation – in the realms of migration control, criminal justice, homeland security, and, to a certain extent, workfare – that the state extends its reach furthest into the private lives of individuals.

Whereas modern states have succeeded in establishing vast coercive bureaucracies, Weber's condition that the exercise of control be recognized as legitimate has presented a much greater challenge to the state. Although few would question the claim that the powers of legitimate coercion should be in the hands of public rather than private actors,[1] the case of coercive social regulation demonstrates that the state's exercise of this authority is in fact highly problematic. The politics of coercive social regulation is regularly marked by intense contestation that can put into question the legitimacy of state intervention.

What renders policies of coercive social regulation so susceptible to conflict is the scope of their societal reach. Importantly, the state's coercive authority is most vulnerable to challenge in liberal democracies. Democratic institutions provide a multitude of opportunities for the representation of societal interests across the various stages of the policy process. In fields of coercive social regulation, the incentive to mobilize against state intervention is particularly strong because state officials impose severe costs upon clearly identifiable individuals (Wilson, 1980). It follows that, because the pluralist institutions of liberal democracy are highly penetrable by those bearing concentrated costs, state actors are regularly confronted with efforts to obstruct the exercise of coercive regulation.

It is not only the openness of its processes, however, that facilitates political challenge to the liberal state's coercive interventions. Democratic institutions are also designed to give expression to fundamental values of liberalism. In the policy realm of social regulation, this discourse plays a particularly pronounced role as opponents of regulation appeal to liberal values in order to denounce state intervention, specifically to the principles of human dignity and individual freedom, and to the proportionality between the means and the ends of state action. Insofar as antiregulatory interests succeed in portraying state intrusions as violations of human dignity, as an excessive infringement of personal freedom, or as the imposition of disproportionate costs upon individuals, they will undermine the legitimacy of state coercion.

In their quest for political influence, both proponents and opponents of state regulation focus their mobilization efforts on the public arena. Crucially, their ability to secure support depends upon the "sensibilities" of the public (Tonry, 2004, p. xii). Not only do mass attitudes toward socially coercive regulation vary over time as periods of relative tolerance alternate with episodes of social backlash (Tonry, 2004), they also differ across social target groups. Not all those subject to regulation, then, are equally likely to appeal successfully to the public. For instance, society is consistently more

---

[1] Where private actors legitimately hold powers of coercion – as is the case with private prisons or detention centers in the United States – this power has to rest on explicit and clearly circumscribed delegation by the state.

likely to throw its support behind nonviolent individuals than behind violent offenders. At the same time, public sympathy for a particular social group is deeply susceptible to political manipulation. It follows that for antiregulatory interests to successfully challenge the legitimacy of coercive social regulation, advocates must strive to "humanize" regulated individuals as deserving community members who are worthy of public support. Proponents of regulation, in turn, stand most to gain from "demonizing" particular social groups as threats to their communities.

This tug-of-war between pro- and antiregulatory interests is the driving force behind the politics of coercive social regulation. And, crucially, the conflict surrounding the legitimacy of state control does not end with the passage of regulatory laws, nor with the judicial review of administrative decisions. Instead, even where administrative decisions have passed legal scrutiny, their legitimacy continues to be questioned. State coercion thus is regularly challenged as illegitimate even where its exercise is legislatively and judicially sanctioned.

Although political contestation is evident across all stages of the policy process, certain interests enjoy their comparative advantage at distinct stages of the policy process. To the extent that a debate frames regulation in generalizing terms – a frame typically employed during the stage of legislative agenda-setting – the demonizing arguments of proregulatory actors are most likely to garner public support. Conversely, where socially coercive regulation is framed in terms of its implications for the individuals concerned – as is the case at the stage of implementation – antiregulatory interests regularly succeed in mobilizing the public.

These forces render the politics of coercive social regulation distinct from other types of public policy. To a much greater extent than is the case with other issue areas, social regulatory policies reflect profoundly normative assumptions. Rules that regulate individual behavior not only "regulate a harm done to society and place a normative value on that harm" (Haider-Markel, 1998, p. 72) but also establish the boundaries between the rights of the individual vis-à-vis the rights of both the state and the larger community. The ensuing conflict is frequently forceful because the costs imposed by the state are not only concentrated, they are also severe. Measures of coercive social regulation, unlike few other interventions of the state, profoundly disrupt the lives of individuals and their families. Furthermore, the normative nature of this conflict has implications for its venue. By contrast to measures of economic regulation, whose subjects prefer to exert political influence privately, the targets of social regulation and their advocates strategically use the public arena to make their case. It is when antiregulatory interests succeed in appealing to the humanitarian values of the public that they stand the best chance of achieving their goals.

Regulatory policies, whether directed at individuals or firms, all hold in common the imposition of concentrated costs. What renders policies of coercive social regulation distinct, however, is the varying salience of policy costs and benefits across policy stages. Whereas at the legislative stage, proregulatory interests typically mobilize the public around the benefits of social regulation, at the stage of implementation, it is antiregulatory interests that instead dominate political debate by drawing attention to regulation's costs. This shift in public attention from policy benefits to costs, then, puts antiregulatory interests in a strong position during the implementation phase and can pose a formidable challenge to state actors charged with the enforcement of such policies. It is to this challenge, and to the conditions underlying state capacity at the various policy stages, that we will now turn.

STATE CAPACITY AT THE STAGE OF LEGISLATION

In order to conceptualize legislative state capacity, we can begin by conceiving of the relationship between the public and legislators as one of principal and agent (Strøm, Müller, & Bergman, 2003). In an ideal-type democracy, legislation arises from voters' delegation of policy-making powers to elected representatives. Although principal–agent models certainly do not require legislative acts to be mirror images of citizens' preferences – even in cases where "the people's will" is clearly discernable – the concept of democratic delegation fundamentally rests on the assumption that lawmakers are in some discernable way responsive to broad public demands. In particular, once legislators identify and endorse a given public mandate – by making corresponding campaign promises, for instance, or by modifying their party platforms – democratic delegation stipulates that, when it comes to writing laws, legislators prioritize the preferences of their public principal over alternative, potentially competing, interests.

Of course, both the concept of "public mandate" and the notion of government responsiveness have been the subject of heated debate among democratic theorists. To avoid conceptual confusion, this study places stringent conditions on the use of "public mandate." Accordingly, the term will only be employed where the presence of a public mandate is generally accepted, that is, where actors across the political spectrum concur that a substantial majority of the electorate holds a clearly identifiable policy preference. Similarly, in order to steer clear of normative debates on the extent of desirable government responsiveness, this analysis will limit itself to instances where legislators have not only recognized the presence of a public mandate but have also expressed a commitment to fulfilling it. Based on these conditions, we will conceive of legislative capacity as the capacity of elected officials to respond to public mandates with laws that reflect these demands in their choice of policy measures.

Interest Articulation in the Politics of Coercive Social Regulation

Legislative behavior is strongly conditioned by the distribution of interests in a given policy area. In fields of coercive social regulation, marked by the diffuse distribution of benefits and the concentrated distribution of costs, legislators are regularly confronted with the competing demands of the public as the unorganized policy beneficiary on the one hand, and on the other hand the claims of well-organized policy losers. Significantly, the strategic advantage of the latter – characteristic of entrepreneurial policy fields more generally – presents a serious challenge to legislators intent on fulfilling public mandates.

The lobbying efforts of opponents of regulation, however, are not the only obstacle in the way of legislating socially coercive policies. Because of their intrinsically normative nature, political battles surrounding these issues also constitute struggles about ideology. Therefore, in addition to facing the opposition of well-organized policy losers, legislators in political systems with strongly programmatic parties may be ideologically constrained in their response to public calls for strict regulation. We will now take a closer look at the distribution of interests in the legislative politics of coercive social regulation.

Proregulatory Preferences of Unorganized Policy Beneficiaries

In fields of coercive social regulation, public opinion is consistently biased against what Arnold calls "politically repellent groups" (1990, p. 80) – welfare recipients, illegal immigrants, and criminal offenders, among others. At the agenda-setting stage, policy issues are typically framed in proregulatory, rights-restricting ways, with public discourse often approximating what sociologists have termed "moral panic" – popular mobilization based on the claim that a particular social group poses a menace to society (Welch, 2002). Given that the targets of coercive policies are individuals "whose claims on public resources are suspect" (Hargrove & Glidewell, 1990, p. 5), demands for stricter regulation of these groups are quickly established (Melnick, 1994).

In their study of agenda-setting, Baumgartner and Jones have used the term "policy image" to describe "how a policy is understood and discussed" (1993, p. 25). In addition to communicating important empirical information, a policy image conveys "emotive appeals" that, the authors argue, make up the "tone" of the image (1993, p. 26). We can thus postulate that, in the legislative arena, coercive social regulatory policies will lend themselves to the employment of policy images that favor the imposition of strict control measures on particular groups. Emphasizing the costs that these groups impose upon society, the tone of policy images will be stigmatizing and punitive.

At the same time, legislative statutes in social regulatory fields often fail to reflect the ardently proregulatory policy preferences of the general public. For instance, in the area of immigration, mass opinion research in the United States has consistently exposed a sizeable gap between restrictionist, proregulatory public opinion, on the one hand, and "expansive" proimmigrant legislation on the other (Simon & Alexander, 1993; Freeman, 1995; Lee, 1998; Gimpel & Edwards, 1999; Fetzer, 2000) – a pattern that Freeman has called the "expansionary bias" of immigration politics (1995). This gap is also evident in Germany and other European countries, yet is somewhat smaller there (Fetzer, 2000; European Monitoring Centre on Racism and Xenophobia, 2001). How can we account for this expansionary bias in the field of immigration? Under what conditions will elected representatives respond to popular demands and pursue coercive regulatory policies?

In fields of coercive social regulation, political conflict, which calls into question the legitimacy of the state's exercise of violence, is fundamentally conditioned by the imposition of overwhelming, and concentrated, costs. James Q. Wilson, in his taxonomy of policy types, which distinguishes policies by the distribution of their costs and benefits, argues that these distributional patterns give rise to distinct political dynamics (1973, 1980). Socially coercive regulatory policies constitute a clear case of entrepreneurial politics. In the case of deportation, regulation imposes high and concentrated costs on immigrants and their families, whereas the purported policy benefits – restoring the integrity of the immigration system, public order, or homeland security – are highly diffuse and difficult to measure (Freeman, 2002).

Significantly, the distribution of costs and benefits in fields of entrepreneurial politics hampers the pursuit of proregulatory policy reform. Because of the diffuse distribution of potential gains, the general public, although overwhelmingly in favor of stricter regulation, is only moderately invested in asserting its interests. In the field of immigration, which is marked by a geographic concentration of immigrants and, correspondingly, popular backlash (Money, 1997), sustained calls for regulation are further limited to particular locales. Consequently, Wilson argues that the unorganized public depends upon political entrepreneurs to represent its interests by drawing attention to particular issues and mobilizing support for reform. These entrepreneurs employ the media and other public forums to raise awareness of the need for stricter regulation and the dangers inherent in the underregulated status quo.

Adding to the diffuse distribution of benefits, public mobilization in social regulatory fields is further hindered by the elusive nature of policy goals. Douglas Arnold argues that where the causal chain linking policy adoption to policy outcome has multiple stages, that is, where "a series of intermediate steps ... must occur before the intended effects can be achieved" (1990, p. 20), policy benefits are highly uncertain, and as a result, citizens are less likely to mobilize. Policy goals such as immigration control and crime reduction constitute multistage policies par excellence, marked by complex causal chains and uncertain outcomes. Multistage policies also render problematic the traceability of any negative policy consequences, that is, the question of whether "a citizen can plausibly trace an observed effect first back to a governmental action and then back to a representative's individual contribution" (1990, p. 47). To the extent that policy consequences are not traceable, Arnold argues that legislators face few incentives to pursue reform measures even when they enjoy broad public support.

Antiregulatory Preferences of Organized Policy Losers

At the same time as the general public faces a collective action problem in asserting its interests, individuals bearing the burdens of regulation face strong incentives to mobilize. As Wilson argues, "when a specific, easily identifiable group bears the costs of a program conferring distributed benefits, the group is likely to feel its burdens keenly and thus to have a strong incentive to organize in order that their burdens be reduced, or at the very least not increased" (Wilson, 1973, p. 334). As a result, legislators who pursue restrictionist regulatory reform will be quickly faced with political opposition by well-organized interests.

What is more, because socially coercive policies naturally conflict with values of individual freedoms and rights, their pursuit regularly triggers ideological conflict. This is particularly pronounced in political systems where parties compete on the basis of programmatic platforms. In these systems, legislators from parties that espouse libertarian or socially progressive ideologies will be further constrained from responding to public calls for harsh regulations.

Given the dual and contradictory demands for both stricter and more lenient regulation, when will legislators pursue socially coercive policy reform? I postulate that, once policy entrepreneurs have succeeded in placing the need for stricter regulation on the political agenda, representatives have at their disposal two distinct strategies of legislative reform. First, representatives can pursue what I call public interest policies: reforms that reflect the substantive interests of the unorganized public. Should legislators pursue public interest policies, they have little choice but to impose significant costs upon organized opposition interests and, in some cases, contend with ideological conflict within their own party. The successful pursuit of public interest policies in contexts marked by clear public mandates thus presents an unequivocal case of legislative capacity.

Alternatively, representatives can pursue private interest policies, which, while being broadly responsive to proregulatory electoral pressure, minimize the costs borne by organized private interests and eschew ideological internal party conflict. In the case of private interest policies, legislators will deflect attention from their failure to legislate public mandates effectively, by including regulatory policy provisions that will nevertheless allow for electoral credit-claiming. For instance, representatives may engage in pork-barreling by authorizing additional fiscal resources for districts in which regulatory demands are strongest. Similarly, elected officials may adopt single-stage policies that will provide short-term, and highly visible, results. However, by eschewing measures of social regulation that would impose significant costs upon organized interests, private interest policies tend to be marked by low levels of policy efficacy.

Under what conditions, then, will legislators opt to impose costs upon concentrated interests by pursuing public interest policies, rather than settling for private interest policies? I contend that we should see public interest policies where the mode of political contestation shifts from entrepreneurial to interest group politics, that is, where well-organized interest groups represent both the losers and winners of policy reform.

Intergovernmental Groups as Public Interest Lobbies
Whereas immigration scholars such as Money (1997, 1999) have focused on voting as a means of public preference articulation, this analysis examines an alternative avenue of interest representation: the lobbying efforts of intergovernmental actors. Because the origins of coercive social regulation are

public in nature, public lobbies perform a crucial function in interest representation. In contrast to private interest groups, these organizations serve as
lobbyists for "a collective good which will not materially benefit only the
members or activists" (Berry, 1977, p. 7). Among public interest groups,
subnational governments fulfill this role best. As Anne Marie Cammisa
points out, "state and local government interest groups are made up of
elected officials who represent the interests of their constituents in contrast
to private lobbying groups whose interests are confined to a more narrow
area" (Cammisa, 1995, p. 16).

Subnational governmental actors can also be powerful agents of public
interest articulation in contexts where political responsiveness is hindered by
ideological conflict. The lower the level of decision-making, the lower is the
likelihood of ideologically driven partisan conflict. Electoral competition at
the municipal level in particular tends to be highly personalized, even in
political systems with strong parties (Wessels, 1999). More generally,
because local – municipal and county – and state governments are most
directly confronted with the costs of regulation and nonregulation alike,
their policy preferences tend to be more pragmatic and less marked by
principled ideological positions (Wells, 2004).

Under what conditions, then, will subnational governments step onto the
stage to act as effective agents of public interest articulation? Drawing on
Campbell and Morgan (2005), we can postulate the following conditions
under which intergovernmental actors are likely to compensate for the
weaknesses of public mobilization and counter the obstruction attempts
of organized policy losers and ideologically driven parties.

First, the preferences of subnational governments need to correspond to
the interests of the unorganized public. It is not essential that intergovernmental actors and the public share the same motivations – what matters here
is convergence at the level of policy preferences. For instance, although
public reactions to immigration may be driven by the perception of cultural
threat, subnational governments may be concerned with reducing the associated fiscal costs. What counts is that, regardless of motivation, both groups
are likely to espouse strong demands for stricter immigration regulation.

Second, in order for subnational governments to compensate for weaknesses in public mobilization, they have to be tightly organized. Moreover, in
cases where public engagement is hindered by the uneven geographic impact
of (non)regulation, intergovernmental actors – local and state officials – can
only overcome this collective action problem if they succeed in forming strong
coalitions across spatial jurisdictions. Finally, a well-developed organizational
infrastructure is of little benefit if it is not matched by political leverage at the

national level. This condition is most likely to be fulfilled in political systems where subnational governments enjoy institutionalized and privileged access to national policy-makers, rather than just being one interest group among many others. Given these characteristics of the politics of coercive social regulation, we can now specify the set of actors whose interests and strategies will fundamentally shape the exercise of legislative capacity.

Actors in the Legislative Politics of Coercive Social Regulation

The legislative politics of coercive social regulation is shaped by the interventions of four sets of actors.

The Public

The general public overwhelmingly supports the coercive regulation of those social groups considered to pose a threat to the common welfare. The strength of public preference articulation, however, depends upon the perceived concentration of the costs of nonregulation. According to Arnold (1990), public preference formation is strongest where (i) the magnitude of costs is high, (ii) citizens live in close proximity to others similarly affected, and (iii) a public instigator (the Wilsonian policy entrepreneur) draws attention to the costs borne by the public.[2] In the case of immigration regulation, these factors most likely apply in locales with high concentrations of immigrants. Citizens in these locations can be said to constitute what Arnold has called attentive publics: they are likely to actively support proregulatory policy initiatives and call for concrete remedial measures.

Although publics in locales with fewer immigrants are more likely to be "inattentive," under certain conditions their "potential" policy preferences (Arnold, 1990) can nevertheless render them influential players in the politics of coercive social regulation. According to Arnold, potential preferences matter politically to the extent that they constitute "preferences which legislators believe might easily be created either by interested parties dissatisfied with legislators' decisions or by future challengers searching for good campaign issues" (1990, pp. 10–11). Although the electorate in locales with low immigrant concentrations is less likely to mobilize in favor of stricter social control, we can assume that its potential preferences will be supportive of

---

[2] Arnold adds a fourth factor, the timing (early- or later-order) of a specific cost or benefit. Because this factor pertains to costs and benefits associated with a concrete proposed policy measure, it is excluded from this discussion.

tighter regulation (Money, 1997). Whether or not national policy-makers take these preferences into account will depend upon the presence of "interested parties" to take on the role of public interest actor.

Public Interest Groups

Intergovernmental actors constitute a public interest group whose interests are closely aligned with those of the broad public. Significantly, groups of subnational governments play a dual role in the politics of coercive social regulation: at the same time as they lobby higher levels of government, they themselves are the target of lobbying efforts by members of the public (Cammisa, 1995). As elected officials, intergovernmental actors are lobbied by taxpayers protesting the costs – both fiscal and nonmaterial – associated with the presence of particular social groups. As intergovernmental lobbies, subnational governments thus face strong incentives, first, to demand increased national resources to meet these costs and, second, to lobby for the stricter regulation of these groups at the national level.

Private Interest Groups

Groups targeted by social regulation face strong incentives to mobilize against coercive measures. Although the targets usually lack the material and political resources for effective lobbying, in many cases, they can rely upon organized advocates to represent their interests. These private interest groups, however, face a distinct disadvantage at the agenda-setting stage where criminalizing policy images dominate and render illegitimate antiregulatory claims. Politicians, eager to appear responsive to the restrictionist demands of the broad public by placing regulatory reform on the legislative agenda, at this stage are unlikely to be receptive to the antiregulatory demands of organized interests. As Arnold argues, "[t]he power of the electoral connection may ... be greater at earlier stages of decision-making, when legislators are deciding which problems to pursue or which alternatives to consider, rather than at the final stages, when legislators are voting on particular amendments, or on a bill's final passage" (1990, p. 269). We can therefore expect the demands of advocates to be most influential at those later stages of the legislative process, which are less exposed to public scrutiny (Guiraudon, 1997).

Legislators

Elected representatives are primarily motivated to pursue strategies that will maximize their opportunity for electoral credit-claiming. As Arnold argued in the context of congressional politics in the United States, "members of

Congress care intensely about reelection. Although they are not single-minded seekers of reelection, reelection is their dominant goal. This means simply that legislators will do nothing to advance their other goals if such activities threaten their principal goal" (1990, p. 5). Accordingly, when weighing the restrictionist demands of the public against the antiregulatory preferences of organized lobbies, or against their party's ideological platform, legislators will carefully consider the electoral implications of their decisions. I argue that as long as public preferences are only weakly articulated, in the final analysis legislators will opt in favor of private interest policies. Private interest policies seek to regulate without imposing significant costs on key organized interests, and they do not require shifts in party ideology. These policies allow representatives to have their cake and eat it too: legislators can engage in electoral credit-claiming without alienating organized interests, or contradicting longstanding party platforms.

Under one condition, however, legislators will pursue public interest policies that do not shy away from imposing policy costs upon organized constituencies, or from imposing ideological costs upon their own parties. For public interest policies to defeat private interest alternatives, intergovernmental lobbies as public interest actors must exercise leverage sufficiently strong to offset the political costs incurred by legislators through the imposition of concentrated costs or the departure from party ideology.

Determinants of Legislative Capacity

Legislating policies of coercive social regulation is a decidedly risky political endeavor that requires elected officials to impose concentrated costs upon organized constituencies and face the prospect of protracted internal party conflict. Our discussion so far has concluded that the pursuit of public interest policies is most likely to occur in contexts where the public is able to piggyback on the lobbying activities of better-organized actors with comparable policy preferences. In the realm of coercive social regulation, subnational governments are most likely to fulfill this role. Once intergovernmental actors exert upward leverage in support of stricter social control, legislators stand to gain politically from pursuing regulatory policies despite the opposition of well-organized private interest actors.

Intergovernmental Relations and Public Interest Articulation

Under what conditions are subnational state actors in a position to exert upward political leverage? At the most basic level, the power of intergovernmental lobbies is determined by the structuring of the vertical relations of government. At one extreme, in unitary states where all constitutional powers are vested in the central government, decentralized units of government often operate at the whim of central policy-makers. In federal states, by contrast, the constitutional protection of subnational (in some cases even local) powers has allowed these governments to develop institutionalized mechanisms for the representation of their spatial interests.

Although all federal systems hold in common the constitutionally enshrined powers of independently elected subnational governments, there is enormous cross-national variation in the precise balance of this vertical separation of powers. Drawing upon Campbell and Morgan (2005), I will examine two distinct aspects of institutional variation that have important implications for the political leverage of intergovernmental lobbies in federal systems. First, there is variance in the capacity of state governments to overcome collective action problems and pool their resources to defend their interests vis-à-vis federal policy-makers. Second, federal systems differ in the degree to which state governments hold institutionalized access to crucial forums of federal decision-making.

The ability of subnational governments to jointly defend their interests at the federal level is principally hindered by the fact that few of the social and economic challenges facing state governments are evenly geographically distributed. As a result, where problems are geographically concentrated, subnational governments that are relatively unaffected have little reason to demand that scarce federal resources be earmarked for issues which are prominent elsewhere. However, some federal systems have in place burden-sharing mechanisms that help states overcome this collective action problem. Among the most prominent of these tools is the horizontal redistribution of tax revenue. Accordingly, where money resources moves from richer to poorer jurisdictions, state governments face strong incentives to pursue collective action because all states share the costs of a particular region's challenges. Horizontal redistribution thus serves to turn a spatially concentrated problem into the problem of all. By contrast, in federal systems where no mechanisms for horizontal redistribution are in place, there are much stronger incentives for "individual states to game the system and maximize federal aid" (Campbell & Morgan, 2005, p. 889).

The capacity to overcome collective action problems is a necessary, but not sufficient, condition for effective intergovernmental lobbying. In order to assert their interests in the federal arena – where policy parameters are largely determined – state actors require institutionalized access to federal policy-makers. Intergovernmental lobbying is therefore most likely to succeed when state governments hold, and routinely exercise, veto power over federal legislation. This is the case where the heads of state governments are either represented in formal intergovernmental decision-making bodies, or hold seats in the federal legislature. On the other hand, where state governments are not institutionally represented in the central policy-making process, their lobbying efforts are likely to fail once they encounter opposition in the federal arena.

Before we put these arguments to the test, the second part of this chapter will examine the question of state capacity at the stage of implementation. Under what conditions, we will ask, will bureaucrats be able to implement policies of coercive social regulation in the face of organized opposition?

STATE CAPACITY AT THE STAGE OF IMPLEMENTATION

A fundamental challenge of representative democracy is to ensure that statutes not only reflect the preferences of the electorate but also are implemented in ways that mirror legislative intent (McCubbins, Noll, & Weingast, 1987). While the first part of this chapter focused on the relationship between the public and its agents in the legislature, this second part treats legislators as principals who delegate the task of implementation to their bureaucratic agents.

Elected Principals and Bureaucratic Agents

As elected principals delegate authority over lower-level decision-making and policy enforcement to bureaucratic agents, statutes oftentimes specify these mandates in great detail. This specificity, of course, does not ensure that bureaucrats will always follow the letter of the law in their day-to-day enforcement routines. On the contrary, as principal–agent scholars remind us, the relationship between legislators and officials is rife with conflict and frequently characterized by divergent preferences. Bureaucratic agents will opportunistically pursue their own interests – leisure (Strøm, Müller, & Bergman, 2003) and budget maximization (Niskanen, 1971), or deviating policy preferences (Huber, 2000) – and shirk implementation unless effectively constrained by their principals (Weingast & Moran, 1983; McCubbins & Kiewiet, 1991). Importantly, control over bureaucratic agents is complicated through agency losses such as moral hazard[3] because much of public

---

[3] The risk that agents will change their behavior after the conclusion of the contract in ways that conflict with the interests of the principal.

servants' action is hidden from the principal (Strøm, Müller, & Bergman, 2003). Policy implementation, it follows, crucially depends upon the principal's postlegislative ability to monitor and intervene in bureaucratic decision-making.

Coercive social regulation should face this dynamic as much as any policy field. Applying the assumptions above to the case of deportation, for instance, we would expect to find a higher likelihood of legally mandated deportation in cases where political principals are able to observe and influence bureaucratic decision-making. However, it is crucial to note that this expectation is based on two key assumptions. First, principal–agent models presume that bureaucrats, left to their own devices, will either shirk implementation altogether, or implement in ways that compromise the goals of the principal. Second, principals are assumed to hold constant preferences that consistently favor the implementation of legislative mandates. The relationship between principals and agents, however, will look quite different wherever either or both of these assumptions do not apply, that is, where bureaucrats are self-motivated to carry out legal mandates or where principals' preferences change.

I argue that in socially coercive policy fields, these two basic assumptions are in fact violated. First, in line with studies of street-level bureaucracy (Kaufman, 1967; Feldman, 1989; Weissinger, 1996), I postulate that bureaucrats are inherently more interested in "working" (Brehm & Gates, 1997) than "shirking." In a second departure from principal–agent models, I contend that, in these policy fields, the postlegislative preferences of principals will systematically differ from their prelegislative preferences. Where agents favor working and where principal preferences are unstable, the institutional conditions favoring successful implementation are naturally very different from those derived from the standard principal–agent model.

The Law Enforcement Preferences of Bureaucrats

The principal–agent literature generally considers the predisposition of the agent to shirk implementation as the key predicament of delegation. With few exceptions,[4] principal–agent scholars have specified bureaucratic unwillingness, rather than incapacity, as the key problem of nonimplementation. As McCubbins, Noll, and Weingast state in their synopsis: "The fundamental premise of this literature is that bureaucrats have personal preferences which conflict with members of Congress and the President.

---

[4] Most notably Huber and McCarty (2004), see also Lupia (2003).

The policy choices of the latter are disciplined by the requirement that periodically they seek ratification of their performance in office by their constituents. The choices of agency officials are not subjected to electoral discipline. Consequently, in the absence of effective oversight, they are likely to reflect personal preferences, derived from some combination of private political values, personal career objectives, and, all else equal, an aversion to effort, especially effort that does not serve personal interests" (1987, p. 247).

However, the premise that the preferences of bureaucrats are incongruent with the implementation of legislative mandates is not supported by the findings of empirical research into public agencies. In what may be the most comprehensive study of bureaucracy to date, Wilson points to the observation – in the light of the principal–agent literature, surprising – that most bureaucrats work, rather than shirk, and attributes this to "[their] desire to do the job" (1989, p. 156). Feldman's study of policy analysts in the Department of Energy is likewise particularly instructive: even though these federal bureaucrats were charged with writing policy memoranda that were unlikely to be read, Feldman found analysts "working hard to produce the information they claimed would be ignored" (1989, p. 1). The observation that social workers in public welfare agencies are strongly motivated to serve their clientele is a well-established finding of the street-level bureaucracy literature (Peabody, 1964; Weatherly, Byrum Kottwitz, Lishner et al., 1980; Goodsell, 1981; Lipsky, 1983; Brehm & Gates, 1997). In a similar vein, studies of coercive bureaucracies reveal intrinsic motivation to fulfill law enforcement mandates. George Weissinger's study of U.S. immigration investigators (1996) finds that street-level officers possess a strong enforcement ethos. Numerous studies of police behavior provide evidence for a strong service commitment among police officers (Reiner, 1992; Etter, 1993) to the extent that law enforcement considerations can take precedence over the protection of civil rights (Skolnick, 1966; Manning, 1977; Manning & Van Maanen, 1978; Skolnick & Fyfe, 1993). Although violent police behavior is clearly problematic, the problem is not one of bureaucratic shirking. In sum, what these empirical studies of administrative behavior hold in common is pervasive evidence in favor of bureaucratic "working," rather than shirking.

Instead of considering bureaucratic agents as primarily motivated by shirking, I propose that their behavior is driven instead by mandate fulfillment. This concept corresponds to what John Brehm and Scott Gates have termed "functional preferences" that describe bureaucratic behavior "where the subordinate acquires utility by performing the very things that he is supposed to do" (1997, p. 75). Provided that legislative mandates conform to the overall mission of the agency, I argue that gaps in implementation will be a function of the incapacity, rather than the unwillingness, of bureaucrats to implement policies. Consequently, effective delegation does not primarily rest on the principal's ability to detect and sanction agent shirking but rather on the principal's extension of support to constrained bureaucratic agents.

The Inconsistent Preferences of Elected Officials

The elegant simplicity of the principal–agent model is compromised by the recognition that the empirical reality of delegation tends to involve several principals. In the American separation of powers system in particular, where this model was initially developed, bureaucratic agents are subject to authority divided not only between the President and the two branches of Congress, but also between the federal and the state governments. As a result, as McCubbins, Noll and Weingast argue, "because they represent different interests, the elected officials in each of these institutions, acting as principals with respect to the agency, will likely seek to influence an agency's policy choices in different directions" (1987, p. 248). In addition to varying across political institutions, the preferences of principals can change over time. This threat of "coalitional drift" means that "the enacting coalition in the statute game must, at the time of enactment, ... consider the prospect of subsequent plays of the status game" (Shepsle, 1992, p. 114).

Although the literature has largely examined coalitional drift in the context of the electoral turnover of principals, we will here examine the problem of principal drift across policy stages. Importantly, although the principal–agent model assumes that the preferences of a given principal are internally consistent and that divergent preferences are the result of multiple principals, I contend that the problem of inconsistent preferences is neither limited to situations that involve multiple principals across different institutions nor to instances of principal turnover. Rather, in fields of coercive social regulation, the preferences of legislators will vary systematically across the stages of legislation and implementation.

Why should the policy preferences of legislators vary across policy stages? Eric Patashnik has argued that the problem of "time-consistency" – politicians reversing course "even when sticking to the original policy would be socially optimal" (2003, p. 209) – results from the difficulty of entering into credible commitments. I propose that, in areas of coercive social regulation, differences in prelegislative and postlegislative preferences can be understood as the result of a systematic change in policy image, and a concomitant shift in public attention, as issues move through the policy cycle. Although the demonizing terms of debate during the legislative stage serve to focus public attention on the benefits of regulation, implementation draws attention to its costs: it brings to the fore the individuals affected by coercive state interventions, many of whom do not fit the criminalizing policy images that dominated prior political debate. To return to the example of deportation, it is at the level of implementation that the human costs of expulsion – the forceful uprooting of persons from their communities, families, and workplaces – become visible.

In a consequential pattern, shifts in policy images regularly "presage changes in patterns of mobilization" (Baumgartner & Jones, 1993, p. 26). As the fates of regulated individuals begin to attract public attention, their advocates will promote and utilize new policy images to augment public support. Significantly, as lobby groups avail themselves of humanitarian policy images to mobilize opposition to social regulation, administrative decisions that may be legally and procedurally correct are reframed as violations of shared norms of human rights and reciprocity. This process of reframing serves to undermine the legitimacy of bureaucratic decisions and, ultimately, threatens the political sustainability (Patashnik, 2003) of socially coercive regulations.

Importantly, although public support is the most critical asset for advocacy groups, it is rarely a sufficient condition for preventing implementation. It is also crucial that antiregulatory interests groups are able to bring public opposition to policy enforcement to the attention of elected officials. Accordingly, those targeted by coercive bureaucratic action stand most to gain by, for instance, calling upon the constituency services provided by their elected representatives. Because casework presents an opportunity for easy electoral credit-claiming, elected officials are likely to be responsive.

Principal–agent scholars have conceived of constituency service as a "fire-alarm" type of control where elected officials rely on members of the public to bring to their attention grievances against administrative agencies (McCubbins & Schwartz, 1984). However, in keeping with the political dynamic of (re)distributive policy areas, this use of the fire-alarm model presumes that the rendering of constituency service will reinforce legislative mandates of service provision. In contrast, I argue that in the case of coercive policies where bureaucrats impose costs, rather than benefits, constituency service creates pressure for nonimplementation.

If it is the case that constituency service promotes nonimplementation, then the assumption of time-inconsistent principal preferences presents a fundamental challenge to the standard principal–agent model. Although the model considers constituency service as a means for reducing bureaucratic shirking, this analysis suggests that, in socially coercive fields where the state imposes significant costs upon its targets, principal–agent models have the dynamic precisely backwards: nonimplementation can in fact be understood as the result of control efforts by elected officials. It follows that bureaucrats are more likely to implement contested policies when they are politically insulated from the interventions of elected officials.

Actors in the Executive Politics of Coercive Social Regulation

The politics of implementation in coercive social regulatory fields is thus shaped by the interaction of four sets of actors.

Advocates

Advocates for regulated groups pursue the nonimplementation of particular policies by means of what I will refer to as "case mobilization." The term describes advocacy efforts by segments of the organized public – for instance, immigrant rights groups – to appeal to bureaucratic actors to exempt particular individuals from enforcement. Because in this conflict, officials, authorized by legislative mandate and executive regulation, hold a structural advantage, regulated individuals and their advocates will attempt to draw previously uninvolved actors into the arena of implementation – a strategy E.E. Schattschneider famously termed the "socialization" of conflict (1975). However, not all socialization is equal. As we will see, advocates are most likely to succeed when they can secure the support of elected officials. In particular, advocates will try to exploit the incentives that elected representatives have to invest in the provision of constituency service – incentives observed across advanced democracies (Norris, 2003). Significantly, because individuals stand to lose a great deal from the implementation of coercive policy measures, those targeted by bureaucratic action are particularly likely to call upon the constituency services provided by their elected politicians.

Not all those subject to regulation, however, stand to gain from case mobilization. The success of case mobilization depends on the ability of advocates to portray regulation as an inhumane act of state coercion. Case mobilization thus will have more efficacy for those whose characteristics most easily lend themselves to humanitarian arguments in favor of clemency.

Elected Politicians

Politicians are primarily motivated by the electoral payoff of their actions (Downs, 1997). However, I contend that the policy preferences deriving from electoral motivations are not constant but vary across the stages of the policy process. In the legislative arena, politicians respond to the pro-regulatory preferences of a majority of the unorganized public by voting in favor of the general principle of coercive regulation. As the issue of social regulation moves downward to the level of implementation, however, the fate of the individual becomes salient. By focusing attention on the disproportionate human costs of policy enforcement in specific "deserving" cases, advocates are able to switch criminalizing policy images dominant at the legislative stage with humanitarian images far less favorable to aggressive social regulation. Thus, to the extent that politicians consider case mobilization as an opportunity for blame-avoidance or even credit-claiming, they will place pressure on bureaucrats to refrain from policy enforcement.

Street-Level Bureaucrats

Bureaucrats at the front lines of implementation most clearly embody Wilson's ideal of "careerists" (1980, p. 375). Careerists distinguish themselves first, by identifying their careers with the agency and its mission. As Weissinger's study of U.S. immigration investigators (1996) shows, careerists in coercive bureaucracies – immigration officers and their mid-level managers – share a strong law enforcement ethos. This conception of public officials fundamentally contradicts the standard principal–agent model's assumption of shirking as a key attribute of bureaucratic behavior. Second, careerists do not stand to gain professional rewards from external constituencies like advocates, instead placing a high premium on autonomy from nonbureaucratic actors (Wilson, 1980). It follows that because case mobilization presents a threat to both their professional norms and their decision-making autonomy, bureaucrats will try to resist attempts by nonbureaucratic actors to intervene in case decisions.

Executive Agency Leaders

Once case mobilization has raised the political salience of a particular case, bureaucratic decision-making shifts from the street level up to the level of senior executive decision-making. Executive agency leaders, unlike the street-level bureaucrats they oversee, are primarily concerned with the political implications of their decisions. Their survival in office depends on the fortunes of an electoral coalition, on the support of their party in the legislature, or on maintaining good relations with important legislators. To the extent that the implementation of contested decisions undermines these sources of support, senior executives will rule in favor of nonimplementation.

Given this constellation of actors, preferences, and strategies, the likelihood of implementation in conflictual situations should depend upon two factors: first, the degree to which bureaucracies are insulated from the interventions of elected officials; and, second, where bureaucratic insulation is strong, the incentives of agency leaders once the case decisions have shifted to higher administrative levels. Accordingly, executive capacity will be strong if bureaucratic agencies are politically insulated and if their leaders have reason to favor unwavering implementation. Conversely, if neither condition holds, executive capacity should be weak. Finally, to the extent that proregulatory executive policy preferences can offset the lack of bureaucratic insulation, and vice versa, we should observe an intermediate level of executive capacity in cases where only one condition is present.

Determinants of Executive Capacity

Institutions, by structuring the horizontal and vertical relations of power in political systems, place constraints on the ability of individual actors to pursue their own preferences (Weaver & Rockman, 1993). Let us then examine the institutional configurations that will maximize executive capacity, first, by insulating bureaucratic agencies and, second, by providing their leaders with incentives to proceed with policy enforcement even in high-conflict situations.

Agency Insulation

What institutional structures most clearly define the relationship between bureaucratic agencies and their elected principals? The first, and most obvious, variable of interest is the institutional structuring of executive–legislative relations. This relationship most distinctly varies between separation of powers systems, on the one hand, and parliamentary systems, on the other, though we can also expect to find significant variation within each of these two systems of government.

To put it simply, parliamentary systems are marked by executive dominance (Lijphart, 1999) because the executive shares its constituency with the parliamentary majority and because the cohesive powers of party discipline enable the executive to rely in general upon the loyalty of its parliamentary party group. Whereas a parliament has the right to dissolve a government through a vote of no confidence, party discipline and the threat of new elections tend to prevent legislators from using this ultimate constitutional weapon against ministers of their own party. And although there are limits to how far governments can go in pursuing legislative agendas that are not endorsed by their parliamentary party group, executives have little to fear from the particularistic demands of individual legislators – in particular backbenchers – as the powers of the latter's are highly circumscribed. In parliamentary democracies, then, legislative oversight is exercised by parties, rather than by individual parliamentarians. Significantly, party oversight rarely presents a threat to the decision-making autonomy of bureaucratic agencies. At the same time as governing parties have few incentives to flex their muscles of oversight – except, maybe, behind closed doors – opposition parties lack the political power for effective control, except in the unusual case of minority government.

In presidential systems, by contrast, executives cannot consistently rely upon the support of their legislative copartisans because they hold separate electoral mandates from legislators and usually operate in the absence of party cohesion. Individual representatives, however, greatly benefit from the legislature's decentralized structure that affords them significant political powers through, for instance, committee leadership positions. Executive agency leaders, who need to secure the support of individual legislators to enact their policy programs, will often find it necessary to accommodate their particularistic requests (Cain, Ferejohn & Fiorina, 1987). As a result, we would expect senior executives in presidential systems to be less insulated from individual legislators than executives in parliamentary systems. In turn, organized interests opposed to socially coercive interventions should have greater success in curbing implementation through pressure on elected officials in presidential than in parliamentary contexts.

A second and a closely related institutional factor is the strength of political parties. Differences in party strength give rise to variation not only in the intensity of elected officials' motivations to provide constituency service, but also in their capacity to do so. First, in parliamentary systems, parties function as gatekeepers to the resources that constituency service would require. Because of their pivotal function in mediating political careers, parties "[restrict] access to resources and opportunities that would allow legislative members to build strong personal ties to their constituencies" (Cain, Ferejohn, & Fiorina, 1987, p. 15). Second, the careers of legislators in strong party systems depend primarily upon the electoral strength of their parties and on the support of their party leaders, and to a much lesser extent on personalized links with the electorate (Persson, Roland, & Tabellini, 1997). As a result, elected representatives in polities with strong parties face weaker incentives to engage in constituency service than do their counterparts in weak party systems, even when controlling for differences in electoral rules (Cain, Ferejohn, & Fiorina, 1987).

In presidential systems, by contrast, legislators operate within decentralized legislative structures that are highly penetrable to the particularized interests of individual legislators. Representatives receive weak support from their party organizations, are less dependent on these organizations for resources, and find their electoral fortunes only moderately tied to the popularity of their party label. In this more personalized environment, incumbents not only are strongly motivated to engage in electoral credit-claiming by means of casework, but are also more likely to have direct access to the necessary material resources.

Because of the stronger motivations and greater opportunities for constituency service in presidential systems, executive agencies will be more exposed to the intervention of elected officials than their counterparts in parliamentary polities. To the extent that there is institutional variation in strength of party affiliation across and within parliamentary systems, we should observe more activist constituency service – and, thus, lower degrees of agency insulation – in jurisdictions where elected officials have weaker party ties.

Agency insulation within a given political regime is not always constant. Specifically, where implementation is under the jurisdiction of subnational governments, bureaucratic insulation is likely to vary across jurisdictions. What matters here is the locus of political scrutiny – the level at which elected officials exercise oversight over bureaucrats. The locus of oversight shapes the scope of agency insulation by determining the ease with which advocates can gain access to the constituency services of elected politicians. *Ceteris paribus*, the more local the level of oversight, the easier it will be for advocates to mobilize elected representatives. Because personalized links between elected officials and their constituencies are the strongest at the local level (Norris, 2003), advocates will find access easiest there. Case mobilization should thus be most successful where oversight is exercised by local politicians. Having specified the institutional conditions under which we can expect agency insulation from the particularistic demands of elected officials to be strongest, we will turn to a second condition of executive capacity: the ideological incentives of agency leaders to pursue the consistent implementation of coercive policies.

Party Ideology

The implementation of coercive policies, I have argued, will be most likely in institutional contexts where bureaucratic agencies enjoy substantial autonomy from the particularistic demands of their elected overseers. We would therefore expect executive capacity to be strongest in parliamentary systems with powerful and cohesive political parties. At the same time, predicting how agency leaders in parliamentary contexts will exercise this autonomy requires us to take into account a noninstitutional factor: party ideology. Although senior executives need not heed the particularistic requests of parliamentarians, they do have strong reasons to make policy decisions that tend toward their parties' ideological center of gravity. Sharp divergences with their parliamentary group can risk broad revolt that will threaten their government's tenure in office, their own tenure and advancement within cabinet, and their government's support within its electoral base.

It follows that to the extent that policy positions vary across parties, ministers affiliated with parties that espouse libertarian or socially progressive positions on coercive regulation are less likely to endorse the contested decisions of street-level bureaucrats than are ministers from parties with socially conservative platforms. It is crucial to note the difference between this dynamic and the dynamic of political interference in presidential systems. In parliamentary contexts, ministerial efforts to temper bureaucratic zeal will derive not from the need to serve small groups of constituents but from generalized pressures to preserve ideological consistency within the party.

Having specified the conditions under which we should expect legislative and executive state actors to wield their powers of coercive social regulation, the following chapters will apply this theoretical framework to the politics of deportation in Germany and the United States. Chapter 2 investigates the capacity of elected representatives to legislate policies of coercive social regulation, while Chapter 3 examines the logic of senior executive decision-making when selecting for implementation some legislative provisions over others. Finally, Chapter 4 looks at the difficult challenges faced by street-level bureaucrats when implementing deportation orders.

2

The Legislative Politics of Migration Control

Nobody wants to be seen as soft on crime and illegal immigration.
(Former legislative director for Congressman Ed Bryant, (R-TN), Washington,
D.C., August 26, 2006)

In the early 1990s, widespread anti-immigration backlash propelled the issue of migration control onto the legislative agendas of the German Bundestag and the U.S. Congress. In both countries, public debate was dominated by vociferous claims that the state had lost control over its borders: in Germany, calls for stricter regulation converged on the rapidly expanding number of asylum seekers, whereas in the United States, protests targeted the country's growing population of undocumented immigrants. Importantly, legislators in both contexts were exposed to strong pressures to enact restrictionist immigration reform.

This, however, is where the cross-national similarities end. Even though immigration control featured saliently in public debates in both countries – a condition that might lead us to expect corresponding legislative responsiveness (Soroka & Wlezien, 2004) – the outcome of subsequent reform initiatives differed substantially. In Germany, legislators enacted public interest policies – statutes that corresponded to the substantive concerns of the public and that provided for the appropriate measures to achieve their goals. By categorically excluding migrants from certain countries from access to the system, German parliamentarians enacted a drastic measure – even clearing the hurdle of constitutional reform – that succeeded in lowering the number of asylum seekers and defusing widespread anti-immigrant backlash. The U.S. Congress, by contrast, while passing one of the most draconian immigration control bills in the nation's history, eschewed exactly those policy provisions that would have best met public demands for reducing illegal immigration: measures designed to deter the employment of undocumented immigrants. Confronted with opposition by organized interests to stricter worksite enforcement, legislators decided to settle for what I call private interest policies. Skirting measures that would impose concentrated costs on private interests, Congress instead increased control provisions that allowed for credit-claiming without alienating organized constituencies.

This chapter pursues the argument that the capacity of legislators to enact public interest policies can be best understood in terms of the availability of institutionalized channels of public interest articulation. Owing to the inherent collective action problem described in the previous chapter, there were no public interest groups that could match the organizational and political resources of private interest lobbies. In both countries, subnational governments stepped into the void and took on the role of public interest actor. In Germany, the institutional ordering of intergovernmental relations allowed state actors to pool their resources and use their veto power to lobby effectively for the restrictionist demands of the public at the federal level. In the United States, by contrast, subnational governments struggled to overcome internal conflicts of interest and at the same time lacked political clout at the federal level. As a result, Congress passed a bundle of private interest policies that differed fundamentally from the public interest reforms enacted by the German Bundestag.

This chapter's substantive scope will be considerably wider than that of the remaining empirical chapters. Although the study of implementation can be easily limited to the case of deportation, in the legislative realm there is no such thing as deportation law. Instead, the removal provisions that are the subject of inquiry in Chapters 3 and 4 were passed as a much larger body of immigration law. In order to understand the legislative politics of deportation, then, we need to study the larger enterprise of immigration reform.

THE LEGISLATIVE POLITICS OF IMMIGRATION CONTROL IN GERMANY

In 1993, after one of the most heated debates in the history of postwar Germany, the two houses of parliament passed the supermajority hurdle of constitutional reform and enacted far-reaching measures of immigration control. In a move that had seemed inconceivable only a year earlier, the Social Democratic Party (SDP) departed from its longstanding ideological opposition to amending the Basic Law's asylum provisions and acquiesced in a reform effort that was to transform Germany's asylum system from one of relative openness to one of tight closure. The following analysis will examine the factors underlying this remarkable development.

The Public Mandate for Asylum Control

With the fall of the Iron Curtain, the number of asylum seekers crossing into Germany soared. Although numbers had been rising steadily throughout the previous decades – annual applications averaged at 5,000 in the 1960s, 17,000 in the 1970s, and 78,000 in the 1980s – the demand placed on the asylum system in the early 1990s was unparalleled in its magnitude: applications more than quadrupled between 1988 and 1992, culminating in a historic high of 438,200.[1] This upsurge in the population of asylum seekers presented municipalities and counties with daunting policy challenges. Charged with providing public housing and income support for applicants, many local communities struggled to find the resources at a time when they were also facing rising public assistance caseloads. The fiscal strain on local communities is clearly reflected in municipal social expenditure data: whereas, between 1981 and 1991 annual increases in municipal social spending ranged between 6 and 9 percent, expenditures in 1992 increased by 24 percent over the previous year and continued to rise by 16 percent in 1993 (Schwarze, 2000).

This dramatic development sparked a national debate that distinguished itself, by its scope and intensity, from earlier episodes of backlash against asylum seekers. This discussion was driven by grassroots public demands for a more restrictive asylum policy – demands that were reflected in opinion polls, articulated at elections, and most problematically, expressed through violent means by right-wing fringes of society. This debate was propelled by vociferous calls for a crackdown on "asylum abuse" by "economic migrants" (*Wirtschaftsflüchtlinge*) and "bogus asylum seekers" (*Scheinasylanten*). Correspondingly, in a 1991 poll by the weekly *Der Spiegel*, a staggering 96 percent of respondents expressed support for keeping out "economic migrants" (Marshall, 2000). In a 1992 survey by the magazine, 77 percent of those surveyed thought that foreigners abused the welfare system, 74 percent agreed that they worsened the housing shortage for

---

[1] Bundesamt für Migration und Flüchtlinge, "Asyl in Zahlen 2006," http://www.bamf.de/cln_006/nn_442496/SharedDocs/Anlagen/DE/DasBAMF/Publikationen/broschuere-asyl-in-zahlen-2006,templateId=raw,property=publicationFile.pdf/broschuere-asyl-in-zahlen-2006.pdf

native Germans, and 59 percent concurred that foreigners were "a danger on the streets" (Steiner, 2000). In October 1992, another survey by the same magazine showed that "getting the problem of foreigners under control" had become the single most important issue to Germans in the West and second only to "economic development" to East Germans (Steiner, 2000). Most disconcerting for the mainstream political parties, 16 percent of respondents in 1992 stated that they considered the anti-immigrant extreme right *Republikaner* party to be most competent in dealing with the "foreigner problem" (Steiner, 2000).

Meanwhile, the public used local and Land-level[2] elections to register their discontent with the status quo. Two electoral trends in particular served as wake-up calls to the political mainstream. First, there was a substantial amount of protest voting in favor of previously unrepresented extreme parties, sending the *Republikaner* and the DVU (*Deutsche Volksunion*) into several Land parliaments and municipal councils. Second, among the two major parties, electoral losses were particularly pronounced for the Social Democrats (SPD) who – in line with longstanding ideological commitments – were running on a less restrictionist immigration platform than the governing Christian Democrats (CDU/CSU).

In September 1991, the Land and municipal elections in the northern city-state of Bremen sent shockwaves through the political establishment as the neo-Nazi DVU entered the Land parliament with 6.2 percent of the vote. As a single-issue party that had campaigned on a platform of immigration control, the DVU benefited from anti-immigrant grassroots sentiment, in particular in economically depressed districts where the party secured up to 16.8 percent of the vote (*Süddeutsche Zeitung*, October 1, 1991a). The SPD, in stark contrast, lost a staggering 12 percent of the vote, forfeiting their absolute majority for the first time in two decades (Marshall, 2000). Similarly, at the municipal level, the party suffered its worst electoral defeat since 1951.

Subsequent political analyses attributed the SPD's disastrous results to the pervasive public perception that the party's leadership was incapable of adopting sufficiently tough measures to resolve the asylum crisis (May, 1992). The chair of the SPD in Bremen, Ilse Janz, publicly blamed the party's catastrophic election results on its failure to come to terms with the public's concerns about asylum seeking: "We weren't sufficiently concerned. We underestimated it, we didn't take the issue seriously enough" (*Süddeutsche Zeitung*, October 1, 1991a). In a similar assessment, political

---

[2] The state or provincial level.

commentators argued that the success of right-wing parties "show[ed] the danger that the state faces when its democratic parties refuse to move from the stage of empty rhetoric to one of collective and responsible action in the asylum question, to adopt actions that its citizens understand and accept" (*Braunschweiger Zeitung*, cited in *Süddeutsche Zeitung*, October 1, 1991b).

On April 6, 1992, the electorate of the affluent southwestern Land Baden-Württemberg dealt a major blow to the established political parties. Mirroring developments elsewhere, opinion polls leading up to the elections had showed "asylum seekers" to be the most salient concern to the Land's public (Forschungsgruppe Wahlen Mannheim, 1992). Consequently, the extreme-right *Republikaner* party increased their share of the vote from 1 percent to a confounding 10.9 percent and entered the Landtag as the third strongest party group ahead of the Liberals and Greens (*Süddeutsche Zeitung*, April 6, 1992). Although the electoral losses were most pronounced for the ruling CDU/CSU – with a drop of 9.4 percentage points, they lost their absolute majority and were forced to enter into a grand coalition with the SPD – the results were also of particular concern to the SPD: postelection analyses showed that the *Republikaner* had made significant inroads into the SPD's core electorate. Blue collar voters, the values of whom had always been traditionally toward the left, made up over 40 percent of the *Republikaner* votes (Marshall, 2000).

Just as after the success of the DVU in Bremen, the rise of the extreme-right vote in Baden-Württemberg was considered a profound threat to democracy. Dieter Spöri, the leader of Baden-Württemberg's SPD, described the election results as a "serious crisis of the democratic party system of Baden-Württemberg" and a "shot across the bows of party democracy" (*Süddeutsche Zeitung*, April 6, 1992). Finally, just one day after the Baden-Württemberg debacle, elections in Schleswig-Holstein dealt yet another blow to the political establishment. Paralleling the Bremen election, the DVU entered the Landtag with 6.3 percent of the vote, whereas support for the SPD fell by 8.6 percent. In the course of just seven months, electorates across the country had shown consistent backing for right-wing parties, eroding the support base of the CDU/CSU and, most pronounced, the SPD. The timing of widespread defeat could hardly have been worse, given that the parties were facing the "super election year" of 1994 that featured not only federal elections but also Land and local elections in a total of 8 Länder, in addition to European Parliament elections.

While the electorate used Land and local elections as plebiscites on the asylum issue, attacks on foreigners by the radical right surged. Whereas in

1990 about 300 right-wing attacks against foreigners were recorded, by 1992, this number had surged to 2,000. One of the most aggressive of these attacks, a one-week siege by skinheads of two apartment buildings in the Saxon town of Hoyerswerda in September 1991, became the symbol of widespread fears about a further escalation of anti-immigrant violence. Most disturbingly, the siege, which culminated in the firebombing of a dormitory, was cheered by large groups of neighbors. Unable to contain the violence, German authorities bused more than 200 residents of the apartments to secret locations, leaving the town in the words of a jubilant bystander, "foreigner-free." Concerns about the rise of political extremism were not confined to the domestic arena. In a damning analysis of the violence in Hoyerswerda, *The New York Times* denounced the incident as "the first time that political leaders had bowed to the demands of violent racists" (*The New York Times*, October 1, 1991).

Fulfilling the Mandate: Constitutional Reform as Public Interest Policy

The Puzzle of Constitutional Asylum Reform

When a wave of anti-immigrant sentiment swept the country in the post-unification period, it was not the first time that Germany's asylum policy had come under pressure for reform. Since the late 1970s, the politics of migration had been driven by restrictionist – though rarely highly salient – public pressure. The asylum laws in place in the early 1990s were the product of countless incremental reforms, designed to speed up a progressively clogged-up adjudication process and to deter migrants from (ab)using the system for economic purposes. Past reform policies had included measures such as cuts in welfare benefits, work prohibitions, mandatory dormitory accommodation, and the curtailment of procedural rights. Nevertheless, by the early 1990s, there was a general consensus that the system, designed to adjudicate individual claims, was no longer capable of handling the hundreds of thousands of asylum applications.

Although there was agreement on the need for reform, there was no consensus on specific proposals. Parties to the left argued that policy failure was essentially the result of the system's acute shortfall in resources. If policy-makers were to commit a sufficiently large budget and create new positions for adjudicators and administrative judges, party officials contended, the asylum process would be much accelerated and, as a result, would reduce the fiscal strain on local communities. This proposal did not, however, enjoy much popular support. Because the fiscal costs of asylum immigration had been at the very center of anti-immigrant backlash, any policy solution that was to entail a commitment of substantial additional public resources was bound to elicit further protest.

By contrast, parties to the right argued that the system was irreparably broken and subject to extensive exploitation by economic migrants. As the notion of asylum abuse became the linchpin of political immigration debates, conservatives increasingly called for a change to the Basic Law's Article 16. This provision, which stated that "persons persecuted on political grounds shall have the right of asylum," gave eligible foreign nationals a legally enforceable claim against the German state. The constitutionally enshrined right to asylum had been adopted in the light of Germany's Holocaust past and the experience of political exile by the Republic's founding fathers and had been politically sacrosanct until the mid-1980s. As recently as the 1985/1986 parliamentary debate on (statutory) asylum reform, all parties had fully endorsed Germany's constitutional right to asylum.

By the mid-1980s, however, restrictionist policy entrepreneurs – in particular members of Bavaria's conservative CSU (Christian Social Union) – started to publicly call into question the continued viability of Article 16 (Höfling-Semnar, 1995). In 1990, Bavaria's governor Max Streibl (CSU) submitted to the Bundesrat – the parliament's upper house – a bill proposing the abolition of Article 16. Only months later, Baden-Württemberg's governor Lothar Späth (CDU) submitted a similar proposal to the chamber (Höfling-Semnar, 1995). Although at this point there was little doubt that constitutional reform would not attract the necessary bipartisan support, the CDU/CSU nevertheless succeeded in breaking a longstanding political taboo by placing the issue on the public agenda.

By 1991, calls for constitutional change were no longer restricted to the conservative wing of the governing CDU/CSU. Within the CDU, which had initially been reluctant to endorse the policy demands of the Bavarian CSU, a consensus had emerged in favor of amending Article 16. In endorsing this drastic measure of asylum reform, the party could point to overwhelming public support for constitutional change. In a 1991 poll by *Der Spiegel*, 72 percent of the respondents in the West and 77 percent in the East supported restricting the Basic Law's right to asylum (Schwarze, 2000).

However, the rest of the political mainstream – Liberals, Social Democrats, and Greens – maintained their ideological opposition to this policy option. The resistance of these left-of-center parties to constitutional reform was also shared by the Protestant and Catholic churches, by human rights and refugee organizations, and, internationally, by the United Nations High Commissioner for Refugees. These interests fiercely opposed the proposal on the grounds that it would pose a fundamental threat to the principle of refugee protection. The Catholic conference of bishops in 1991 and 1992 passed resolutions that categorically rejected reforming Article 16 (*Süddeutsche Zeitung*, October 5, 1992; September 21, 1992). The prominent refugee lobby "*pro asyl*" sharply attacked the CDU/CSU's policy proposal, arguing that it was "the bloody duty of democrats to protect the Basic Law" (pro asyl, 1992).

Yet, in June 1993, the Bundestag passed the supermajority hurdle and, with the support of the CDU, CSU, FDP, and, most significantly, the SPD, voted for a constitutional amendment to the Basic Law's Article 16. Although preserving the individual right to political asylum, the new Article 16a categorically denied access to certain groups. First, migrants arriving via a "safe third country" could no longer file asylum applications in Germany because, it was argued, they would have had the opportunity to do so in their country of transit. Because all of Germany's neighbors were now considered "safe third countries," this clause in effect barred all individuals entering across land borders from applying for asylum. Second, nationals of "safe countries of origin" were equally denied access to the asylum process. Third, in addition to asylum seekers from "safe countries of origin," individuals whose applications were considered "manifestly unfounded" were now subject to an expedited removal process that precluded access to suspensive[3] judicial review (Nuscheler, 1995).

It was not long before these far-reaching constitutional changes showed their desired effect. By 1994, the number of asylum applications had fallen to just over 127,000 – a drop of over 70 percent compared to 1992. By 1998, the number of applications for the first time in ten years did not surpass the 100,000 mark, and has since remained below this threshold. Although it is not possible to quantify the independent impact of asylum reform on the number of claimants, there is little doubt that its effect has been substantial. For instance, whereas in 1992, over 135,000 Romanians and Bulgarians filed asylum applications, in 1994 – when these countries were considered safe countries of origin and transit – they filed just under 13,000 applications.[4]

The success of the new asylum clause was not limited to its policy efficacy. Most importantly, the reform succeeded in bringing an end to the escalation of anti-immigrant sentiment and right-wing violence. As the

---

[3] Under suspensive judicial review individuals are protected from deportation until their appeal is adjudicated.

[4] Bundesamt für Migration und Flüchtlinge. http://www.bafl.de/template/index_asylstatistik. htm, (accessed December 1, 2004, page now discontinued).

liberal weekly *Die Zeit* commented: "The new law was intended to bring calm to the land. In this, it has succeeded – on the backs of those seeking asylum" (*Die Zeit*, July 1, 1994, cited in Marshall, 2000, p. 96). Opinion polls showed a marked decline in the salience of the asylum issue in the postreform period. Whereas in the summer of 1992, 78 percent of West Germans considered asylum seekers and foreigners "the most important issue," this proportion fell to 32 percent in September 1993, and 7 percent in 1995 (Marshall, 2000, p. 96). Tellingly, attempts by the CSU to return the issue to the political agenda during the 1994 federal elections failed (Nuscheler, 1995), and extreme right parties performed poorly at both the Land and federal levels (Marshall, 2000).

The amendment of the Basic Law constitutes a remarkable development in German immigration politics. As pointed out, from 1949 until the mid-1980s, there was a solid consensus across the mainstream party spectrum on the inviolability of this constitutional protection. Importantly, even after the CDU/CSU had abandoned their unqualified support for Article 16, the SPD's principled opposition – fiercely supported by religious and human rights groups – remained the key obstacle to the passage of constitutional reform. At its party congress in 1989, the SPD affirmed its unconditional support for the asylum clause: "The right to asylum for those fleeing political persecution has to remain an unrestricted entitlement" (cited in Schwarze, 2000, p. 128, my translation[5]). The left wing of the party in particular was unwavering in its support for Article 16, "even if this meant putting principle before electoral support" (Marshall, 2000, p. 93). Vice chairperson Däubler-Gmelin at the party's special congress in 1992 argued that the constitutional right of asylum was an integral part of the SPD's identity: "The constitutional right to asylum for the politically persecuted ... has constituted and continues to constitute an integral part of the identity of the Social Democrats, which we collectively carry on" (*Sozialdemokratische Partei Deutschlands*, 1992, p. 20, cited in Schwarze, 2000, p. 230).

What, then, can account for the SPD's volte-face on the constitutional protection of asylum? Why did the party in its special congress in November 1992 decide to acquiesce to a revision of the Basic Law's Article 16? Given the political costs of curtailing the constitutional right of asylum – the vocal protest of churches and human rights groups, the associated threat of alienating progressive constituencies who would defect to the Greens, and, most importantly, the party's surrendering of a principle central to its identity – the SPD stood to lose much from constitutional reform.

---

[5] All translations from German to English are by the author.

The party's policy reversal in 1992, I argue, can be understood as the outcome of concerted intergovernmental lobbying, facilitated by a particular structure of center–periphery relations. Germany's horizontal burden-sharing arrangements provided the institutional conditions that allowed for the restrictionist demands first expressed at the municipal level to spread across the country quickly. Intergovernmental lobbies of municipal and Land officials shared the public's demands for fundamental reform and, through their lobbying efforts, divided the Social Democratic Party internally. Importantly, as powerful political actors in the policy process, subnational governments were able to shape policy reform enduringly, far beyond the agenda-setting stage.

Intergovernmental Lobbying as a Means of Public Interest Articulation

Whereas federal party politics in the early 1990s was characterized by fierce battles over asylum policy, the municipal level witnessed the emergence of a bipartisan consensus in favor of curtailing the relevant constitutional rights. Among the different levels of government, it was municipal and county politicians who were most exposed to the fiscal and social costs of asylum seeking. Importantly, demands for reform came from politicians across the many municipalities. In accordance with Germany's horizontal burden-sharing arrangements mandated by Article 72 of the Basic Law, which commands "the establishment of equal living conditions throughout the federal territory," asylum seekers had been dispersed across the Länder and local communities since the 1970s (Schwarze, 2000). This administrative arrangement had important political ramifications. Although burden-sharing, which was based on the population size of municipalities, allowed for the even distribution of the fiscal costs of asylum processing across the country, once numbers rose rapidly no region was exempt from the costs of additional social provision. As a result, horizontal burden-sharing created strong incentives for local governments across the country to mobilize and to lobby their demands collectively.

The policy positions of the Christian Democratic Party leadership, who, by the late 1980s, had endorsed the need for more fundamental asylum reform, cannot be understood without reference to the restrictionist demands of their local functionaries. Not surprisingly, it was the Bavarian CSU, the strongly regionally oriented sister party of the CDU, whose demands went furthest and which was the first to propose constitutional change (Schwarze, 2000). By contrast, local party functionaries to the left faced a much longer uphill battle in their attempt to influence the policy positions of their federal party group.

In their role as public interest actors – articulating both their own demands and those of the public – representatives of local governments pursued two complementary strategies. On the one hand, prominent local SPD officials, in particular the mayors of major cities, publicly broke with their party leadership and advocated constitutional asylum reform. On the other hand, local governments collectively voiced their restrictionist demands through influential intergovernmental lobbies, such as the German Conference of Cities (*Deutscher Städtetag*). In each case, politicians used their positions as independently elected representatives of local publics to exert pressure on the Social Democratic Party leadership to consent to constitutional reform.

German political parties have a substantial stake in municipal and county government: politicians who attain prominence in local politics embody powerful interests. They are major assets to their parties, and federal and Land party organizations do well to respect the interests of prominent local officials (Johnson, 1982). Traditionally, this has been particularly the case for the SPD, as Nevil Johnson argues: "No national leader of the Social Democrats . . . can be indifferent to the fact that much of the strength of the party lies in its record in the major cities of the country" (1982, p. 151). At the same time, because mayors are independently elected officials with their own constituencies, federal leaders have limited means at their disposal to enforce discipline on those local officials who stray from the party line.

In the early 1990s, a number of prominent Social Democratic mayors publicly defied their party's position on asylum and instead endorsed the CDU/CSU's demands for constitutional change. During the 1991 municipal electoral campaign, for instance, the SPD mayor of Bremen, Klaus Wedemeier, announced that he would henceforth reject any asylum-mapplications by Polish or Romanian nationals (Schwarze, 2000). Similarly, Georg Kronawitter, the hugely popular SPD mayor of Munich, made national headlines with his statements defying the party line on this issue. In an interview with the prominent weekly *Der Spiegel*, Kronawitter echoed the CDU/CSU's demands to deny nationals from several Eastern European countries access to asylum, arguing that Germany could no longer afford its overly liberal asylum provisions. Unless parliament put a stop to the continued influx of foreigners, Kronawitter warned, "there will be a public uprising." Germany, he argued, could no longer serve as "the dumping ground for the world's poor" (*Süddeutsche Zeitung*, September 7, 1992). When faced with vocal opposition from his Social Democratic copartisans, Kronawitter pointed to his electoral mandate and argued that he, unlike the party leadership, took the public's concerns seriously (*Süddeutsche Zeitung*, December 2, 1992). Kronawitter's opposition to the status quo was not confined to political rhetoric. After the assignment of a large group of asylum seekers to Munich, the mayor announced that the city was confronted with an "acute emergency" and, in a highly provocative move, ordered mobile homes erected on the prominent site of the city's cherished *Oktoberfest* (*Süddeutsche Zeitung*, April 13, 1992).

The CDU/CSU was quick to instrumentalize, and further provoke, these divisions within the SPD. In 1991, CDU secretary-general Volker Rühe sent a letter to all Land, county, and municipal CDU leaders with materials – including press statements, parliamentary questions, and talking points – that could be used to divide local SPD officials against their federal party leaders (Höfling-Semnar, 1995). Outlining this strategy, the letter argued: "the SPD's refusal [to consider constitutional change] ... has a particularly strong impact on local authorities who have to house asylum applicants. It is in cities and local communities that the public is most likely to articulate discontent and a lack of acceptance of the current asylum law" (*die tageszeitung*, October 8, 1991). Not surprisingly, CDU/CSU politicians were quick to adopt this strategy. After Kronawitter's controversial asylum statements, for instance, Bavarian governor Max Streibl from CSU publicly castigated the SPD for double-crossing the German public (*Süddeutsche Zeitung*, March 5, 1992).

At the same time as the party leadership came under increasing pressure from prominent county and municipal SPD mandate holders, these local officials simultaneously pursued their demands through intergovernmental lobbies. In true neocorporatist fashion, peak bodies such as the German Conference of Cities maintain a substantial organization and have close contacts with both houses of parliament where they regularly press their claims on major policy issues (Johnson, 1982). Schwarze (2000), in her comprehensive account of the politics of asylum in Germany, shows that in the early 1990s intergovernmental lobbies – akin to individual local mandate holders – used their connections to the mainstream parties to lobby for reform. As early as 1988–91, the German Federation of Cities and Municipalities (*Deutscher Städte- und Gemeindebund*) used its annual report to blame the country's constitutional right of asylum for the recent increase in applications (Schwarze, 2000, p. 131). In 1991, the organization contended that the scope for statutory reform had been exhausted and that policy-makers needed to seriously consider the possibility of constitutional change (Schwarze, 2000, p. 132).

Intergovernmental lobbies also targeted leading Land government officials. The conference of cities of North Rhine-Westphalia, Germany's most populous Land and a Social Democratic stronghold, had a particularly strong influence on the SPD. In September 1991, North Rhine-Westphalia's interior minister Herbert Schnoor – previously opposed to constitutional reform – commented in a session of the Bundesrat: "There is no ideal way. ... Sometimes it is hard to face the possibility that one will have to correct one's political views in consideration of changing circumstances" (cited in Schwarze, 2000, p. 201). It is not coincidental that calls for constitutional reform in the federal arena first emerged in the Bundesrat, rather than in the Bundestag. As the representative body of the Länder governments, the Bundesrat is more exposed to bottom-up populist demands than the Bundestag and has traditionally assumed the role of pioneering restrictionist immigration initiatives. For instance, as we saw earlier, the governors of Bavaria and Baden-Württemberg used the Bundesrat to spearhead the first legislative proposals for constitutional asylum reform. Importantly, as more and more Bundesrat SPD deputies yielded to popular pressure and started to entertain the option of reform of the Basic Law, the party's leadership could no longer count on its Bundesrat majority for political support on the issue (Schwarze, 2000).

In a pattern typical for anti-immigrant mobilization, then, the mounting pressures for harsher asylum regulation in the early 1990s originated at the grassroots level of the country's towns and counties. Whether mass discontent focused on the strains faced by public service providers, on the social tensions engendered by collectively housing large groups of asylum applicants in relatively homogeneous communities, or whether it simply was an expression of hitherto latent xenophobia, it is always at the local level that the costs of immigration are felt first, most acutely, and most directly. Municipal and county officials – some reluctantly – then gave a voice to these pressures, utilized them for their own electoral gain, and not infrequently poured oil into the fire of public discontent by portraying asylum seekers as economic opportunists intent on exploiting Germany's generous asylum system and welfare state.

In August 1992, neo-Nazi attacks on an asylum hostel in Rostock, which the police only managed to contain after one week, once again sent shockwaves through the nation. In a television interview, the mayor of Rostock described the town as a "civil war area" where the police had to suffer for the incompetence of federal politicians (Schwarze, 2000, p. 222). In the aftermath of the attacks, intergovernmental lobbies argued that the violence was a clear indication that municipalities were no longer able to cope with the arrival of new asylum seekers. Local authorities insisted that nationals from "safe countries of origin" be categorically excluded from asylum and urged federal politicians to respond to demands for constitutional change (Schwarze, 2000).

In the weeks following the attacks, the SPD party executive under the leadership of chairman Björn Engholm authored an emergency program that came to be known as the Petersberg Resolutions (*Petersberger Beschlüsse*). This program constituted a major milestone on the road of asylum reform as it marked the party leadership's decision to consider a change to the Basic Law. The following weeks were marked by intense debate within the SPD as the policy turnaround was met with bitter opposition by many Bundestag deputies and Land groups. Under crossfire, supporters of constitutional reform justified their position by pointing to the demands of intergovernmental lobbies. In the words of one influential Social Democratic parliamentarian: "these positions are composed by bodies of elected individuals who are members of the SPD and who have received their mandate through the votes of citizens. This means that, as far as we are concerned, these votes should have the same importance as any party conference resolution" (cited in Schwarze, 2000, p. 225).

The Christian Democratic Bundestag group, meanwhile, contended that the country was in the middle of a "national and constitutional crisis" and argued that the SPD would have to be held accountable for the failure of asylum reform (Schwarze, 2000, p. 228). In November, the secretary-general of the CDU Peter Hinze asked all SPD party members in an open letter "to exert pressure on the SPD leadership so that they will vote in favor of constitutional reform" (cited in Schwarze, 2000, p. 229).

In November, the SPD held a special congress in order to reach agreement on the Petersberg Resolutions. Even though the actual vote on constitutional reform would have to be taken by the Bundestag's party group, the special congress was intended to legitimate this decision with the grassroots base (Schwarze, 2000). The congress' outcome was highly uncertain, not least because a decision in favor of the Resolutions would signify a historic break with human rights lobbies and the churches. In the end, although the party emerged from the congress still divided, discipline had been sufficiently strong to secure a vote in favor of the Petersberg Resolutions. Their proponents had devised a policy compromise: in return for the summary exclusion of particular groups from asylum, the party leadership agreed to retain the Basic Law's individual right of asylum. Moreover, the recognition that similar policy developments were taking place at the level of the European Union gave the amendment an air of inevitability and helped hesitant delegates to justify their acquiescence to constitutional reform.

Negotiations between the federal party groups took place in December. The party leaders, in what came to be known as the "Nikolaus compromise," agreed on amending, rather than abolishing (as the CSU had demanded) Article 16, thus allowing the SPD to save some face with prorefugee interests. In return for its consent to amend Article 16, the SPD prevailed with its demand to create a separate civil war refugee status in the light of contemporary developments in the Balkans. Despite harsh criticism of the compromise by several prominent SPD politicians, including chairperson Herta Däubler-Gmelin, it was passed by a majority of the party's parliamentary group. By this point, as Schwarze argues, the SPD "was principally interested in presenting the public with a collective negotiation result that constituted a political solution, thereby demonstrating its capacity to act" (2000, p. 238). Had the "Nikolaus compromise" failed, she contends, the ruling CDU/CSU would have had ample ammunition to hold the SPD accountable not only for any subsequent increase in asylum applications, but also for any future neo-Nazi violence.

The parliamentary debate on the amendment of Article 16, which took place on May 26, 1993, was one of the longest and most heated in the Bundestag's history. While parliamentarians debated for thirteen hours, the Bundestag building was guarded by the largest police force ever employed in Bonn (Steiner, 2000). Within the Social Democratic Party, the opponents of the asylum compromise contended that the proposed law was discriminatory and repressive. For instance, Deputy Detlef von Larcher warned of a "dangerous rightist tendency in our society that weighs its own well-being so absolutely that the solidarity with persecuted people who come to us in need is lost" (cited in Steiner, 2000, pp. 88–9). Social Democratic legislators who supported the compromise once again justified their position by pointing to the concerns of grassroots actors. Cornelie Sonntag-Wolgast, a prominent SPD home affairs expert, argued: "The many mayors, local politicians, and heads of welfare agencies who consider the status quo as unsustainable are no right-wing rowdies. They deserve our understanding and they deserve our solidarity" (cited in Schwarze, 2000, pp. 245–6). Similarly, the leader of the SPD's parliamentary party group Ulrich Klose argued: "The people who live in areas with high numbers of asylum-seekers are not xenophobic, but their standard of living is dropping in an often dramatic manner; they feel themselves threatened, personally and socially. It would not be right to deny this, and it would be dangerous to stand idly by and let things go on" (cited in Steiner, 2000, p. 86).

In the end, the Bundestag passed the constitutional amendment by a clear two-thirds majority; within the SPD, 133 deputies voted in favor, 96 against the compromise (*Neue Zürcher Zeitung*, May 27, 1993). Two days later, the Bundesrat passed the amendment with the required supermajority – only those Länder ruled by coalitions with the Greens did not vote for it

(*Süddeutsche Zeitung*, May 29, 1993). Thus, after over two years of political debate, the two chambers acceded to the demands of the public and of intergovernmental lobbies and took the drastic step of constitutional reform to curtail Germany's once sacrosanct asylum protections.

Even though the reforms of 1993 targeted the regulation of entry into – rather than the departure from – the territory, the reforms had far-reaching implications for the direction of deportation policy. Most importantly, in passing the compromise legislators sent a clear signal to both the public and administrators that the problem of immigration control was essentially one of asylum control. As we shall see in Chapters 3 and 4, in curtailing access to the asylum system, the 1992 reforms not only increased the pool of deportable asylum seekers, but, most importantly, firmly established their removal as a political imperative.

THE LEGISLATIVE POLITICS OF IMMIGRATION CONTROL IN THE UNITED STATES

When, after two years of a highly politicized debate, Congress enacted the Illegal Immigration Reform and Immigrant Responsibility Act in 1996, it passed one of the most restrictionist pieces of immigration legislation in the nation's history. And yet, once we examine the Act's substantive provisions, they bear little semblance to the demands voiced by the electorate and by public interest actors throughout the reform process. Instead of passing worksite enforcement provisions that probably would have reduced illegal immigration, members of Congress opted to reinforce controls at the U.S.–Mexican border instead – a strategy few policy-makers considered effective for reducing the numbers of undocumented migrants. Moreover, at the same time as legislators skirted the issue of worksite enforcement, they imposed stunningly harsh control measures on a migrant group much different from undocumented workers: criminal offenders. Why did members of Congress forge a legislative deal that had moved so far from the concerns which were salient to the public? In other words, why is the outcome of immigration reform in the United States so different from the path of public interest reform taken by legislators in Germany?

The Public Mandate for Illegal Immigration Control

Just as the contentious issue of asylum immigration featured prominently on Germany's political agenda in the early 1990s, the United States witnessed equally intense demands for immigration control in the mid-1990s. Again, the costs of immigration borne by local communities became the linchpin of restrictionist popular demands. Unlike Germany, however, it was undocumented immigrants, rather than asylum seekers, who bore the brunt of the backlash. Even though estimates of the magnitude of illegal immigration are much harder to obtain than data on asylum immigration, there is a general consensus that, throughout the 1990s, the population of illegal immigrants in the U.S. was expanding quite drastically. The Pew Hispanic Center, a nonpartisan research organization, estimates that the annual increase in the number of "unauthorized migrants"[6] more than doubled in the early 1990s. According to Pew's calculations,[7] the number of unauthorized migrants grew by 180,000 a year in the 1980s, then rose by 400,000 per year between 1990 and 1994, and by 575,000 per year between 1995 and 1999 (*Christian Science Monitor*, May 16, 2006).

Unlike asylum seekers in Germany, illegal immigrants in the United States are not equally distributed geographically nor are there horizontal burden-sharing mechanisms in place that could compensate states with disproportionate illegal populations for related social expenditures. This has far-reaching implications, given the heavy geographical concentration of illegal immigrants in some parts of the United States. In 1990, California was home to a staggering 42 percent of the country's illegal population. The estimated 1.5 million undocumented immigrants amounted to 6.5 percent of the state's total population and, by 2000, had increased to over 2.2 million. Further, illegal immigrants in the top five states – California, Texas, New York, Illinois, and Florida – accounted for over 77 percent of the country's undocumented population in 1990 (U.S. Immigration and Naturalization Service, 2003b).

Anti-immigrant backlash is closely related to the costs incurred as a result of particular migrant groups.[8] As I already argued, the backlash against asylum seekers in Germany was triggered by soaring numbers in the early 1990s and the related fiscal costs of providing housing and basic welfare support for this group. In the United States, by contrast, the numbers of asylum seekers remained much lower during this period, while those individuals who did file for asylum were barred from access to public housing and income support. Undocumented immigrants, however, not

---

[6] This includes some migrants who have temporary permission to live in the United States or whose immigration status is unresolved.

[7] Pew bases its numbers on a monthly assessment of about 50,000 households conducted by the U.S. Census Bureau and the U.S. Bureau of Labor Statistics.

[8] At the same time, concomitant benefits are often ignored, as is the case with the economic benefits arising from the employment of undocumented workers.

only made up a much larger and faster growing population in the United States but also enjoyed access to certain public services, in particular emergency health care.[9]

Not surprisingly, then, it was the governors of states with the highest proportions of illegal immigrants who most vocally called attention to the strain that this population placed on their budgets. California's governor, Pete Wilson (R), estimated that the state's spending on health care for illegal immigrants had increased eighteenfold between 1990 and 1994, whereas education and prison costs for this population had "simply exploded" (*Christian Science Monitor*, February 1, 1994). Illinois' governor, Jim Edgar (R), contended in 1994 that the state spent over $140 million annually to provide federally mandated education, emergency health care, and prison space for its illegal population. In a similar vein, Florida's governor Lawton Chiles (D) protested that the state spent $739 million annually on social service provision to illegal immigrants (*Chicago Sun-Times*, January 31, 1994). It is important to note that where public debate focused on the population of immigrant offenders – as it did in the context of soaring prison costs – these concerns centered on incarcerated illegal immigrants, rather than on immigrant offenders with legal immigration status.

As in Germany, public discourse on immigration during this period came to be dominated by negative and demonizing policy images. In California in particular, local protest concerning the fiscal impact of illegal immigration was powerfully articulated by means of anti-immigrant political initiatives. Most prominently, in the early 1990s, former INS official Harold Ezell founded a grassroots organization called "Save our State" and mobilized the Californian public in support of Proposition 187. The initiative sought to deny public, social, educational, and health services to undocumented immigrants in the state. In 1994, the issue of immigration control quickly came to dominate the state's gubernatorial race as incumbent governor Pete Wilson threw his support behind Proposition 187. His electoral fortunes threatened by economic slump and gaping budget shortfalls, Wilson effectively made the restriction of immigration the centerpiece of his reelection campaign – a strategy that would return him to office.

Opinion polls at the time clearly confirmed the salience of illegal immigration to the Californian public. When asked about their perceptions of the seriousness of the problem in the state, 77.6 percent of respondents in 1993

---

[9] Although most illegal immigrants in the United States pay taxes, this disproportionately benefits the federal purse and leaves municipalities and states to absorb the bulk of the fiscal costs of service provision.

considered the situation to be "very serious" (The Odum Institute, August 1993). Similarly, in 1994, 61 percent of Californians who were surveyed reported they were "extremely concerned" about illegal immigration (The Odum Institute, July 1994). Considering these data, it came as no surprise when Proposition 187 passed with an overwhelming 59 percent majority, and, although later ruled unconstitutional, it played an important role in maintaining the political salience of the immigration issue. Governor Wilson, aware of the likelihood of judicial defeat, astutely argued that the Proposition's passage would nevertheless send a powerful message to federal legislators that the public was no longer willing to pay for the costs of illegal immigrants (*The San Francisco Chronicle*, October 15, 1994).

On November 9, the Republicans swept into Congress, gaining their first majority in the House since 1954. The Republican Party, riding a wave of public backlash against the Clinton Administration, was buoyed by the ideological unity that the "Contract with America" had brought to political campaigns across the country. However, unlike other prominent social issues such as crime and welfare reform, the Contract did not include the issue of immigration control in its policy agenda. Crucially, although the national public consistently espoused restrictionist immigration preferences, the salience of these preferences varied by state. Although Californians were highly mobilized on the issue of illegal immigration, at the national level crime and welfare reform featured more prominently on the public's mind. A nationwide NBC News/*Wall Street Journal* survey in October 1994 showed that 20 percent of respondents placed illegal immigration at the top of their lists of pressing issues, trailing behind crime and welfare reform (cited in Tichenor, 2002, p. 277). As a result, "it was difficult to excite members of Congress from interior states about campaigning on reforming the nation's immigration law" (Gimpel & Edwards, 1999, p. 212).

However, the clear endorsement of Proposition 187 effectively propelled immigration reform onto the national policy agenda. As recalled by a political consultant instrumental in the success of Proposition 187: "We've had phone calls from at least 15 states about how to get a 187 movement going. We remind them that the goal, ultimately, is not just to cut off aid to illegal immigrants but to put pressure on Washington to do something about illegal immigration in general" (*The New York Times*, December 4, 1994). Most importantly, political observers attributed Wilson's gubernatorial victory to his decision to run his campaign on a restrictionist immigration platform. In view of the 1996 presidential elections, neither party could afford to ignore a state with fifty-four electoral votes. As a policy analyst argued, "if Clinton is to have any chance of winning reelection in '96, he is going to have to find ways of appealing to the electorate in California and Texas. .... For now he is demonstrably on the wrong side of the most pressing issue, immigration. By fundamental actions, not mere tinkering, he must be prepared to make up for the rhetorical mistakes of attacking [Proposition] 187" (Alan Heslop, cited in *Christian Science Monitor*, November 14, 1994). Immediately after the 1994 congressional elections, the Clinton administration decided to withdraw its initial immigration reform proposal in order to tighten up its enforcement provisions (*St. Petersburg Times*, November 20, 1994).

Meanwhile, the new Republican majority in the House took Proposition 187 – together with opinion poll trends – as an unmistakable mandate for comprehensive immigration reform. In response to the lobbying efforts of the California and Texas delegations in particular, Speaker Newt Gingrich (R-GA) set up a special task force on immigration reform to be chaired by Californian immigration hardliner Elton Gallegly (Tichenor, 2002). In a parallel development, Republicans in the Senate mobilized to draw up their own immigration bill. Majority leader Robert Dole (R-KS) publicly protested the disproportionate immigration costs borne by California, Florida, and Texas, and blamed policy-makers for being "not willing to protect our borders" (cited in Reimers, 1999, p. 134). In the minds of many political observers, there was little doubt that the 104th Congress, with both houses firmly under Republican control and prominent hardliners chairing the immigration subcommittees, would bring about fundamental reform in this area (Tichenor, 2002).

Skirting the Mandate: Immigration Reform as a Private Interest Compromise

The Puzzle of Partial Immigration Reform

The immigration bill that was drawn up by the House subcommittee in the spring of 1995 under the leadership of Lamar Smith (R-TX) closely mirrored the recommendations of the presidential Commission on Immigration Reform's final report on illegal immigration (U.S. Commission on Immigration Reform, 1994). The bipartisan commission, established under the 1990 Immigration Act and chaired by former representative Barbara Jordan (D-TX), championed a comprehensive approach to immigration control. Although its recommendations included better border management, the detention and removal of criminal offenders, federal reimbursements of certain immigration-related state and local costs, denial of welfare benefits to illegal immigrants, and stronger sponsoring requirements, the report's most fundamental provision concerned the issue of worksite

enforcement. Proposing the establishment of an electronic worker verification program that would draw on INS and Social Security Administration data to verify worker eligibility, the Commission laid out its
basic approach to immigration control:

> The Commission believes that reducing the employment magnet is the linchpin
> of a comprehensive strategy to reduce illegal immigration. The ineffectiveness of
> employer sanctions, prevalence of fraudulent documents, and continued high num-
> bers of unauthorized workers ... have challenged the credibility of current worksite
> enforcement efforts.
>
> (U.S. Commission on Immigration Reform, 1994, p. xii)

The Jordan Commission's recommendations were based on the recognition
that the sanctions introduced by the 1986 Immigration Reform and Control
Act (IRCA) had failed to discourage the employment of illegal immigrants. Not
only were employers not required to verify the authenticity of job applicants'
documents, but IRCA's approach to worksite enforcement was based on voluntary compliance. In conjunction with the fact that the INS' worksite enforcement divisions were severely underresourced, these factors had discouraged
systematic enforcement and prevented the imposition of substantial fines for
noncompliance. In fact, the number of INS investigations even declined
between 1989 and 1995 from 14,706 to 5,963, as the agency shifted its focus
to other enforcement activities such as deporting criminal offenders (*The San
Francisco Chronicle*, March 18, 1996). Moreover, during this period the
average fine had amounted to $1,612 – hardly enough to act as an effective
deterrent (*The Washington Post*, February 2, 1995). When challenged about
this policy, INS spokesman Russ Bergeron defended the low penalties as a
strategy to induce cooperation, stating that the agency prefers "not to assume
an adversarial relationship to the business community" (*Rocky Mountain
News*, December 10, 1995).

Among the members of the immigration subcommittee there was
bipartisan agreement with the Commission's approach. Howard Berman
(D-CA) remarked: "You can talk about Proposition 187s and we can fight
about benefits and we can talk about them, but unless you've dealt with the
issue of verification, all those initiatives and all those propositions and all
those proposals are really meaningless" (cited in Gimpel & Edwards, 1999,
pp. 224–5). Similarly, chairman Lamar Smith, (R-TX) endorsed the worksite enforcement provisions. Smith himself had long held restrictionist views
that reflected the concerns of his constituents in southern Texas on
immigration: "People back home are aware of the people trafficking, the
drug trafficking, the overcrowding, and the other problems associated with

immigration. My constituents want to talk about immigration more than any other issue" (cited in Gimpel & Edwards, 1999, p. 213).

Smith recognized the 1994 Republican electoral landslide as a rare window of opportunity for the pursuit of comprehensive restrictionist immigration reform. The ensuing subcommittee's bill contained five titles pertaining to immigration control measures,[10] which included border security, human trafficking, the deportation of illegal and criminal immigrants, employer sanctions and verification, and eligibility for benefits and sponsorship (Gimpel & Edwards, 1999). Importantly, the employment verification system proposed by the Jordan Commission was incorporated in the form of a telephone system that would require employers to call a toll-free number to corroborate any potential employee's eligibility.

In the Senate, the immigration subcommittee was chaired by Alan Simpson (R-WY), an experienced restrictionist who had been instrumental in drafting previous acts in this policy area, including IRCA. Simpson and ranking Democrat Edward Kennedy were in basic agreement over key policy measures such as worksite enforcement, verification of work eligibility, and employer sanctions (Gimpel & Edwards, 1999). Like the House immigration subcommittee, the Senate subcommittee's bill was modeled after the recommendations of the Jordan Commission, and, as a result, its enforcement provisions largely corresponded to those put forward by Lamar Smith in the House (Tichenor, 2002).

Not only did the House and Senate subcommittees principally agree on key measures of immigration control, but the Clinton Administration also shared Smith's and Simpson's conviction that the Jordan Commission's recommendations – including the employment verification system – should form the basis for legislative reform. Tellingly, before the November Republican landslide, the Administration – although in general agreement with Jordan on the need to better enforce employer sanctions – had rejected the Commission's proposals for an electronic verification system, echoing the privacy concerns of ethnic minority and civil liberties lobbies. However, it was not long after the November elections that the Administration withdrew its immigration bill. President Clinton, famously concerned with opinion polls, understood that far-reaching control measures were deeply popular, in particular in California where his electoral margin in 1992 was not sufficiently large to guarantee the state's electoral votes in the upcoming presidential elections (Gimpel & Edwards, 1999). Consequently, when Howard

---

[10] The bill further included titles on the restriction of legal immigration. For an excellent account of the failure of legal immigration reform, see Gimpel and Edwards (1999).

Berman (D-CA) reintroduced the Administration's bill, it overwhelmingly focused on curbing illegal immigration and, most significantly, included provisions for an electronic work verification system.

Finally, several governors from states with large populations of illegal immigrants vocally supported the idea of an employment verification system. Remarkably, Florida's governor Lawton Chiles (D), an outspoken opponent of California's Proposition 187, even went beyond the Commission's recommendation by calling for a national identity card. Arguing that "as long as an immigrant can get a job, you will have two more coming tomorrow," Chiles responded to polls that showed that a majority of American-born residents and legal immigrants favored the introduction of a national identity card (*The Tampa Tribune*, July 13, 1995). Similarly, Pete Wilson during his gubernatorial campaign focused on this measure and demanded that all Californians be required to present identity cards when seeking employment, entering school, or applying for nonemergency health care (*The New York Times*, October 26, 1994). After his Democratic opponent branded his proposal as a case of "Big Brother, Big Government," Wilson in a letter to the editor of *The New York Times* toned down his demands, but insisted on the need for a "tamperproof system for verification of legal residency" (*The New York Times*, December 4, 1994).

As the congressional immigration subcommittees deliberated on immigration reform, there was general agreement that the 104th Congress was in a historic position to overhaul the nation's immigration system and legislate the public's demands for more effective immigration control. Frank Sharry, executive director of the National Immigration Forum and one of Washington's most influential immigrant advocates, recalls:

> In the spring of 1995, we didn't think we could turn the restrictionist tide, couldn't stop the reform juggernaut, and it looked like something close to zero immigration was on the verge of being enacted. The current system would be gutted, the safety net for legal immigrants would be shredded, and a national work verification system would be imposed... Lamar Smith has a capable staff and they came roaring out of the blocks. Smith wrapped himself in the Jordan Commission's cloak and wanted to get the bill to the floor by the end of the year.
>
> (cited in Gimpel & Edwards, 1999, p. 225)

It thus came as no surprise that the Illegal Immigration Reform and Immigrant Responsibility Act (IIRIRA), enacted in late September 1996, was heavily enforcement-oriented. IIRIRA sought to curb illegal immigration by stepping up government activity along the U.S.–Mexican border, including the construction of a border fence near San Diego and the hiring of 1,000 additional border patrol agents. Concerning deportation, the Act mandated the detention of most removable criminal offenders, drastically expanded the range of deportable crimes, and rendered these provisions retroactive. IIRIRA further provided for the "expedited removal" of non-citizens who entered through ports of entry without valid documents. Finally, the Act tightened immigrant sponsor requirements, obligated family sponsors to assume financial responsibility for their relatives, and provided for federal hospital reimbursement of emergency health care costs associated with illegal immigrants.

What was conspicuously absent from the Act, however, was the original emphasis on worksite enforcement. The proposal of a nationwide employment verification system – the Jordan Commission's "linchpin" of immigration control – instead had been watered down to a pilot program that would allow employers to check employees' immigration status electronically on a purely voluntary basis. Given the widely acknowledged failure of permissive approaches to worksite enforcement, why did the 104th Congress decide against more forcefully addressing what was considered one of the central causes of illegal immigration? I argue that the failure of reform in this area is best understood as the inability of proregulatory intergovernmental lobbies – as the "most likely" public interest actor – to counteract the demands of opposing private interest lobbies. Instead of legislating measures that corresponded to the public's demand for effective immigration enforcement, congressional decision-making was strongly shaped by private interest actors who were resolutely opposed to the regulation of irregular employment.

Immigration Reform in the Absence of Effective Public Interest Lobbies

In a pattern resembling the initial stages of immigration reform in Germany, immigration reform in 1996 was initiated from the bottom-up, as governors from states with high levels of illegal immigration placed the issue onto the federal agenda. In contrast to Germany's Land-level politicians, however, when it came to lobbying for specific policy measures, governors were unable to overcome the collective action problem that reflected the uneven geographical distribution of illegal immigrants. Although they could agree on the issue of federal reimbursement for the locally incurred costs of illegal immigration – a demand that carries through most policy areas – no consensus was reached on virtually any other aspect of immigration control. For instance, Illinois' governor Jim Edgar (R) commented in 1994: "The key is the money, as far as I'm concerned. I'm not trying to suggest that we come up with any tough new immigration policies" (*Chicago Sun-Times*, January 31, 1994). In a similar vein, governors William Weld (R) of Massachusetts and Christine Todd Whitman (R) of New Jersey – both strong supporters of demands for federal reimbursement for immigration-related expenses – remarked that they did not support initiatives like Proposition 187 because their states were not subject to levels of illegal immigration as high as those of California (*The Washington Post*, November 22, 1994).

Clearly, spatially diverse interests are unlikely to be represented by lobbies – such as the National Governors' Association – that operate on the basis of unanimity. Although individual governors often succeed in placing their policy demands on the legislative agenda, their influence rapidly wanes once policies move beyond the agenda-setting stage. For instance, when in early 1994 six governors[11] met with federal budget director Leon Panetta to lobby their case for federal reimbursement, they were told that, in order to stand any chance of getting these demands met, they must first mobilize the support of states with smaller illegal populations (*The San Francisco Chronicle*, February 1, 1994).

In order to assess the significance of the absence of powerful intergovernmental lobbies from the legislative politics of immigration control, we will examine the evolution of the House and Senate bills after leaving their respective subcommittees. In the House, the Immigration in the National Interests Act's provision of a nationwide work verification system sustained its first blow when the judiciary committee approved an amendment introduced by Steve Chabot (R-OH) to implement the program in the form of pilots in the five states with the largest illegal populations. This was the first, if relatively minor, success of a broad coalition of private interest lobbyists that included business, libertarian, and immigrant interests. Representative Chabot characterized the telephone verification system as "1-800-Big-Brother" and warned that it would represent unduly invasive state regulation of private enterprise (Gimpel & Edwards, 1999). Nevertheless, although the Chabot amendment weakened its worksite enforcement measures, the bill left the committee with its core provisions largely intact.

In the Senate, by contrast, the Immigrant Control and Financial Responsibility Act's judiciary committee markup resembled, in the words of James Gimpel and James Edwards, "major surgery, if not complete dismemberment" (1999, p. 252). It was in this committee that an antiregulatory coalition of private interests groups first revealed its political clout. On the business side, the coalition was led by Jennifer Eisen, lobbyist for the computer hardware giant Intel, who convened regular meetings with established interest groups such as the National Association of Manufacturers and the

---

[11] Representing California, Florida, Texas, Illinois, Arizona, and New Jersey.

U.S. Chamber of Commerce to devise an effective strategy (Gimpel & Edwards, 1999). At the same time, ethnic organizations such as the National Immigration Forum, the National Immigration Lawyers Association, the National Council of La Raza, and the Mexican American Legal Defense and Education Fund recognized that they would have few inroads into a Republican-dominated Congress unless they entered into a coalition with the well-financed and well-connected business community. The resulting left–right coalition of ethnic lobbies and business was eventually facilitated by immigration experts from the libertarian CATO Institute (Gimpel & Edwards, 1999).

The private interest coalition successfully engineered the break between several Republicans in the committee who had strong ties to business, most prominently Senator Spencer Abraham (R-MI), and Simpson's ambitious restrictionist agenda. Although the coalition's most striking success was their "split-the-bill" strategy, which separated the issue of legal immigration from the illegal immigration reforms – a move that cleared the way for the ultimate defeat of the former provisions – their influence was also palpable in the markup of worker verification measures. Once again, business led the fight against this part of the bill, criticizing it as imposing massive burdens on the private sector (*The Tampa Tribune*, September 24, 1995). The committee adopted amendments by Senators Hatch (R-UT) and Kyl (R-AZ) that not only weakened penalties for hiring illegal workers, but also prevented the INS from retaining most of the funds raised by employer sanctions – a provision that, its opponents argued, would have led to "overzealous enforcement." Finally, the amendment eliminated the imposition of civil and criminal penalties on employers who had knowingly employed undocumented immigrants (Gimpel & Edwards, 1999; Masci, March 16, 1996).

As Lamar Smith prepared to introduce his immigration bill on the floor of the House, he realized that the lobbying efforts of the antiregulatory coalition threatened to defeat his bill's legal immigration restrictions and provisions for worksite enforcement. Smith knew that he had no powerful advocacy groups to rely on – the only active and well-organized group was the restrictionist Federation for American Immigration Reform (FAIR), which at the time was still on the fringe of the political mainstream (Gimpel & Edwards, 1999). Before the bill came up on the floor of the House, Smith, in a preemptive strike, moved to make participation in the employment verification pilot program voluntary. The tactic was successful: a subsequent amendment by Steve Chabot (R-OH) to eliminate the now-voluntary program was defeated. In an attempt to return some effectiveness to the much weakened measure, Florida's Bill McCollum (R) introduced an amendment

that called for a tamper-resistant social security card as the basis for employment verification. However, the amendment was voted down with well-
rehearsed arguments that a tamper-resistant Social Security card would
ultimately give rise to a national identity card and thereby infringe on individual liberties (Idelson, March 23, 1996).

The Senate voted in favor of retaining Simpson's employment verification
provisions after Spencer Abraham had unsuccessfully introduced an amendment to eliminate the pilot programs altogether. Simpson had resolutely
fought Abraham's opposition to a program that not long before had been
considered the crux of the illegal immigration reform. As the Senate and
House bills moved on to the conference committee, both included provisions
for a pilot employment verification system. However, unlike the Senate, the
House had settled for making participation voluntary (Idelson, May 4,
1996). Significantly, in the House–Senate conference committee, this difference was ultimately resolved in favor of the House version. Business lobbies,
in particular the National Federation of Independent Business, the U.S.
Chamber of Commerce, Employers for Responsible Immigration Reform,
and Americans for Tax Reform had demanded the elimination of the provision of mandatory participation (Gimpel & Edwards, 1999).

In the spring of 1996, just months before the passage of the IIRIRA, an
editorial in *The Washington Post* argued optimistically:

In contrast to 10 years ago when they were given a generous amnesty, there is today
very little sympathy in Congress for illegal aliens. The bills now being considered
would beef up border control, strengthen employer sanctions and provide some relief
for the handful of states that attract almost all these aliens. There may be some
debate about the system now proposed for verifying job eligibility – a call-in system
similar to that now used to check credit card validity – but that system has been
tested in pilot projects and found to be easily implemented and effective.

(*The Washington Post*, March 3, 1996)

In the end, however, despite what initially had appeared to be a bipartisan consensus on the need for more effective worksite enforcement, the
verification system, as enacted in IIRIRA, fell far short of the original proposal to establish a nationwide, mandatory employment verification program. Even though the provision was passed in the form of a voluntary pilot,
a chain of amendments had created sufficient loopholes to raise serious
doubts as to its policy efficacy. Hardly surprisingly, when the pilot employment verification systems expired in 1999, the House allowed the program
to end (*Progressive Punch*, October 28, 2003).

The case of employment verification demonstrates the incapacity of U.S.
legislators to impose costs upon organized interests in the absence of public

interest lobbies. In some respects, the failure of worksite enforcement reform did not come as a surprise – it has long been recognized that, "unlike slashing benefits to illegal immigrants or beefing up the border, taking aim at employers has profound economic consequences" (*The San Francisco Chronicle*, March 18, 1996). There is no doubt that, in the United States, the pursuit of immigration control has always been hampered by the country's dependence on cheap migrant labor. The very real economic costs of worksite enforcement have presented a particular dilemma for the Republican Party because of its closer ties to business. As Republican lawmakers struggle to cater to both business and populist calls for law and order, they run the risk of alienating one or the other. Even where leaders are determined to override the preferences of business, these attempts are often foiled by the lack of party discipline. As we saw, Smith and Simpson were unable to reign in their defecting fellow partisans and, as a result, the party squandered the political capital of a Republican-controlled Congress.

However, as the case of Germany has demonstrated, the presence of formidable political opposition does not necessarily have to end in reform failure. Although legislators who sought to overhaul Germany's asylum system did not have to contend with staunch business opposition, they faced a formidable challenge of a different kind. In agreeing to constitutional reform, the Social Democratic Party was forced not only to give up a principle at the heart of its identity but also to take the risk of alienating its traditional allies, the churches and human rights lobbies. Yet, because intergovernmental lobbies were well positioned to articulate the public's demands for reform, the political costs of skirting public mandates surpassed the costs of alienating antiregulatory interests.

Although worksite enforcement reforms were doomed to failure in the United States, restrictionist demands that did not face the opposition of well-organized interests were translated into corresponding legislation. Because the 1996 Immigration Act entailed a plethora of control provisions, the failure of employee verification did not prevent legislators from claiming credit for "cracking down" on illegal immigration. Significantly, policy-makers at the time recognized that the efficacy of measures such as the border fence at San Diego was very limited (Andreas, 2000; *The Washington Post*, May 5, 1994). What made these measures attractive, however, was their political compatibility: because border fortification presented a single-stage, highly visible measure that targeted areas with particularly intense anti-immigrant backlash, its credit-claiming dividends were substantial. At the same time, because illegal migrants at the border have much weaker constituencies than undocumented immigrants within the country, border control measures allow politicians to safely walk the tightrope of appeasing public demands without alienating organized constituencies.

The political maneuvers of Senator Spencer Abraham (R-MI) are particularly instructive in this respect. As the above analysis showed, Abraham was the most effective ally of business: not only was he responsible for splitting the legal immigration provisions from the Senate bill, he also was one of the fiercest opponents of the employment verification program. As the Senate and House bills moved to the conference stage, Abraham used his influence with the Republican precommittee's chair Orrin Hatch (R-UT) to drastically toughen provisions pertaining to criminal offenders, such as the provision of mandatory deportation for immigrants on one-year suspended sentences, and the mandatory preremoval detention of most immigrant offenders. A former counsel of Lamar Smith and to the House immigration subcommittee recalls:

And then Senator Abraham sticks it to criminal aliens, really gets tough with them. He did this very strategically to contradict his anti-restrictionist legal immigration views. Then it got really nasty. Republicans planted against Republicans. There was an editorial in the *Washington Times* that accused us as being "soft on criminal aliens." It was all planted. ... They really were demagogues on the issue. ... At the time I felt that if somebody has been admitted and then commits a crime, we need to be tougher on them, but they are also members of the community. Some misdemeanors and minor drug crimes don't warrant deportation.

(Former Counsel to the House Subcommittee on Immigration and Claims, Washington, D.C., August 20, 2002)

There is little doubt that Abraham's punitive initiative was a strategic move to claim credit with the restrictionist public. At the time, there was a general consensus that both bills' existing criminal alien provisions were sufficiently tough – not even the ultrarestrictionist Federation for American Immigration Reform pushed for further changes.[12] However, because "there was no constituency for criminal aliens,"[13] immigrant offenders presented the perfect target for congressional entrepreneurs like Abraham who wanted to appeal to the public without alienating organized constituencies. Because labels such as "criminal alien" convey powerful messages concerning the threats posed by particular social groups, proponents of restrictionist regulation can pursue their agendas largely unobstructed. A congressional

[12] Personal interview, Federation for American Immigration Reform, Washington, D.C., August 19, 2002

[13] Personal interview, former Counsel to the House Subcommittee on Immigration and Claims, Falls Church, VA, August 20, 2002

staffer reflects on the political risks of sponsoring less restrictionist legislation pertaining to immigrant offenders:

It's a real electoral gamble, because you can just see the headlines: "Senator X supports criminal aliens and aggravated felons!" It's politically untenable. ... People always hear the word "aggravated felon" and think of bad criminals. ... The problem is that most people we are talking about here have committed non-violent drug crimes.

(Counsel to Barney Frank (D-MA), U.S. House of Representatives, Washington, D.C., August 21, 2002)

To conclude, when we compare IIRIRA with its original proposals, drawn up at a time of intense anti-immigrant backlash, a clear pattern emerges. Provisions that were not resisted by the private interest coalition – including the fortification of the U.S.–Mexico border, the expedited removal of immigrants without documents at ports of entries, and the mandatory detention and deportation of criminal offenders – were either kept intact or even further tightened as the provision moved through the legislative process. By contrast, measures that were ardently opposed by the coalition were either significantly weakened (for example, the employment verification system) or fully defeated (for example, a cutback in legal immigration). As a result, what started out as a comprehensive reform package poised to lower illegal immigration ended up as a bundle of legislative provisions marked by both severe punitiveness, on the one hand, and policy inefficacy, on the other. Whereas estimates for the annual increase in the number of unauthorized migrants were at 575,000 for the period 1995–9, they had increased to 850,000 between 2000 and 2005 (*Christian Science Monitor*, May 16, 2006).

How significant, then, is the absence of powerful intergovernmental lobbies in accounting for the outcome of U.S. immigration reform? Speculating about a hypothetical scenario in which the National Governors' Association (NGA) was in agreement on the need to pursue fundamental reform in the area of illegal employment, would this have been sufficient to counter the opposition of the expansionist coalition? As studies of U.S. welfare reform have shown, the influence of the NGA – the most powerful of intergovernmental lobbies in the U.S. – has been substantial in areas marked by agreement between governors and Congress (Weaver, 2000). Because of the national prominence of its members – many of whom have political aspirations beyond the governorship – the NGA can exert substantial pressures on Congress to pursue favored policy measures. At the same time, the literature on welfare reform has also shown that in instances where the interests of governors do not correspond to those of members of Congress, their leverage is quite limited (Cammisa, 1995; Weaver, 2000).

Intergovernmental lobbies in the United States do not have institutionalized access at the federal level that would provide them with a permanent seat at the decision-making table. To borrow from Campbell and Morgan, "while German Länder are a regular bargaining partner of federal policymakers, the American state governments are one interest group among many that must vie for influence in a competitive, pluralist environment" (2005, p. 896).

Instead, frustrated with repeated congressional failure to legislate worksite enforcement[14] and unable to exert leverage at the federal level, states have begun to take advantage of what limited jurisdiction they have over immigration-related law-making. In 2007, state legislatures enacted 170 immigration bills, two and half times more than in the preceding year (*The New York Times*, August 6, 2007). Many of these new laws concerned worksite enforcement, with Arizona passing the most far-reaching provisions. In July 2007, Democratic governor Janet Napalitano signed into law the Legal Arizona Workers Act, which required all businesses to verify the status of job applicants with an electronic verification system run by the Department of Homeland Security (*The News Herald*, January 2, 2008). Employers who knowingly hired illegal immigrants were to face suspension of their business license for a first offense and its permanent loss for a second offence committed within three years (*The New York Times*, August 6, 2007). In early 2008, a federal judge dismissed a legal challenge by Arizona employer associations, arguing that under federal immigration law, states have the power to sanction business licenses (*Phoenix Business Journal*, February 8, 2008). Thus, states have stepped into the vacuum created by the failure of federal public interest reform and have focused their efforts on compensatory law-making at their own level. As Timothy Bee, Republican president of the Arizona Senate, argued: "The message loud and clear from our constituents was their frustration that the federal government has not taken the necessary action to secure the border" (*The New York Times*, August 6, 2007).

The legislative pursuit of immigration control, like other measures of coercive social regulation, is hampered by its particular distribution of costs and benefits. Because the costs of restrictionist policies are concentrated and their benefits diffuse, the proregulatory preferences of the public are frequently not reflected in statutes. The capacity of legislators to translate

---

[14] Most recently in 2007.

public mandates for immigration control into law is greatest, I have argued, where intergovernmental lobbies mobilize and, as public interest actors, use their political resources to lobby in favor of regulation. However, both the likelihood and the efficacy of such campaigns are largely shaped by the institutional arrangement of intergovernmental relations. In Germany, where horizontal burden-sharing arrangements allow subnational governments to overcome collective action problems arising from the spatially concentrated patterns of costs, intergovernmental lobbies face lower hurdles in pursuing common lobbying strategies. Further, because of their representation in the Bundesrat, these public interest lobbies have institutional leverage in pressing their demands in ways that intergovernmental lobbies in the United States do not.

Having examined the dynamics driving the politics of legislative reform in the area of migration control, we will now move on to the next link in the policy chain: implementation. The next chapter will investigate the decision-making processes of senior executives who are charged with drafting regulations and setting implementation priorities for the street-level bureaucracies they oversee. Do these officials have the capacity to ensure the implementation of deportation mandates, even where this requires the imposition of significant costs upon organized interests?

3

Deportation and the Executive Politics of Implementation

> The problem with working at headquarters is that you always get called up from people higher up than you in the Administration, or from Congress, and you need to drop everything and respond to them.
>
> (Personal interview, deportation officer "M," INS San Diego, August 1, 2002)

Once the ink has dried, even the most hotly contested of immigration laws are likely to disappear from public view – at least until they reach the stage of field implementation. Between the highly visible policy stages of legislation and street-level enforcement, however, lies the regulatory realm occupied by senior executives. The day-to-day tasks performed by these leaders of executive agencies, cabinet ministers, and their immediate staffs range from choosing implementation priorities and corresponding performance indicators to deciding on budget allocation, drawing up agency rules, and supervising field offices. In fields of coercive social regulation, the executive politics of implementation, which largely takes place outside of public view, is a venue of conflict in its own right: ultimately, the setting of enforcement priorities determines who will be within, and who will be outside, the coercive reach of the state.

While few policy areas are immune to lapses in implementation, fields of coercive social regulation are particularly vulnerable to the emergence of implementation gaps. For one, policy goals such as immigration or crime control are simply too resource-intensive to allow for close-to-perfect enforcement. As Joel Migdal reminds us:

no matter how vaunted the bureaucracy, police, and military, officers of the state cannot stand on every corner ensuring that each person stop at the red light, drive on the right side of the road, cross at the crosswalk, [or] refrain from stealing and drug dealing ... (Migdal, 2001, p. 251)

Given that complete implementation is beyond their reach, leaders of coercive bureaucracies are faced with a choice as to which legislative provisions to enforce, while exempting others from implementation. Whereas the constraint of resource scarcity is universal across bureaucratic contexts, the substance of implementation decisions is not. In this chapter, I will pursue the argument that implementation priorities vary systematically across institutional contexts, and that this variation is indicative of differences in executive capacity.

Bureaucratic enforcement decisions are closely related to state capacity because they have far-reaching implications for the political sustainability of migration control policies. The notion of political sustainability describes "the capacity of any public policy to maintain its stability, coherence, and integrity as time passes, achieving its basic promised goals amid the inevitable vicissitudes of politics" (Patashnik, 2003, p. 207). Wherever programs impose concentrated costs and diffuse benefits – as is the case with coercive social regulation – this problem is particularly pronounced. Because policy beneficiaries face higher hurdles to organization than losers, reform initiatives will struggle to survive with each successive stage in the policy cycle. In fact, the collective action problem faced by beneficiaries – the mass public – is most daunting at the stage of executive policy-making because of its insulation from public view. Socially coercive regulations are costly, and policy losers face strong incentives to seek the support of elected representatives to pressure bureaucrats to refrain from implementation. Given that the setting of implementation priorities is largely hidden from public view, when push comes to shove legislators will be unlikely to prioritize the weakly mobilized preferences of policy beneficiaries – the general public – over the vocal demands of well-organized opponents.

Turning to the preferences of senior executives, what are the incentives that guide decision-making by those in charge of overseeing implementation? The top executives of the U.S. Immigration and Naturalization Service and of Germany's interior ministries straddle the difficult divide between the often disparate worlds of administration and politics. Where they enjoy autonomy, these senior officials are likely to "go native" and pursue policy goals expressive of their agency's mission (Heclo, 1977). At the same time, the top echelon of immigration executives – the holders of (often appointed) executive schedule positions – are politicians in their own right who "see themselves as having a future in elective or appointive office outside the agency. . . . The maintenance and enhancement of their careers outside the agency is of paramount importance" (Wilson, 1980, p. 373). By contrast to lower level careerists with a future (and tenure) within the civil service, these executives cannot afford to stay clear of the vicissitudes of politics. This is particularly true for Germany and the United States, where agency leaders share a degree of politicization not commonly found in other Western civil service systems (Aberbach, Derlien, Mayntz et al. 1990).

Despite these similarities, however, German senior executives have little in common with Hugh Heclo's "government of strangers" of relatively inexperienced, short-term U.S. executives (1977). Not only is the number of political appointments in the German senior bureaucracy much smaller, but appointees do not share the rather transitory public service career of U.S. bureaucrats without tenure (Derlien, 1988; Aberbach, Derlien, & Rockman, 1994). For instance, the highly influential, appointed positions of "political civil servants" (*politische Beamte*), designed to bridge the gap between ministers' political needs, on the one hand, and the career principles espoused by subservient civil servants, on the other, are occupied by individuals with long-standing experience in the civil service (Mayntz, 1984). Most importantly, the politicization of the German senior bureaucracy does not give rise to the centrifugal tendencies of executive politicization in the United States. Although the preferences of both groups are shaped by aspirations reaching beyond the agency they serve in, in Germany these goals are funnelled through the discipline of partisanship. American executives, by contrast, do not stand to gain from party loyalty when pursuing their political and business aspirations; instead they are left to fend for themselves when seeking to establish networks with influential interests.

The institutional weakness of American agency leaders is further augmented by the separation of powers system in which they operate. The U.S. senior bureaucracy, caught between competing pressures that emanate simultaneously from the White House and from Congress, is deeply exposed to the vicissitudes of an executive–legislative conflict that is rarely constrained by partisanship. By comparison, German top level administrators operate in a much more sheltered environment: directly accountable only to a government that can rely on the political support of the parliamentary majority, they benefit from the restraint of partisanship. Although opposition parties will be keen to engage in oversight for political reasons, they have at their disposal only limited means of control and rarely present a threat to senior executives.

These institutional arrangements have far-reaching behavioral implications. Because of their lack of political insulation, U.S. senior executives

often go to great length to avoid public controversy and to engage in anticipatory conflict management (Aberbach, Putnam, & Rockman, 1981).
Richard Rose has described this reaction as "government by directionless
consensus ... In the absence of a forceful partisan initiative, providing both
protection and direction, the simplest course of action is for administrators
to seek out the lowest common denominator of opinions among affected
interests" (1969, p. 442). German agency leaders, by contrast, are much
more insulated from legislative interference and, as a result, have far less
reason to dodge political conflict. Given these institutional differences, it is
not surprising that cross-national survey research has found significant variation in the experiences of federal senior public servants in the two countries. For instance, in an influential comparative study on bureaucratic
behavior, Joel Aberbach et al. found that although 54 percent of U.S. executives agreed that "Congress too often interferes with the work of the
agencies," only 31 percent of German officials complained about a similar
phenomenon (Aberbach et al. 1990, p. 10).

In this analysis we will more closely examine the proposed relationship
between the institutional structuring of executive–legislative relations, executive capacity, and the choices of senior immigration executives. To do so,
we will focus on the politics of legislative oversight as the focal point of
interaction between elected principals and bureaucratic agents. I argue that,
in the sphere of coercive social regulation, representatives' scrutiny regularly
presents bureaucrats with two contradictory sets of incentives. Collective
forms of legislative oversight that appeal to the concerns of the public at
large, such as public committee hearings or parliamentary questioning, are
likely to scrutinize the effectiveness of immigration agencies in fulfilling
overarching goals of immigration control, thereby creating pressure for
more stringent enforcement. Because in this scenario, representatives are
driven by electoral credit-claiming and blame-avoidance, their substantive
demands closely resemble the public mandates articulated at the early legislative stage. The partial exception to this pattern occurs in contexts marked
by strong party discipline, where scrutiny that appeals to the public at large
will closely follow partisan lines. Accordingly, although parties to the right –
which typically endorse restrictionist immigration platforms – will exercise
public forms of oversight in ways that will create pressure for stricter
enforcement, parties to the left will push for a more liberalized implementation practice.

The second set of bureaucratic incentives flows from individual, rather
than collective, forms of legislative control. At the same time as representatives collectively monitor agencies in ways that appeal to the public at large,

individual politicians – in particular if relatively unconstrained by party discipline – pursue oversight activities that respond to the demands of organized policy losers. These more particularistic forms of scrutiny – most prominently the provision of constituency service – will closely match the demands of private interests expressed during the process of legislation and will place pressure on agency leaders to refrain from implementation.

What, then, are the implications of this institutional dynamic for executive decision-making on matters of immigration control? Agency leaders, dependent upon the technocratic expertise of lower level career civil servants, will pursue the law enforcement mandate of their organizations as long as this course of action does not present a political liability. In other words, where executives enjoy a strong degree of decision-making autonomy, they will select for implementation policies which are most congruent with the overarching, and, by necessity, cost-inflicting, mandate of immigration control. By contrast, in contexts in which agency leaders lack political capacity, they will set implementation priorities that can accommodate the demands arising from particularistic forms of oversight. Therefore, to the extent that enforcement undermines vital sources of support such as good relations with key legislators – and, by extension, powerful societal interests – senior executives will favor for implementation policies that are most congruent with the political constraints placed upon them by their elected principals.

This chapter argues that the deportation outcomes outlined in the introductory chapter are best understood in terms of the executive–legislative dynamics already described. Although senior immigration executives in Germany have tenaciously pursued the public mandate of returning failed asylum applicants – regardless of the political costs incurred in the process – U.S. agency leaders have resorted to a particularistic mode of implementation instead. Because of opposition by organized interests to the deportation of undocumented immigrants – mediated through congressional oversight – top U.S. executives have targeted for removal individuals without constituencies, in particular criminal offenders and migrants at ports of entry. We will now turn to our empirical analysis, starting with the executive politics of implementation in Germany's interior ministries.

THE EXECUTIVE POLITICS OF IMPLEMENTATION IN GERMANY

In Germany, jurisdiction over the implementation of deportations is shared between the interior ministries of the sixteen Länder and the Federal Ministry of the Interior. Although the Länder hold the constitutional mandate for policy implementation, in the sphere of deportation, they share this authority with the Federal Interior Ministry. To the extent that enforcement involves officers of the Federal Border Police – as is usually the case with air deportations – it is the federal ministry that issues regulations and decides over matters of implementation. It follows that to gauge the capacity of immigration executives, we will need to pay close attention to the relationship between both federal and Länder interior officials with their respective elected overseers.

The Politics of Parliamentary Oversight

We will now take a closer look at the dynamics of parliamentary oversight over the federal and Länder immigration bureaucracies. After examining the politics of oversight at the federal and subnational levels, we will investigate to what extent the identified patterns hold even under the restrictive conditions of administrative scandal.

The Immigration Bureaucracy under Federal Parliamentary Oversight

In contrast to the United States, where congressional committees are the most prominent agents of legislative oversight, bureaucratic control does not feature prominently among the day-to-day activities of the Bundestag's committees[1] (Johnson, 1979). Parliamentary control of administrative actions is therefore exercised most visibly on the floor of the Bundestag. Because of the interdependence of the government and the majority party group, however, control of executive actions on the Bundestag floor is effectively the task of the opposition. Accordingly, the Bundestag's politics of administrative control can be broadly characterized as driven by partisan politics, with the opposition availing itself of means of control available to party groups such as interpellations, question hours, and parliamentary questioning.[2] Control measures that require a floor majority, in contrast, are rarely employed because of the reluctance of the governing party coalition to join in the public exercise of administrative control.[3]

---

[1] With the partial exceptions of the petitions and appropriations committees, as well as the nonstanding investigatory committees.

[2] With the entry of the Greens as a second opposition party into the Bundestag in 1983, the use of these measures intensified notably as electoral competition within the opposition increased (Ismayr, 1992; Saalfeld, 2003).

[3] Between 1949 and 1990, the Bundestag voted in favor of summoning a member of government (*Zitierrecht*) fourteen times – about once every three years. Even more pronounced, of the twenty motions of censure (*Missbilligungsanträge*) put forward by the opposition during this period, not a single motion was passed (Ismayr, 1992).

In what ways, then, do these oversight procedures shape the activities of the executive branch? Given that governing parties rarely choose to employ these measures, does the scrutiny by the parliamentary opposition provide significant checks on bureaucratic decision-making at the federal level? An examination of questions submitted for both verbal and written reply during the 13th (1994–8) and 14th (1998–2002) Bundestag on issues relating to deportation policy reveals three basic findings (see Appendix 1). First, congruent with the literature on parliamentary oversight (Lichtenberg, 1986; Busch & Berger, 1989; Ismayr, 1992), this tool of parliamentary control is largely employed by the opposition parties, accounting for 80 to 95 percent of questions during the 13th and 14th Bundestag, respectively. Second, debates on deportation policy are marked by clear ideological differences between the political parties that persist even after governmental change. Parties to the left are predominantly concerned with the protection of immigrant rights, whereas parties to the right are primarily concerned with implementation deficits, national security, and law and order.

Finally, and most significantly, in the majority of cases bureaucratic responses to parliamentary questions reflect attempts by the interior minister and his representatives to evade oversight. Patterns of evasive behavior include executives' outright refusal to respond to parliamentary questions, withholding substantive information, deflecting criticism, and passing the buck to the Länder governments (see Appendix 1). These findings closely correspond to Wolfgang Ismayr's (1992) assessment of the efficacy of control mechanisms at the disposal of the parliamentary opposition. The ministerial bureaucracy, Ismayr argues, discloses only a modicum of data and frequently refuses to share information pointing to (self-defined) security grounds or a nontransparent "core area of executive 'personal responsibility'" (1992, p. 340). Problematically, senior executives take no risks when sharing data only selectively and inaccurately because the opposition party groups do not have the right of access to government files.[4]

It follows that, at the federal level, parliamentary oversight as exercised by the opposition parties has only limited impact on decision-making by interior ministers who enjoy the political support of the chancellor and, by extension, the majority party. Although senior executives are constitutionally obliged to be responsive to Bundestag oversight, legislators' control efforts have little impact on ministerial decision-making. Despite consistent

---

[4] Access to government files requires a majority vote of the (standing) committee of petitions or a qualified minority vote by a (nonstanding) committee of investigation, see Ismayr, 1992.

parliamentary pressure to ensure the protection of asylum seekers better – in particular until 1998 when the SPD and Greens were in opposition – policy developments during this period clearly reflect the conservative interior ministry's determination to step up enforcement and to target this group for deportation. It comes as no surprise that, just as legislative initiatives by the opposition are seldom successful but instead serve as appeals to public opinion (Mayntz & Scharpf, 1975), the exercise of parliamentary oversight on the floor of the Bundestag is better suited to public attention-seeking and electoral credit-claiming than to influencing administrative decision-making.

Because of the institutional configuration of Germany's political system, then, the exercise of control over the executive largely depends upon the willingness of the governing parties to oversee administrative actions proactively. This willingness is rarely forthcoming, however, because parliamentarians of the majority party have few incentives for monitoring the bureaucracy. As we will see, it is only in the event of political scandal that the governing parties have little choice but to wield their weapons of oversight. Before we turn to an instance of governing party scrutiny, we will examine the position of Land-level executives vis-à-vis their legislative principals in the Landtage.[5]

The Immigration Bureaucracy under Land-Level Parliamentary Oversight

What is true for federal parliamentary oversight also holds for the Landtage: parliamentarians, in particular members of the political opposition, who avail themselves of the tools of oversight are largely wielding a blunt sword. Although the constitutional means of scrutiny provide members of the parliamentary opposition with the opportunity to force issues onto the agenda and to go on record as having challenged government policy, they are ill-suited for influencing administrative policy decisions. The inefficacy of legislative oversight is most clearly evident when examining the use of motions (*Anträge*), a tool of oversight explicitly designed to effect a change in governmental policy. As we will see, motions filed by opposition party groups regularly fail because the governing parties vote as a bloc to withhold the necessary majority support.

To illustrate, during the 12th legislative session (1996–2001) of the Landtag of Baden-Württemberg, the preeminent issue pertaining to

---

[5] Land parliaments.

deportation policy was the return of civil war refugees to the former Yugoslavia. Three parliamentary motions were filed demanding a change in regulations, all of which were rejected by either the interior committee or the
Landtag floor: a motion by the opposition Green party group requesting the
extension of temporary residence permits for Bosnian refugees (Landtag
Baden-Württemberg, 1996), a motion to extend residence permits for Bosnian apprentices filed by the Social Democratic opposition (Landtag Baden-
Württemberg, 1997), and a second Social Democratic motion requesting a
stay of deportation for Kosovar refugees (Landtag Baden-Württemberg,
1998).

The SPD's motion to exempt Bosnian apprentices from deportation is
particularly instructive because it concerns an issue position shared by the
Liberals, the junior partner of the governing coalition headed by the CDU.
Significantly, when the motion was debated on the Landtag floor, the Liberals, who have traditionally held libertarian and rights-oriented positions on
immigration, adhered to their coalition partner's restrictionist party line and
helped defeat the motion, thereby contravening their own policy position.

However, in a striking policy reversal, in January 2001, the Land's interior ministry issued regulations concerning civil war refugees from the former
Yugoslavia (Innenministerium Baden-Württemberg, 2001) that exempted
from deportation certain qualified workers in medium-sized firms (*Bleiberechtsregelung*). This turnaround was not the result of political pressure from
the Landtag floor, however. Rather, it was a concession by the CDU to their
junior coalition partner – traditionally the advocate of medium-sized business – which was negotiated behind closed doors. As an insider recounts,
"the *Bleiberechtsregelung* ... in Baden-Württemberg was forced by the Liberals. In December 2000, the cabinet decided to interpret [a federal regula-
tion] in a way that took into account regional economic interests."[6]

In sum, executive policy change at the Land level can be attributed to the
influence of political actors within the governing coalition. Importantly, the
Land government's eventual liberal interpretation of federal regulations
pertaining to Bosnian civil war refugees did not come about because of
oversight by opposition parties on the Landtag floor. Instead, when faced
with scrutiny by the SPD, the Liberal Party chose to shield the coalition
government from criticism even at the cost of contravening its own party
platform. Because of the community of interest between the government
ministries and the members of the parliamentary majority parties, the

---

[6] Personal interview, former civil servant in Baden-Württemberg's interior ministry, Landtag
Baden-Württemberg, Stuttgart, January 11, 2002.

Landtag opposition thus has little leverage when it comes to forcing an administrative change. This pattern largely mirrors the politics of oversight at the federal level where senior executives operate with a great degree of political autonomy from parliament. However, whereas federal opposition representatives have the opportunity to pursue policy change by way of negotiating legislative compromise in standing committees, Land politicians end up empty-handed because immigration law is federal law. We will now return to the federal level and investigate the politics surrounding administrative scandal as a "most likely case" of effective parliamentary oversight.

Parliamentary Oversight under Administrative Scandal

On May 30, 1999, a Sudanese national Aamir Ageeb, wearing a helmet[7] tightly strapped onto his head and escorted by officers of the Federal Border Police, died of asphyxiation during his deportation aboard a flight from Frankfurt to Cairo. Ageeb's death turned out to have major ramifications for the administration of air deportations by the Federal Border Police. It resulted in the unusual decision of federal minister of the interior Otto Schily (SPD) to suspend escorted air deportations temporarily, followed by a substantial revision of federal regulations and the prosecution of the three escorting officers. Importantly, Ageeb's death not only attracted sustained media attention but also led to a flurry of parliamentary oversight activity, both on the Bundestag floor and in the interior committee. In addition to a number of parliamentary questions and a series of minor appellations, the interior committee requested a written report from the ministry, and summoned the interior minister and several senior civil servants to testify before the committee. In response, the ministry submitted a detailed report that included a comprehensive account of the events of May 30, measures taken by the ministry to prevent the occurrence of future deaths, and various statistics on air deportations, including those on the use of helmets (Bundesministerium des Innern, 1999). Strikingly, federal officials under previous parliamentary questioning had denied the availability of these data.[8]

---

[7] Helmets are used to protect escorting officers from bites by individuals who resist deportation.

[8] When in 1996 Green Bundestag delegate Manfred Such asked for statistics on the use of physical means of coercion during deportations, parliamentary state secretary Horst Waffenschmidt replied: "The repatriation by the Federal Border Police of foreigners who physically resist deportation can require the use of physical force. Because we do not collect statistical data on the use of physical force, we cannot provide answers to your question" (*Deutscher Bundestag*, February 7, 1996, 7476, author's translation).

This case of executive responsiveness to legislative oversight, I argue, must be understood in the context of control exerted by the governing coalition's parliamentary party groups. Because of the ideological leanings of the SPD and especially the Greens, who had run on a platform of an expansionist, compassionate immigration policy, parliamentary control in this instance was liberal in nature. At the same time, although there is no question that legislative oversight had a discernible impact on administrative practice, it did not serve to undermine executive capacity. Although deportations were temporarily suspended and the resumption of removals made contingent on stricter regulations for escorting officers, the longer-term repercussions of Ageeb's death were more complex. On the one hand, the new regulations succeeded in curtailing the discretion of Federal Border Police officers and in sensitizing law enforcement officers to the risks of physical coercion. For instance, the following interview quote by a senior border police officer reflects a new awareness of the perils of physical force.

Since the Ageeb case, we have become very careful. As soon as a deportee tells us that he won't cooperate, we abort the deportation, provided the plane hasn't taken off yet. We don't want to get into trouble.
(Personal interview, senior Federal Border Police officer "A," regional Federal Border Police office, October 2001)

On the one hand, the political repercussions of Ageeb's death have served to curtail bureaucratic discretion by limiting the range of options available to officers for enforcing physical compliance. At the same time, however, the scandal provided ministry officials with a renewed impetus to develop alternative deportation strategies. In consequence, the German immigration bureaucracy has increasingly come to rely upon private employees for air escorts, in particular foreign airline personnel. After Ageeb,[9] we observe an

---

[9] Ageeb was not the first person to die in the custody of the Federal Border Police: in 1994 a Nigerian national, Kola Bankole, died on his flight to Nigeria after having received a large dose of sedatives. Bankole's death, however, never reached the same level of politicization, and thus had only minor administrative ramifications. What distinguished Ageeb from Bankole was in part the coincidence of timing: Ageeb's death occurred in the wake of two fatal deportations in neighboring countries. Less than a month before, the death of a Nigerian asylum seeker in the custody of Austrian authorities triggered a political scandal in Vienna, while in September 1998, the death of a Nigerian refugee in Belgium even forced the resignation of interior minister Louis Tobback (Fekete, 2003). In a second difference between the incidents of 1994 and 1999, Bakole's death took place under Christian Democratic hardliner interior minister Manfred Kanther, whereas Ageeb's transpired under Social Democratic minister Otto Schily whose red-green coalition had run a platform of liberalizing the country's immigration policy.

increase from 13.9 percent (1999) to 20 percent (2000) for those air deportations escorted by foreign airline personnel (*Deutscher Bundestag*, December
30, 1999; March 30, 2001). By de facto contracting out the politically
sensitive tasks of physical coercion to foreign actors, German executives
not only have reduced the risk of public exposure of violent incidents, but
also have evaded legal liability.[10]

Yet another strategy for dealing with physical resistance has been the use
of charter planes for group deportations. The most important characteristic
of such removals is that they take place out of public view: because there is
no third party to be mobilized on behalf of the deportees, charter deportations render physical resistance virtually ineffective.[11] Moreover, as the
following statement by a senior border patrol officer shows, this practice
also reduces the constraints on officers employing physical force to secure
compliance.

Of course there is the issue of group deportations. Some time ago we sent 30
deportees, escorted by 60 border police officers and a medical doctor, to Romania.
In these cases we can exert more force – I can openly admit to this – the deportees get
shackled at their hands and feet and can also get pushed down, but of course not in a
way that could lead to asphyxiation.
(Personal interview, senior Federal Border Police officer "A," regional Federal
Border Police office, October 2001)

In 2000, the Conference of Interior Ministers decided to make use of
small charter planes when deporting individuals who were considered particularly violent. Even more than is the case with charter deportations, the
rationale of invisibility justifies the enormous fiscal costs of this strategy.

We started with small charter planes in 2000. We use those with really difficult cases,
for one or two persons. Mostly we use them for safety reasons. ... The advantages
are clear: the pilot will definitely cooperate, and there is no public who can take the
side of the deportee.
(Personal interview, senior civil servant, Federal Ministry of the Interior, Berlin,
November 13, 2001)

Our discussion of the politics of parliamentary scrutiny has yielded two
important insights which, as we will see, clearly distinguish German immigration executives from their American counterparts. First, although members of the Bundestag opposition are highly proactive in employing
oversight, the impact on executive decision-making is negligible. Because

[10] For a similar argument, see Lahav & Guiraudon (2000).
[11] By contrast, deportations on commercial flights are often aborted if passengers and pilots
object to the use of coercion.

of the community of interest between the government and the parliamentary majority – joined by party discipline and the imperative of staying in office – German senior officials have little to fear from attempts by the parliamentary opposition to intervene in bureaucratic decision-making in ways that might constrain executive policy.

Second, in the event of effective legislative oversight – which is limited to scrutiny by the governing party – senior executives stay on their chosen course of action. The political scandal following Ageeb's death clearly demonstrates executive responsiveness to parliamentary concerns in conjunction with the capacity to devise new strategies that serve to restore the political capacity to implement contested policies. Rather than abandoning escorted air deportations, federal ministry officials adopted new implementation strategies that since have facilitated the removal of asylum applicants by circumventing specific political obstacles. In other words, interior officials have unwaveringly pursued their legislative mandate of controlling asylum immigration, despite pressures for less rigorous implementation exerted by left-of-center parliamentary parties.

What has been absent from our analysis, thus far, are attempts of individual legislators to intervene in bureaucratic decision-making. By contrast to the politics of congressional oversight in the United States, policy-related concerns of legislators in the Bundestag and the Landtage have to be funneled through their parliamentary party group. This was evident in our discussion of the *Bleiberechtsregelung* in Baden-Württemberg, where the lobbying efforts of midsize business to exempt Bosnian employees from deportation were placed on the Landtag's agenda by the Social Democratic and Liberal party groups. However, as far as lobbying efforts that focus on individual cases – as opposed to more general policy issues – are concerned, parliamentarians rarely play a significant role. Whereas federal legislators hold no jurisdiction over the case-by-case implementation decisions of immigration bureaucrats, Land parliamentarians are too politically feeble to intervene in administrative decision-making on a case-by-case basis. One important caveat applies, however. Although bureaucrats rarely have to fear the interventions of parliamentarians when making case decisions, particularistic pressures can have a significant impact on decision-making at the local level. The oversight activities of municipal politicians are beyond the analytical scope of this chapter but we will return to this dynamic in Chapter 4.

What, then, are the implications of these patterns of executive–legislative relations for executive decision-making? In the following section, we will identify executive implementation priorities by investigating the deportation of three administrative groups: asylum, illegal, and criminal migrants. The data clearly show that officials have strategically focused their removal efforts on asylum seekers. By studying these groups in terms of the demands that their deportation places upon bureaucratic agencies, I provide evidence that the administrative targeting of asylum seekers is contingent upon strong executive capacity.

Setting Implementation Priorities

Asylum Applicants

There is little question that, in recent decades, the forced removal of rejected asylum applicants has been at the forefront of implementation efforts across the interior ministries. Whereas in the late 1970s asylum seekers accounted for roughly 5 percent of deportations from Germany, by the late 1990s this group made up over a half of all deportations (see Figure 2, Introduction). In absolute numbers, the annual number of deported asylum seekers increased thirty-six-fold between 1978 and 1998, from about 500 to 18,000.[12] Moreover, the immigration bureaucracy raised the (approximate) asylum deportation rate from below 5 percent in the late 1980s to between 15 and 20 percent in the mid- and late 1990s.[13]

Significantly, these statistical findings closely correspond to alternative indicators of executive priority-setting. Looking at recent instances of institutional innovation, for instance, we find that, in every case, the creation of new administrative deportation structures has been designed with asylum seekers in mind. Most significant has been the establishment of central immigration authorities – to be examined in Chapter 4 – which the Land interior ministers decided upon at their conference in June 1989 (Nuscheler, 1995). The model central authority was to include an immigration agency, a satellite office of the federal refugee agency, a reception center for asylum applicants, and a satellite office of the regional administrative court. By combining these offices as part of a single institution, it was argued, all administrative tasks pertaining to the processing of asylum applicants – their registration, initial housing, the asylum hearing and decision, court appeals, and, in cases of rejection, their deportation – could be performed with a minimum of delay.[14] Even though the timing and size of these centralized

---

[12] Source: Data provided to author by the Federal Ministry of the Interior and Federal Border Police Directorate, Koblenz; also Munch, 1993.
[13] Author's calculations.
[14] Personal interview, deportation officer "A," regional immigration authority, Karlsruhe (Baden-Württemberg), January 25, 2002.

institutions has varied across the Länder, all Länder have established central immigration institutions of some kind.

Although this leaves close to half of all deportations accounted for by groups other than asylum seekers, it is crucial to note that the administrative effort required for the repatriation of these groups is disproportionately small. For reasons to be explained below, the administrative and political resources required for asylum deportations far outweigh those involved for the forced removal of any other migrant group. There is little doubt that the executive focus on asylum seekers cannot be explained in terms of bureaucrats taking the path of least resistance – on the contrary, asylum deportations regularly elicit intense proimmigrant mobilization. Instead, I contend that the bureaucratic targeting of asylum seekers is indicative of the capacity of agency leaders to pursue deportations even when these meet with organized opposition. Importantly, these executive priorities closely correspond to the substantive nature of earlier rounds of public mandate oriented immigration reform.

Illegal Immigrants

Compared to asylum seekers, illegal immigrants[15] residing in Germany without work or residency authorization are at lower risk of deportation. As we saw in the Introduction (Figure 2), in the 1990s the proportion of nonasylum deportations ranged from 23 to 53 percent of total deportations, averaging at around 42 percent. It is only when we add to this number the returns conducted by the Federal Border Police on the basis of apprehension near the border[16] (Figure 5) that repatriations of illegal immigrants exceed the number of asylum deportations by a substantial margin. However, returns by the border police have more in common with removals at ports of entry (to be discussed in the U.S. case) than with deportations from within the country, both with regard to the ease of apprehension, immigrants' ties to their host country,[17] and, finally, their procedural and substantive rights. The population of interest to the current analysis – illegally resident, rather than entering or transiting, migrants – is subject to arrest by the Länder police forces, rather than by the Federal Border Police. Although there are no

---

[15] The relevant administrative distinction between asylum seekers and illegal immigrants is whether or not the individual has filed an asylum application.

[16] The Federal Border Police are authorized to apprehend noncitizens within a 30-km radius of the border and at points of international transit such as train stations. Apprehensions in the interior are under the jurisdiction of the Länder police.

[17] The Federal Border Police are only authorized to apprehend and repatriate noncitizens who have been in the country for less than six months.

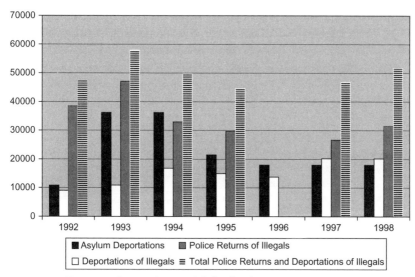

FIGURE 5. Germany, deportations and federal police returns, 1992–1998.
Source: Bundesministerium des Innern, Bundesgrenzschutzdirektion.
(No data on police returns available for 1996)

reliable statistical data on the size of this group, there is little doubt that it is substantial and growing, with estimates ranging from over half a million to well over 1.5 million illegal residents (Alt, 1999, p. 50).

Most importantly, comparing the typical profile of Germany's undocumented immigrants – Eastern European and former Soviet nationals who entered and/or worked illegally – with those of rejected asylum seekers, many of whom originate from Asian or African countries, it is evident that the administrative efforts required for asylum removals, in particular the procurement of identity documents, far outweigh the challenge of deporting undocumented immigrants, both in terms of legal proceedings and travel arrangements. The fact that less than half of all deportations are accounted for by this sizeable and easily deportable group is thus worth noting.

The relative neglect of undocumented immigrants by law enforcement authorities is reflected in the absence of specific administrative infrastructures designed for their arrest and repatriation. The central immigration agencies in Länder such as Baden-Württemberg, designed to facilitate and speed up deportations, deal nearly exclusively with rejected asylum seekers. In order to deport illegal immigrants, then, municipal immigration authorities depend upon the police for apprehension. Although there tend to be few problems of interagency cooperation between immigration authorities and the police – both operate under the supervision of the Länder interior ministries – the latter do not consider the apprehension of illegal immigrants a priority for law enforcement. Most importantly, police officers stand to gain few professional rewards from the apprehension and processing of undocumented immigrants.[18] For instance, the police in Stuttgart, Baden-Württemberg's capital, have transferred the apprehension of illegal migrants out of their (prestigious) criminal division down to officers on the beat, thereby indicating its lower status.[19] Similarly, the following quote by a Bavarian deportation officer attributes the relative neglect of undocumented immigrants to a lack of public concern:

> In my opinion, the second biggest problem [after getting travel documents] is the fact that today illegal residence is considered a trifle offense. It used to be different; when people heard about an illegal immigrant, they thought, "He must be a thief." Today we don't consider it a crime any more; society tolerates it. Being illegal no longer violates our sense of justice.
>
> (Personal interview, deportation officer, local immigration authority, Augsburg/Bavaria, February 19, 2002)

Why is it, then, that in the eyes of both the public and policy-makers the deportation of rejected asylum seekers trumps that of illegal immigrants? A closer examination of the issue of illegal immigration exposes a striking vacuum in German political debate. For instance, a contents search of all electronically available Bundestag and Bundesrat transcripts from 1990 to 2002 yields only ten hits for illegal immigrants,[20] whereas asylum-related keywords result in 416 hits.[21] This pattern is confirmed when we investigate the substantive focus of parliamentary questions pertaining to deportations. Examining the substantive foci of questions submitted for verbal and written reply to the Federal Interior Ministry during the 13th (1994–8) and 14th (1998–2002) Bundestag, among those questions that explicitly referred to an administrative deportation category, 86 percent (13th Bundestag) and 64 percent (14th Bundestag) concerned the removal of asylum seekers. Illegal immigrants, in contrast, did not feature notably during parliamentary questioning (0 and 7 percent, respectively) (see Appendix 1).

---

[18] An important exception to this is human traffickers, whose arrest is considered a priority in law enforcement.

[19] Personal interview, deportation officer, local immigration authority, Stuttgart (Baden-Württemberg), January 8, 2002.

[20] If we add "illegal employment," a term that often but not always pertains to immigrants, the number of hits increases to thirty-five.

[21] Dokumentations- und Informationssystem für Parlamentarische Vorgänge, http://dip.bundestag.de, accessed March 2004.

The reason for the relative neglect of undocumented immigrants and the concomitant targeting of asylum seekers by German law enforcement authorities lies in their different fiscal impact on local communities. Unlike asylum seekers who qualify for public assistance, basic health care, housing benefits, and public education, illegal immigrants have no access to public services with the exception of emergency health care. As I argued in Chapter 2, the widespread backlash against asylum seekers in the early 1990s was largely a response to the fiscal costs borne by municipalities and counties. The costs incurred by the presence of illegal immigrants in contrast, are less quantifiable, particularly in the bifurcated German labor market where fewer natives compete with illegal migrants for unskilled jobs than in the United States. In Germany, then, widespread demands for increased deportations have focused on asylum seekers. As a result, immigration bureaucracies do not have a strong mandate to allocate their resources in ways that prioritize the return of illegal immigrants. In other words, the bureaucratic neglect of undocumented migrants reflects the lack of a popular and legislative mandate, rather than the lack of executive capacity.

Criminal Offenders

Unlike the U.S. immigration service, German immigration authorities have not rigorously pursued the return of criminal offenders, with the important exception of criminal asylum seekers. When the Conference of Interior Ministers decided it was safe to resume the deportation of Bosnian and Kosovar civil war refugees, the Länder did single out criminal offenders for early return. However, beyond the group of asylum seekers – and paralleling the situation of illegal immigrants – interior ministries have devised no specialized administrative structures for the deportation of immigrant offenders more generally. As a result, the deportation of convicted criminals has remained exclusively in the hands of municipal and county authorities, with important consequences.

Because the Länder interior ministries have made no concerted effort to set up structures of interagency cooperation paralleling the regional deportation authorities for asylum seekers, local immigration officers often struggle to establish close working relationships with prison personnel and public prosecutors. In interviews, deportation officers repeatedly voiced frustration with the lack of cooperation by public prosecutors in particular:

Sometimes inmates get released before their sentence is up. That usually comes as a surprise to us. ... In the ideal scenario, the public prosecutor informs us of the upcoming release of somebody under our jurisdiction. The person is released, and

we decide whether or not to deport. However, often we only get informed on the day of release, and then it's simply too late [to initiate deportation proceedings].
(Personal interview, deportation officer, local immigration authority,
Forst/Brandenburg, November 19, 2001)

The deportation efforts of local authorities are not only hampered by a lack of interagency cooperation but also struggle to acquire the necessary legal expertise to tackle the repatriation of criminal offenders. In distinction to U.S. immigration law, German law affords immigration bureaucrats substantial discretion when deciding on whether or not to deport a legal resident convicted of a crime. Interview respondents repeatedly emphasized the need for well-trained officers in the field of criminal deportations. Explains a member of an interagency pilot project that was set up by the police and designed to increase deportations of serial immigrant offenders:

We can really focus on our task. This is why we can work intensively; we stick with cases, regardless of how difficult they are. We do whatever the law allows us to do. . . . If someone from a municipal immigration authority tries to do this, they give up quickly, because they have other things to take care of. We initiate a case, and then we want to see results, of course.
(Personal interview, police officer, Joint Working Group on Serial Offenders,
Frankfurt am Main, January 22, 2002)

It is important to note that the challenges posed by criminal deportations do not stem from a lack of political capacity. Unlike asylum removals, they do not require much in the way of political capacity to succeed. Because criminal offenders have few advocates, their deportation rarely triggers the kind of mobilization that could provide a challenge to bureaucratic agents:

Public protest simply is not an issue for us. Not a single time. Even we are surprised about this. I think that this is because we're dealing with serial offenders: nobody contests their deportation.
(Personal interview, police officer, Joint Working Group on Serial Offenders,
Frankfurt am Main, January 22, 2002)

Rather, the relative neglect of criminal deportations reflects the absence of a parliamentary mandate for focusing infrastructural resources on this group. Although the German public undoubtedly supports the removal of offenders, anti-immigrant backlash has been directed against asylum applicants, and deportation resources have been targeted accordingly. The relative lack of political concern with immigrant offenders is clearly reflected in the substantive focus of legislative oversight. Looking at parliamentary questions, for instance, immigrant offenders were the subject of only 14 percent of deportation questions during the 13th Bundestag. In the 14th Bundestag they only featured significantly when the conservative CDU/CSU engaged in opposition politics (29 percent).[22]

Once we retrace our steps to the point of agenda-setting, it is evident that deportation policy in Germany is marked by a remarkable degree of political sustainability. The implementation priorities set by senior executives are strongly aligned with the policy concerns of earlier rounds of reform, and, by extension, the substantive focus of public debate, which made the issue of immigration control politically salient in the first place. In contrast to their American counterparts, German immigration executives enjoy a substantial degree of autonomy. Despite determined attempts by opposition parties to use their powers of parliamentary oversight to force senior officials to adjust their implementation priorities, the institutional logic of parliamentarianism renders this weapon comparatively powerless. It is only the rare occasion where policy implementation erupts into a high-profile political scandal that the governing parties will curb executive autonomy. At the same time, even these instances of governing party oversight are unlikely to have a long-term negative impact on bureaucratic capacity. We will now turn to the United States to examine the factors driving the executive politics of implementation in an institutional context much at variance from that shaping the behavior of immigration executives in Germany.

THE EXECUTIVE POLITICS OF IMPLEMENTATION IN THE UNITED STATES

Because the INS is a federal agency, legislative oversight is within the sole jurisdiction of the U.S. Congress. In contrast to the legislative scrutiny in the Bundestag, congressional oversight is exercised most powerfully in committees and subcommittees: it is in committee that legislators debate bureaucratic performance, commission reports by the General Accounting Office[23] and other investigatory government bodies, as well as stage hearings to query agency leaders. At the same time, immigration executives are subject to oversight interventions by individual members of Congress. And, as we shall see, to a vastly greater extent than is the case in Germany, individual legislators hold considerable political power when setting out to intervene in administrative decision-making.

---

[22] Dokumentations- und Informationssystem für Parlamentarische Vorgänge, http://dip.bundestag.de, accessed March 2004.

[23] The General Accounting Office is the investigatory arm of Congress. Its main task is to examine the use of public funds by auditing and evaluating federal programs and activities.

The Politics of Congressional Oversight

In this analysis of the politics of oversight, we will begin by examining the activities of congressional committees as the dominant form of collective legislative control, before moving on to examine the more particularistic forms of oversight exercised by individual members of Congress. What bureaucratic incentives flow from these forms of congressional control, and how do these shape executive decision-making on matters of deportation?

The Immigration Bureaucracy under Congressional Committee Oversight

Beginning in the late 1980s, congressional immigration subcommittees started to systematically, and, oftentimes, aggressively, engage in oversight over the INS. We will examine two measures of legislative oversight which Aberbach (1990) identifies among the most frequently employed means of control: oversight hearings conducted by the House immigration subcommittee,[24] and investigatory reports of the General Accounting Office and the Justice Department's Office of the Inspector General (OIG), commissioned by congressional committees.[25]

Just as the flurry of oversight activities on the floor of the Bundestag can be best understood as appeals to public opinion, so also can congressional committee oversight be considered an important opportunity for electoral credit-claiming and blame-avoidance. As Martha Derthick has argued, committee oversight "yields politically rewarding publicity for the congressional practitioners and public humiliation for the agency" (1990, p. 160). The question of what motivates legislative scrutiny is an important one because these incentives have far-reaching implications for the substantive nature of oversight. It follows that, to the extent that legislators pursue these measures as means of electoral credit-claiming, they will focus on issues that appeal to the concerns of the public at large.

It is therefore not surprising to find that, on issues of immigration, congressional oversight has nearly exclusively concentrated on the agency's law

---

[24] This chapter mostly examines the oversight activities of the House because its members, elected from smaller electoral districts, are more vulnerable to particularistic pressures than Senators. However, although the dynamics described here are more pronounced in the House, they are also observable in the Senate.

[25] In Aberbach's study of legislative oversight, these two measures were exceeded in frequency only by staffers' communication with agency personnel.

enforcement mandate, rather than on its tasks of service provision[26] – a pattern that bespeaks responsiveness to popular demands for stricter immigration control. Between February 1997 and June 2002,[27] a period spanning the 105th and 107th Congresses, the House immigration subcommittee held an impressive total of 46 oversight hearings on the agency's implementation of relevant statutes. This number compares to a total of only 39 oversight hearings conducted by the House Judiciary Subcommittee on Crime over five separate law enforcement agencies during the same period. In those immigration hearings that single out the agency's deportation mandate, we observe a sustained congressional concern with the removal of illegal immigrants, followed by the repatriation of criminal offenders. Between the passage of IIRIRA in 1996 and the break-up of the INS, the House subcommittee conducted four oversight hearings on illegal immigrants (July 1, 1999; June 10, 1999; June 19, 2002; March 18, 1999), two hearings on the issue of criminal aliens (July 15, 1997; July 27, 1998), and two hearings that dealt with both (February 11, 1997; February 25, 1999).

The reports of the General Accounting Office reflect an equally intense interest in the INS's performance: in the course of seven years (1996–2002), the General Accounting Office issued a staggering 39 reports on the immigration agency. The substantive foci of investigatory reports commissioned by Congress confirm a continued interest in both deportee populations. In the aftermath of the 1996 reforms, the General Accounting Office published four reports on the INS' enforcement mandates: one report – mandated by IIRIRA – dealt with illegal immigrants within the United States (U.S. General Accounting Office, 1999b), two reports investigated the implementation of the new expedited removal provisions (U.S. General Accounting Office, 1998, 2000), and one report examined the deportation of criminal aliens (U.S. General Accounting Office, 1999a).[28] Similarly prominent, of the Office of the Inspector General's evaluation and inspection reports for 1994–2003, 38 dealt with the INS, whereas the remaining Justice agencies – the Bureau of Prisons, Drug Enforcement Administration, U.S. Marshals' Service, and the Federal Bureau of Investigations – collectively were the subject of twelve reports. In the OIG reports from 1996 to March 2003,

---

[26] Such as naturalization, visa issuance, and permanent residency.

[27] The first year for which electronic-hearing transcripts are available was 1997; 2002 marks the last year of the INS before the agency's incorporation into the Department of Homeland Security.

[28] Although the reports on illegal and criminal aliens were enforcement-driven, the investigation of the expedited removal program was mandated by the International Religious Freedom Act of 1998 and therefore dealt with human rights issues.

the deportation of illegal aliens features particularly prominently: although three reports dealt with illegal immigrants (U.S. Department of Justice Office of the Inspector General, 1996b, 1997, 2002), only one report focused on criminal immigrants (U.S. Department of Justice Office of the Inspector General, 2001).

It is evident that Congress, exercising oversight through committee hearings and investigatory reports, has singled out the INS among the various law enforcement agencies as a favored target of oversight. In doing so, it has vociferously criticized the agency for its implementation failures and demanded more stringent enforcement of its deportation mandate. Significantly, now that legislative behavior is – as in the early stages of agenda-setting – once again tailored toward public credit-claiming, illegal immigrants resurface as the focus of the congressional control rhetoric. Importantly, as we are about to see, U.S. executive officials are too institutionally exposed to be immune to these blame-casting strategies. The following analysis will examine how these patterns of congressional oversight shape the outcome of policy implementation by molding bureaucratic behavior.

What are the bureaucratic incentives flowing from these instances of committee monitoring? I contend that congressional oversight places significant pressures on agency leaders to rely on measurable indicators of immigration control. Because committee oversight is principally motivated by electoral credit-claiming, legislators require clear assessments of agency performance that allow them to appraise, chasten, and communicate to colleagues and constituents the successes and failures of the bureaucracies they oversee.

How is one to measure an agency mandate as complex and as intangible as immigration control? The INS constitutes what Wilson has called a "coping agency": bureaucracies in which neither the tasks (outputs) nor the results (outcomes) of bureaucratic action are observable. As Wilson contends, legislators who oversee coping agencies "cannot observe the tasks being carried out, unambiguously assess their effect on the organizations' goals, or even state those goals in clear and precise language" (1989, p. 245). Among the range of available tools of oversight, "fire alarms" (McCubbins & Schwartz, 1984) such as constituent complaints and media coverage, while allowing legislators to identify potentially problematic areas of implementation, do not lend themselves to a systematic tracing of agency performance over time. From the point of view of agency leaders, fire alarms are equally undesirable means of assessing agency performance. Given that the agency each year performs tasks of coercive regulation that affect the lives of millions of individuals, clients are likely to contest bureaucratic decisions. And because the attainment of policy goals such as immigration control is inherently elusive, the organization is acutely vulnerable to the raising of fire alarms.

Compared to fire alarm signals, numerical indicators present an alternative and more attractive means of measuring agency performance. Needless to say, statistics on enforcement outputs such as the number of apprehensions, detentions, and removals may not necessarily tell us anything about the efficacy of agency actions. However, legislators and agency leaders may not care too much about whether these indicators are valid measures of effective enforcement – what matters is that these indicators capture activities that can be portrayed as indicative of agency performance. Moreover, statistical data are the nuts and bolts of prominent forms of oversight such as evaluation reports by congressional research agencies. From the point of view of the INS leadership, in turn, quantitative indicators allow for the attainment of discrete performance goals. Like the FBI under the leadership of J. Edgar Hoover, who played the numbers game with enormous zeal (Wilson, 1978), the work of the INS statistical division is driven by congressional data requests.[29]

When it comes to interpreting deportation statistics, effective enforcement bears little relation to the number of removals. Because the pool of deportable individuals is both vast and unknown while agency resources are limited, enforcement necessarily relies upon targeting. Whereas numbers-driven implementation is motivated by maximizing the number of deportations, effective enforcement concentrates on the removal of those individuals whose presence most clearly prejudices the well-being of their communities. This, however, is a resource-intensive standard of performance contingent upon the use of intelligence and surveillance resources. For instance, given the loose label of "criminal alien" – an issue we will return to below – criminal status alone cannot be used as a reliable proxy for "societal threat."

Importantly, neither members of Congress nor immigration executives are sufficiently motivated to prioritize effective enforcement over numbers-driven implementation. Few officials, regardless of the strength of their ideological commitment to migration control, can politically afford to focus on the former. Importantly, a shift from quantifiable to effective enforcement would reduce the number of deportations, at least in the short term. In contrast, an upsurge of deportations reflects well not only on the INS, but also on committee members overseeing the agency.

What kinds of evidence should we expect to see in support of this claim of numbers-driven enforcement? Principally, we would expect both legislators

---

[29] Personal interviews, Statistics Division and Division on Business Systems and Analysis, INS Headquarters, August 26–27, 2002.

and immigration executives to explicitly frame agency performance in quantitative terms. This claim is corroborated by the data. Like countless others, the following statement by the chairman of the House immigration subcommittee Lamar Smith during an oversight hearing on the Institutional Hearing Program[30] defines bureaucratic accountability in terms of the number of deportations performed:

> In order to make progress, all parties involved have to focus on several key factors. First, we have to focus on the percentage of eligible criminal aliens who are actually removed from the United States pursuant to IHP [Institutional Hearing Program]. The current rate of 25 to 30 percent must be increased. As a measure of accountability, we will have to see significant increase in this percentage.
>
> (July 15, 1997, pp. 4–5)

Congressional attempts to measure bureaucratic accountability in terms of ever increasing deportation numbers have resulted in a strong emphasis on statistics as preferred performance indicators. The following excerpt from the opening statement of Paul Virtue, Acting Executive Associate Commissioner for the INS in 1997, indicates that the agency itself is also party to this numbers game:

> With the strong support of the Congress and the administration, INS has raised the number of removals to record levels 3 years in a row, and has worked to restore the integrity of the deportation process. This fiscal year we'll see an increase in detention space to over 12,000 beds, and an unprecedented effort to remove at least 93,000 aliens ordered deported and excluded. That's a 37-percent increase over last year's total of 68,000.
>
> (February 11, 1997, pp. 17–18)

Significantly, agency leaders in their reliance on enforcement statistics have increasingly based resource allocation decisions on the number of deportations undertaken. The numbers game pervades agency culture down to the field offices, as the following interview quotes by two street-level deportation officers illustrate.

> Right now headquarters tell us that we have exceeded the aim of 102% criminal deportations. They give us certain numbers. We are at a pace of 172%!
>
> (Personal interview, deportation officer "J." INS Miami, May 28, 2002)

> There is only one tangible result, and that is the number of removals. And we have seen these grow.
>
> (Personal interview, deportation officer "L." INS San Diego, July 10, 2002)

---

[30] Later renamed the Institutional Removal Program. The program provides for the deportation of incarcerated noncitizens at the completion of their criminal sentence.

These accounts illustrate that the logic underlying the numbers game has far-reaching implications for the implementation of deportation policy. Most fundamentally, this approach to enforcement strongly favors strategies that produce rapid increases in the number of removals, regardless of their efficacy to further the policy goals of migration control. For instance, in many instances it is easier to locate and deport petty offenders, rather than to go after those with violent criminal records. In a similar vein, removing individuals at the border requires far fewer administrative and political resources than pursuing undocumented immigrants settled within local communities. Before we investigate these implications more closely, we will turn to a second, alternative form of congressional control – oversight activities by individual representatives.

The Immigration Bureaucracy under the Oversight of Individual Legislators

Whether congressional oversight is exercised collectively or individually matters because each form of oversight gives rise to a distinct dynamic of bureaucratic control. Derthick, in her study of the Social Security Administration (1990), found that although Congress as a "legislative institution" restricts eligibility for disability benefits, Congress as a "collection of individual representatives" is committed to helping individuals gain benefits. Importantly, this pattern should extend beyond the case of disability because it follows an institutional logic. Applied to the case of deportation, I argue that legislators are likely to promote the stricter enforcement of removal statutes in their committee work, while through their constituency service exert pressure on bureaucrats to refrain from implementation.

Constituency service provides elected officials with particularly easy opportunities for credit-claiming. In general, legislators will be most responsive to narrow and organized interests in situations where the group's costs and benefits are both visible and traceable to the representative's actions, although the costs and benefits to the larger public are less easily discernible (Arnold, 1990). Clearly, where a member of Congress succeeds in pressuring the INS to withdraw a deportation order, the benefits for their constituents are enormous and, most importantly, can be directly attributed to the representative's intervention. It should therefore come as no surprise that immigration features dominantly on the casework agenda of members of Congress. For instance, in Bruce Cain et al.'s study of constituency service (1987), immigration issues were the second most frequently reported examples for members of Congress.[31] Significantly, examples of "congressional parochialism" (Melnick, 1994, p. 244) are not limited to legislators' interventions in individual case decisions. As we will see, representatives are also quick to respond when agency actions impose costs upon entire communities within their districts. In the words of Wilson, at the same time as congressional committees tell agency leaders to "find and expel illegal aliens," individual representatives demand that the agency "not break up families, impose hardships, violate civil rights, or deprive employers of low-paid workers" (1989, p. 158).

In the American institutional universe, Congress as the overseer and agency executives as the overseen coexist on highly unequal terms. In his influential study of federal bureau chiefs, Herbert Kaufman argued that "even if you define autonomy more narrowly as the ability of chiefs and bureaus to bargain as equals with all those trying to tell them what to do, they were not autonomous. Congress clearly [had] the upper hand in dealing with them, and many other constraints on them sprang from that relationship" (1981, p. 161). Although these are the institutional conditions under which all federal bureaucracies operate, immigration executives lack autonomy to an even greater extent than most other agency leaders (Morris, 1985; Wilson, 1989; Barrios, 1999). Unlike, for instance, the more successful Social Security Administration (Derthick, 1980) and U.S. Postal Service (Carpenter, 2001), the INS lacks a key condition of strong administrative leadership: a well-organized agency clientele that will mobilize political support for the agency (Barrios, 1999). As Kenneth Meier has argued, agencies that implement distributive and redistributive policies can cultivate the political support of their clientele to whom they provide valuable benefits (1979). The INS as a social regulatory agency, by contrast, has no loyal constituencies because their agents impose concentrated costs upon their clients whereas any associated benefits are widely dispersed and difficult to gauge.

This imbalance of power, which typifies executive–legislative relations in the United States more generally but is particularly pronounced for the INS, has important implications for bureaucratic decision-making. Most importantly, to the extent that executive agency leaders rely upon the support of individual legislators to enact their policy programs, they will find it necessary to accommodate their particularistic requests (Cain, Ferejohn, & Fiorina, 1987). Unable to operate autonomously even in situations where the policy complexity so typical of coping agencies requires the exercise of administrative discretion, INS senior officials resort to a defensive, risk-averse mode of

---

[31] After social security and military or veterans' benefit problems.

implementation that is driven by political crises, rather than policy goals, and characterized by blame-avoidance, rather than accountability. Significantly, a culture of risk aversion arising from a basic lack of political capacity permeates the agency from headquarters to the district level. Thus, as the following statements by immigration lawyers illustrate, even where street-level bureaucrats are authorized by law to employ prosecutorial discretion when making case decisions, they regularly decide not to do so.

INS officers have discretion not to pursue a case, to settle a case, or to drop a case! But they refuse to exercise this discretion. . . . There is no other government agency like the INS with a reluctance as strong to make decisions – we always hear: "I can't decide this, I need to speak to my supervisor." they always need to ask for permission for everything.
(Personal interview, immigration lawyer and human rights advocate, San Diego, July 24, 2002)

When you go to the INS to apply for a waiver, it is extremely hard to get. . . . The INS is scared of being too liberal, because if something goes wrong, the adjudication decision can be tracked down to a particular officer.
(Personal interview, immigration lawyer, Miami, June 12, 2002)

From the immigration agency's perspective, risk-aversion reflects a reality of bureaucratic vulnerability to aggressive congressional oversight. As Barrios argues in her historical study, "the agency has been the focus of too much congressional attention. Throughout its history, it has been so tightly monitored and closely controlled that INS Commissioner Meissner characterized her agency as 'hooked at the hip with Congress'" (1999, p. 36). From the position of agency leaders, congressional oversight ultimately serves to undermine the agency's enforcement efforts. Although committees fault the agency for insufficiently implementing legislative mandates, the following quote confirms Cain et al.'s finding (1987) that individual members of Congress – even sponsors of restrictionist legislation – freely lobby the immigration causes of individual constituents.

We often write letters to district offices . . . There is little hesitancy on our part to put in a call on behalf of constituents.
(Personal interview, Legislative Director for George Gekas (R-PA), Washington, D.C., August 19, 2002)

Members of Congress intervene in INS decision-making not only in response to requests by individual constituents, but also to ward off any potential costs from organized interest lobbies. For instance, Miriam Wells, in her study of immigration enforcement in California, chronicles how, in the mid-1990s, Democratic Congressman Sam Farr responded to lobbying efforts by agribusiness and Latino constituencies by brokering a deal with the local INS office in California's Salinas Valley that effectively brought an end to worksite enforcement in the region (2004). The following interview quote by a senior career civil servant at INS headquarters similarly captures the corresponding double bind in which the agency finds itself:

I give you an example about Congress and the INS: Congressman X and another Midwest congressman complained that there were too many illegal aliens. So Investigations develops two operations, visits industries to verify workers. Our officers execute it. They find a lot of illegals. Two weeks later, the same congressman calls up, asking us to stop it. And so the operation closed down.
(Personal interview, senior official "D," INS Headquarters, Washington, D.C., August 27, 2002)

This account parallels the fate of "Operation Vanguard," an INS clampdown on meatpacking plants in Nebraska, Iowa, and South Dakota in 1999:

Nebraska's members of Congress at first called for tougher enforcement, recalled Mark Reed, then INS director of operations. But when the result shut down some plants, 'all hell broke loose,' he said. ... Members of Congress at first hostile to immigrants embraced 'all the same people who were so repugnant to them before,' Reed said, 'and they prevailed.' Operation Vanguard – which was designed to expand to four states in four months and nationwide the next year, eventually including the lodging, food and construction industries – was killed. Congress 'came to recognize that these people . . . had become a very important part of their community, churches, schools, sports, barbecues, families – and most importantly the economy,' Reed said. 'You've got to be careful what you ask for.' The mention of Operation Vanguard provokes strong reactions in Omaha, where people say a similar effort today would still cause trouble.
(*The Washington Post*, June 19, 2006)

These accounts of reluctant worksite enforcement correspond to quantitative patterns of the agency's worksite enforcement activities. Figure 6 shows that from 1992 to 2001 – a period of intense politicization surrounding the control of illegal immigration – the number of employer investigations dropped from 7,000 to just 1,600.

Not surprisingly, then, attempts at aggressive enforcement at the district level that stand to alienate core congressional constituencies run the risk of meeting with disapproval by the agency leadership. A San Diego deportation officer recounts,

The worst thing you can do is to embarrass the agency. Once we sent out letters to people with final removal orders, telling them that they might be eligible for some new relief. Over 50 turned up! And we arrested them. We had it checked with the trial attorneys and with headquarters, we had the go-ahead that this was legal.

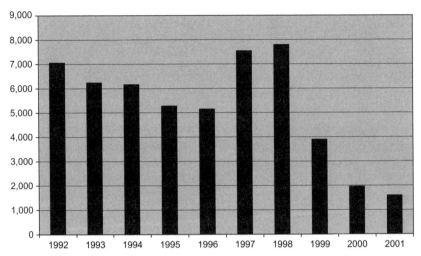

FIGURE 6. INS employer investigations, 1992–2001.
Source: INS Statistical Yearbooks.

Though it didn't go up all the way to the Commissioner. We had a reporter here from the *LA Times* and thought this was a good chance for enforcement coverage. Then, one woman knelt on the floor, crying loudly. Of course, this was the picture that made it onto the front page. This stirred up a lot of trouble. The Commissioner was furious! Now these sting operations have to be approved by the Commissioner.

(Personal interview, deportation officer "M," INS San Diego, August 1, 2002)

Given the political risks entailed in deporting undocumented immigrants, it is not surprising that the significance of immigration-related as compared to criminal deportations has declined over time (see Introduction, Figure 4) and, even after a modest increase in the late 1990s, remained below the level of immigration-related deportations of the 1970s. Figure 7 shows the relative stagnation of immigration-related deportations and monitored required departures[32] from the interior of the United States (excluding removals at ports of entry).

Lacking institutional autonomy from its congressional overseers, the immigration agency is ill-equipped to deal with the double-bind of contradictory congressional expectations. The resultant culture of defensiveness is acutely exposed in the political scandal triggered by a visit of the Republican

---

[32] "Required departures" are monitored returns of individuals who are allowed to depart "voluntarily" and are thus exempt from the statutory reentry bars linked to deportation orders. This provision is only available to certain noncriminal immigrants.

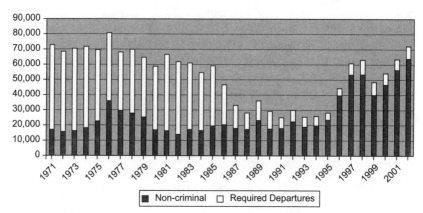

FIGURE 7. United States: noncriminal deportations and required departures, 1971–2002.
Source: INS Statistical Yearbooks/USCIS internal data.

Congressional Task Force on Immigration Reform to the Miami district in 1995. Unbeknownst to congressional delegates, senior managers of the Miami office had taken steps to hide the fact that the district was experiencing major difficulties in discharging its duties. INS managers had ordered the temporary move of detainees to other detention facilities, artificially increased staffing at Krome detention center, and moved foreign nationals out of holding cells at the airport – steps that were designed to conjure up an image of the Miami district as "well-managed, efficiently run, and under control" (U.S. Department of Justice Office of the Inspector General, 1996a, p. 1). Moreover, when, tipped off by a group of whistle-blowers, the Justice Department's Office of the Inspector General started to investigate the incident, senior officials at regional and district levels attempted to obstruct the inquiry.

To the district leadership, the visit of the congressional Task Force was perceived as a serious threat. The feeling of political vulnerability is clearly conveyed in the following email excerpt, sent by Miami District Director Walter Cadman to several program managers and the eastern regional director after meeting with INS Commissioner Meissner in Washington, D.C. to discuss the Task Force's upcoming visit:

During my one-day visit to HQ on Friday, one of the things I found out is that the above-referenced visit by the group of congressional Representatives headed by Rep. Gallegly is considered EXTREMELY important by Commissioner Meissner. ... Apparently, they did the San Diego border tour previously and it went well, but not without a few of the members of this Congressional Asylum Reform group pulling some employees to the side to get the "real story." This, of course, carries with it some real risks. The Commissioner is concerned that it would take very little to put the kiss of death on their views toward INS, with significant adverse consequences for some time thereafter.

(U.S. Department of Justice Office of the Inspector General, 1996a, p. 4, all caps in original)

The deception of Congress by the Miami district is exemplary in revealing just how strongly the INS feels threatened by legislative oversight and fears the political repercussions of negative congressional review. Even though the problems at Krome detention center were at least in part the result of under-resourcing, the district leadership considered it more important to minimize the risk of congressional disapproval than to point to the problem of resource scarcity. And, as we have seen, the same sense of political vulnerability is present at the level of agency leadership in Washington, D.C. Commissioner Meissner, in a policy interview after her tenure as INS Commissioner, succinctly summarized the conflicting position of U.S. immigration executives. When asked whether there were any particular countries whose migration policies or strategies she admired, she replied,

Canada is a country that all countries in the world admire and would want to emulate in terms of the professionalism of the people who deal with immigration. Because a separate ministry handles migration, it gets the political attention within the cabinet that it deserves. ... Because they have a parliamentary system, they can execute their policies without the kind of contentious relationship with the Congress that we have.

(Naím, 2002, p. 34)

I have argued that congressional oversight, set in an institutional context of legislative dominance over the bureaucracy, regularly undermines the immigration service's deportation efforts. In the final part of this chapter, we will take a careful look at the implications of this dynamic for executive decision-making on matters of deportation. How does this "contentious relationship" between Congress and the INS shape the implementation priorities of the INS leadership?

Setting Implementation Priorities

Congressional oversight, I have argued, has generated incentives for immigration executives to select for implementation policies that will maximize the number of deportations while at the same time minimize the risk of conflict with legislators. Policy selection is therefore made on the basis of one essential consideration: is the intervention "politically compatible?" I will offer empirical evidence for the claim that both the disproportionate number of criminal deportations and the high number of expedited removals from the United States are best understood as the result of an enforcement logic that is driven by concerns about political compatibility. Unlike deportations of undocumented immigrants from within the country, criminal and expedited removals are unlikely to meet with political opposition. Immigrant advocates tend to shy away from taking up the cause of criminal offenders for political reasons, while having little control over the fate of migrants at ports of entry.

Targeting Immigrants Without Constituencies

By contrast to German interior ministers, U.S. immigration executives do not possess the necessary political capacity for the steady implementation of contested legislative mandates. Simultaneously faced with congressional pressure for stringent enforcement, on the one hand, and requests for leniency by individual legislators, on the other, agency leaders respond by targeting for implementation those immigrants whose deportation is unlikely to engender political opposition. Immigrants who do not have constituencies likely to mobilize on their behalf best fit this requirement, and two groups of noncitizens meet this criterion particularly well.

First, immigrants who are under deportation orders on criminal grounds rarely elicit the support of immigrant advocates. Just as in the legislative arena public support for "criminal aliens" constitutes a serious political liability, advocates who mobilize on behalf of migrants under deportation orders cannot rely on public support when taking on the cause of criminal offenders. A useful test case for the mobilization potential of "criminal alien" cases is the aftermath of the passage of the IIRIRA and the Antiterrorism and Effective Death Penalty Act of 1996. Not only did these Acts radically expand the category of deportable crimes to include a multitude of nonviolent crimes – including misdemeanors – but they also rendered these provisions retroactive. As a result, after 1996, significant numbers of legal permanent residents faced deportation, many of whom did not fit popular notions surrounding a "criminal alien." In fact, many of these "aggravated felons" had lived in the United States since their childhood and were now facing deportation for nonviolent crimes that they had committed many years ago, when they did not constitute grounds for deportation, and for which they had already been punished.

Given these often tragic circumstances, advocates in many cases did attempt to mobilize to prevent deportation of particularly deserving cases. Although in some cases public and legal advocacy did result in the lifting of deportation orders,[33] these mobilization successes were exceptional and did not reflect the overall experience of advocates, as reflected in the following quote by a San Diego advocate:

Citizens and Immigrants for Equal Justice [a group supporting families affected by deportation] in San Diego disbanded after 9/11. That had partially to do with 9/11, but there also was a feeling that we had done all we could, and wouldn't achieve anything. There was a strong feeling of devastation. A sense of frustration. We took to the street, and we had one proposal after another – and it made no difference. Nothing happened. No one wants to take on the cause of criminal legal permanent residents. ... It has to do with this country's attitudes toward criminal aliens, and these have always been harsh. They contradict many liberal aspects of this society; on this issue this society is so conservative.

(Personal interview, immigration lawyer and human rights advocate, San Diego, July 24, 2002)

Because of public antipathy toward criminal offenders, immigration officers have been able to capitalize on the stigma attached to the labels of "aggravated felon" and "criminal alien" and have used deportation as a way of claiming credit for purportedly effective law enforcement – even when the grounds for these claims were spurious, as the following statement by a Miami journalist illustrates:

James Goldman, the INS Head of Investigations after 1996, told us that they were being aggressive at picking up aggravated felons. They worked through local parole offices to identify people. So they publicized this, they wanted credit. They described the people they had picked up as dangerous, as, I quote, "the worst of the worst." We then checked their criminal records. And there we saw that these people had only committed misdemeanors.

(Personal interview, staff writer, *The Miami Herald*, Miami, June 6, 2002)

It follows that, even in cases where deportation does not constitute effective law enforcement – where its primary impact is the disruption of family and community life, rather than the promotion of public safety – implementing the criminal alien provisions of immigration law is a bureaucratic strategy that carries a minimum of political risk and maximizes the political payoff of implementation. INS leaders have repeatedly justified their decision to focus deportation efforts on criminal immigrants as a responsible use of scarce

---

[33] One of the most high-profile cases was that of German national Mary Anne Gehris who had moved to the United States as an eighteen-month-old adoptee in 1965. When in 1988, Gehris pulled another woman's hair in a quarrel, she was placed on one-year probation for a misdemeanor conviction of simple battery. A decade later, under the retroactive deportation provisions of 1996, the INS initiated deportation proceedings against Gehris. In 2000, the state of Georgia granted her a full pardon after an intense national media campaign, thereby averting her deportation.

resources to remove those individuals most harmful to the public. However, the indiscriminate focus on offenders does not necessarily reflect an effective use of law enforcement powers. The category of "criminal aliens" consists of significant numbers of individuals whose offenses are nonviolent and which under criminal law would only be regarded as misdemeanors. Most importantly, the agency does not prioritize within this group by the severity of the crime. Removal data on the most common categories of recorded offenses support this claim: between 1997 and 2002, violent offenses accounted for only 14.5 percent of all criminal deportations.[34]

It is in large part because of their political compatibility, then, that criminal aliens have become the main target of the INS's Detention and Removal Division. A former INS political appointee under the Clinton Administration confirms this assessment:

This was consistent with what the White House wanted. The White House wanted to be tough on immigration, and it wanted to be tough on crime. Criminal aliens were easiest to remove. . . . On criminal aliens, there was a meeting of the minds between INS and the White House. INS initiated it because it wanted credit for enforcement, and the White House was glad about getting criminal aliens removed.

(Personal interview, former INS General Counsel and Executive Associate
Commissioner for Programs, April 7, 2004)

The importance of political compatibility as a factor steering implementation is evident once we examine the relevant counterexample: the deportation of undocumented immigrants from within the United States – a challenge that will be dealt with in more detail in Chapter 4. Here, implementation efforts consistently meet with political opposition. As the following two quotes demonstrate, not only does its social disruptiveness to local communities render this form of removal highly vulnerable to political conflict, but so does the visibility of physical coercion when removing individuals from their families and homes:

In Miami, there is a focus on criminal aliens. They are not that active in clamping down on employment enforcement because this would be too disruptive. There was a case where the INS was clamping down on a flower business, and people were jumping on cars and everything. They stuck with that case but then tried to stay away from these types of cases.

(Personal interview, immigration lawyer, Miami, July 10, 2002)

---

[34] Source: 1998–2002 Statistical Yearbooks of the INS. The following categories were coded as "violent offenses": assault, robbery, sexual assault, and family offenses. The remaining top crime categories are: drugs, immigration, burglary, larceny, traffic offenses, weapon offenses, fraudulent activities/forgery, stolen vehicles. Where immigrants have committed more than one offense, only the most serious offense is recorded.

We also used to have a program, in 1999 or 2000. But then some family member got pepper-sprayed by mistake, and this put an end to it. . . . We used to go out to [illegal immigrants'] homes and pick people up but were told off by the Clinton Administration because of complaints by Congressmen.
(Personal interview, senior deportation officer "K," INS San Diego,
July 23, 2002)

Just as the deportation of immigrant offenders rarely evokes widespread political protest, neither does the removal of migrants at ports of entry. In 1996, Congress instituted the provision of expedited removal, abolishing the right to a judicial hearing for arriving noncitizens[35] and instead authorized the INS to remove migrants administratively who arrived at ports of entry without travel documents, or who attempted entry through fraud. Because access to ports is highly regulated, advocacy groups are not in a position to monitor removals and, in the vast majority of cases, only hear about removed individuals after the fact. As the following quote reflects, expedited removal officers operate in an environment marked by high levels of political insulation:

We haven't really had problems down here with the press or protest groups. They can get to the border, but not into the port – it's federal property.
(Personal interview, expedited removal officer, San Ysidro Port of Entry,
August 6, 2002)

To sum up, criminal offenders and migrants at ports of entry are particularly convenient targets for removal by an immigration bureaucracy acutely vulnerable to congressional meddling. Because these two groups are unlikely to elicit mobilization, their deportation allows immigration executives to take credit for implementing legislative mandates without alienating important sources of political support. At the same time, the agency has shied away from directing its implementation efforts at the population of resident undocumented immigrants. In the experience of INS executives, to do so is to risk congressional interference in bureaucratic decision-making, which threatens to undermine not only implementation, but also the agency's credibility. It follows that although German and U.S. immigration authorities hold in common a relative neglect of illegal immigrants, they do so for markedly different reasons. Whereas in Germany, illegal immigrants have rarely been the target of popular demands for immigration control, bureaucrats in the United States operate in a

---

[35] With the exception of legal permanent residents.

political environment preoccupied with the issue of illegal immigration. At the same time, however, they lack the political resources to implement measures that would effectively lower illegal immigration.

This chapter has pursued the argument that empirical variation in the distribution of deportations across migrant groups can in large part be accounted for by cross-national differences in the implementation incentives of senior executives. In both Germany and the United States, these incentives are fundamentally shaped by the institutional context in which agency leaders operate. In particular, it is the relationship between immigration executives and their legislative overseers that most strongly shapes the direction policy implementation takes and that affords German immigration executives a degree of political autonomy that is the envy of their American counterparts. In consequence, U.S. executives have opted for numbers-driven and risk-averse enforcement strategies and have targeted for deportation immigrants without organized constituencies – immigrant offenders and migrants at ports of entry – even though public pressure has remained focused on illegal immigrants. German executives, in contrast, have tenaciously pursued the return of asylum seekers, even though this is the migrant group with the strongest support lobby and the highest level of politicization concerning their deportation. In the following chapter, we will further pursue this argument by studying the implementation efforts of deportation officers on the beat.

4

Deportation and the Street-Level
Politics of Implementation

> People support deportation, but not deportation of people who they know
> personally.
>
> (Personal interview, deportation officer "A," INS Miami, June 5, 2002)

Like few other forms of government policy, coercive social regulation calls
upon state actors to impose costs upon constituencies hostile to intervention. And yet, not all exercise of the state's social regulatory authority
presents an equally momentous challenge. The demands of coercive social
regulation vary not only by the constituency targeted, but also over the
course of the policy process. In this chapter, we will study the politics
of deportation at the final and, arguably, most crucial policy stage: that
of street-level implementation. Specifically, we will examine the capacity of
field officers to carry out removal orders when faced with grassroots
opposition.

By studying those actors upon whose shoulders the task of implementation rests, this chapter provides a crucial test case for our theoretical framework of state capacity. Although enforcement gaps abound in most areas of
public policy, few reveal a disparity as drastic as that between immigration
law, on the one hand, and its administration, on the other. To illustrate,
even when we consider that the 115,000 deportations conducted by the U.S.
immigration service in 2002 presented a then-record high in the agency's
postwar enforcement history, the number of legally removable immigrants
the same year ran into the millions. More generally, given the global
proliferation of policy initiatives of stricter immigration control, the presence of millions of illegal migrants across the advanced industrialized world
cannot be understood as arising from a lack of legal instruments to enforce

their departure. Rather, it is the issue of implementation that strikes at the heart of the reality of illegal immigration.

Among the principal challenges faced by deportation bureaucrats are the political costs associated with enforcement. To the extent that removal imposes severe costs upon migrants, it is likely to be marked by high levels of conflict. The politically problematic nature of forced return has been poignantly articulated by Gibney:

Deportation is a "cruel power," one that sometimes seems incompatible with the modern liberal state based on respect for human rights. Deportation tears individuals from families and cruelly uproots people from communities where they may have lived for many years, sometimes banishing them to places where they have few ties or connections. It requires the coercive hand of the state on what are often extremely vulnerable men, women and, perhaps most controversially of all, children. The coercion required for deportation may be contested in the courts or on the street.... Grassroots campaigns can turn local schools, neighborhoods and churches into formidable if unlikely sites of resistance to expulsion. (2008, p. 147)

While few would disagree that, in liberal democracies, the mass expulsion of millions of immigrants does not constitute a feasible policy option, the political precariousness of deportation holds even for individual cases. As this chapter's empirical analysis will show, the forced removal of even a single family from their local community can become a lightning rod for highly visible antienforcement drives that have far-reaching consequences for street-level bureaucrats.

THE CHALLENGE OF CASE MOBILIZATION

Deportation elicits political challenge at every step along the policy chain. At the same time, countermobilization is most forceful during field implementation because it is at this stage that the true costs of removing individuals become evident. For immigrants who have spent years living in local communities, a deportation order constitutes a coercive uprooting from their relatives, workplaces, and neighborhoods. In countless cases, families are broken apart as one spouse remains with the children in the host country in order to hold on to educational and occupational opportunities. Often the deportee may be barred for years – sometimes even for life[1] – from returning, even for the purpose of family visits. If it is the primary breadwinner who is forced to leave, deportation can result in severe financial hardship, especially

---

[1] Permanent reentry bars are more common in the United States. In Europe, reentry bars of five years are the norm.

if – as is often the case – he or she is unable to secure well-paid work after returning to his or her country of nationality. Even in cases where the material losses resulting from forced return are less drastic, the psychological harm suffered by deportees and their families can be devastating. Finally, the costs incurred through deportation are not confined to the families of those who are removed. In cases where long-term residents are targeted for expulsion, forced removal will also have consequences even for migrants' wider social networks and workplaces. Thus, the list of policy losers will extend beyond the immediate circle of family and friends to include community groups and employers.

Although government removal data do not record the length of residence, there is no doubt that, in both countries, many expelled migrants have well-established community ties. In their study of Salvadoran deportees, Jacqueline Hagan et al. (2008) found that 54 percent of respondents had resided in the United States for more than five years prior to deportation, whereas 38 percent had lived there for over ten years.[2] Importantly, the surveyed sample included expedited removals – had they excluded this group, the percentage of deportees with long-term ties to the United States would have been significantly higher. In Germany, similarly, a large proportion of asylum seekers live in the country for years before a negative administrative decision becomes legally binding. The reality of long-term residence for many applicants is evident from the fact that in 2000, in 43 percent of cases, it took administrative courts over two years to adjudicate asylum appeals alone (Unabhängige Kommission Zuwanderung, 2001).[3] As a result, by the time they are issued their deportation orders, many asylum seekers have become well integrated members of their local neighborhoods.

As the costs borne by these individuals and their communities become apparent, mobilization drives by immigrant advocates – usually amplified through local media coverage – can piggyback on the tacit support of a large segment of the general public. The following statement by a senior civil servant in one of Germany's Land interior ministries illustrates how the enormous costs of deportation that surface during implementation can turn law enforcement into a highly unpopular intervention:

It is unbelievably difficult to convey deportations to the public. This is because it impinges on human dignity, and because of all the emotions involved. It is a difficult

---

[2] Fifty percent had lived in the United States for less than five years, 4 percent did not report length of residence.

[3] This period does not include the actual adjudication of claims.

situation for those affected. No matter where they return to, their lives will deteriorate.

(Personal interview, senior civil servant, Interior Ministry of Baden-Württemberg, Stuttgart, January 7, 2002)

Because cases of forced repatriation often lead observers to conclude that the costs of enforcement are vastly incommensurate with any associated benefits, implementation allows for a humanitarian reframing of deportation. The new humanizing frame starkly contrasts with earlier debates in the legislative stages that were dominated by generalized and demonizing claims regarding, for instance, the economic threat posed by "illegal aliens."[4] As a result, although in the legislative arena proregulatory pressures tend to prevail, implementing bureaucrats are likely to encounter antiregulatory demands instead.

Where deportation is perceived to impose unduly harsh costs on immigrants, or where its criminalizing discourse does not fit the profile of a particular individual, we are likely to observe a form of public mobilization that I call "case mobilization." This concept describes advocacy efforts by segments of the public to appeal to bureaucratic actors to exempt particular people from deportation. To illustrate, such opposition may mobilize in support of a family who have resided in a local community for many years. The family originally entered as asylum applicants (as is often the case in Germany), or undocumented immigrants (more frequently the case in the United States), and are now issued with a deportation order. Included may be small children born in the host country – those born in the United States are citizens by birth – who are well integrated in kindergarten or school and are better versed in German or English than in their "native" language. Their parents may be actively involved in the life of the community, coaching the soccer club or volunteering in a local church congregation. What happens next is succinctly summed up by a German street-level bureaucrat:

There is a lot of public pressure ... The longer that immigrants have been here, the bigger the problem gets. All legal recourse has been exhausted ... administrative proceedings are over. And then the church gets involved, or fellow pupils

---

[4] A similar pattern has been observed by Magaña in her descriptive study of immigration policy and the INS. She cites a senior INS officer as arguing: "People want to control immigration when it is faceless, but when someone has a friend who needs immigration help, people have no problem calling us for assistance or asking us to make exceptions" (2003, p. 30). Magaña uses the quote to illustrate that the public does not understand the mission of the agency.

in school.... There is no legal basis for this. But these instances of mobilization occur on a daily basis.

(Personal interview, deportation officer "D," local immigration authority, Brandenburg, November 19, 2001)

A corresponding dynamic has been identified by Wells in her recent research on grassroots immigration politics in San Francisco, California. Writing in the context of local understandings of civic membership, she explains:

Immigrants' day-to-day involvement in economic life, in religious, educational, and political institutions, and in neighborhood activities [...] can generate felt solidarity, responsibilities, and mutual dependencies that themselves become a basis for asserting and securing immigrants' rights. In such contexts, a range of community members, interest groups, and authorities – from employers, unions, and civil rights organizations, to politicians, religious leaders, school administrators, and co-ethnic legal residents – can come to perceive illegal immigrants as part of the public that the locality is pledged to protect. (2004, pp. 1314–5)

These community ties play an important role in facilitating case mobilization, which fundamentally depends upon the willingness of local people – nursery school teachers, neighbors, pastors, or established advocacy groups – to stage campaigns on behalf of particular immigrants and organize letter-writing drives to politicians, orchestrate public demonstrations, and in some cases even offer church sanctuary.

It is at this point that case mobilization begins to interact with executive–legislative relations as advocates appeal to elected officials to intervene in bureaucratic decision-making on behalf of particular "deserving" individuals. And, significantly, politicians stand much to gain – and little to lose – from being seen as protecting these immigrants from the interventions of unpopular coercive bureaucracies. Given the low costs of approaching bureaucrats – and the significant associated public benefits of doing so – few elected officials, even those with modest constituency service resources, will choose to run the risk of being perceived as indifferent toward the plight of a sympathetic deportation case.

Immigration bureaucrats, of course, face strong incentives to try to ward off these attempts at political interference. Street-level officers in law enforcement agencies typically fit the pattern of "careerists" outlined by Wilson (1980, p. 375). They tend to closely identify with their organization, its mission and its rules, and will be hostile to interference by elected officials, which they will perceive as illegitimate political meddling in administrative affairs (Weissinger, 1996). Careerists not only prefer the predictability and accountability associated with bureaucratic regulations, they also jealously guard their turf and resent external requests to bend the rules on behalf of purportedly "exceptional" cases. The following statement by a German immigration bureaucrat illustrates the careerist's law enforcement mentality:

> Our benchmark is the law. If we depart from it in one case, then we are no longer credible. There are good reasons for emphasizing humanitarian considerations, but it is our obligation to follow the law.
>
> (Personal interview, director, local immigration authority, Ostprignitz-Ruppin/Brandenburg, November 27, 2002)

Case mobilization, it follows, constitutes a substantial threat to the autonomy of street-level bureaucrats.

Before we continue our empirical analysis, a caveat is in order: not all deportation cases are equally likely to benefit from public campaigns. Advocates will be careful to select cases in which "deservingness" is beyond dispute, while staying well clear of individuals whose personal history may tarnish their reputations – such as immigrants with criminal records or similar social stigmas. Those who become the beneficiaries of case mobilization need not be the most deserving in terms of the objective impact that deportation may have, nor need these individuals be victims of egregious administrative practice (though both help). What is most important for the purpose of case mobilization is the likelihood that deportation will elicit public support – a condition present where, for instance, school children are involved, or where the person to be deported has been actively involved in his or her community, such as in a local church congregation.

FOUR EMPIRICAL CASES OF STREET-LEVEL IMPLEMENTATION

Once we take a closer look at the dynamics shaping the implementation of deportations, we find that instances of case mobilization abound in both Germany and the United States. And, strikingly, across the two countries, efforts to mobilize the public are based on the same rationale, advanced with the same arguments, and carried out by means of similar strategies. Yet the empirical evidence presented in this chapter shows that the capacity of bureaucrats to carry out deportation orders in the face of case mobilization is far from constant. On the contrary, when interviewed about the challenges of implementing removal orders, field officers in different locales provided noticeably different assessments of the scope of their executive capacity.

Taking a closer look at these interview data (see Appendix 2), we find that executive capacity is by far the strongest in the centralized, conservative

German Land of Baden-Württemberg, where not a single deportation officer considered case mobilization a significant obstacle to implementation. Bureaucrats in the decentralized Land of Brandenburg display the second strongest degree of executive capacity: 70 percent of interviewed officers considered case mobilization to be a constraint on enforcement. By contrast, executive capacity is weakest in U.S. bureaucracies: in Miami, all interviewed deportation officers considered campaigns supporting individual immigrants as an impediment to repatriation. Even in jurisdictions where such opposition was relatively weak, as the case of San Diego demonstrates, executives were likely to abandon implementation once confronted with sustained opposition. The remainder of this chapter will carefully examine the politics of case mobilization in these four locales. In doing so, we will closely analyze not only the scope of enforcement capacity in each case, but, most importantly, the conditions that have generated such striking cross-national and subnational divergence in executive capacity.

Two German Cases: Regional versus Municipal Implementation

In Germany, the constitutional powers of policy implementation rest with the governments of the sixteen federal Länder; as a result, there is considerable subnational variation in how legislation is administered. In 1989, Baden-Württemberg, located in the southwest of the country, pioneered the centralization of removals as it shifted implementation from approximately 120 municipal and county immigration authorities to four regional authorities. The purpose of this centralization was to allow for more consistent enforcement of deportation orders issued to rejected asylum applicants, according to a senior civil servant who had been instrumental in overseeing this process:

In the late 1980s, the number of asylum seekers increased rapidly ... and hardly anyone got deported .... We then decided to move decision-making up to the regional level .... The main reason for this reorganization was the systematic enforcement of the [rejected asylum seeker's] duty to leave Germany.
(Personal interview, deportation officer "A," regional immigration authority, Karlsruhe/Baden-Württemberg, January 25, 2002)

In an important decision, these newly established regional authorities were not, as had been the case with local immigration agencies, headed by elected officials. Instead, the centralized agencies came to operate under directors appointed by the senior executive of the Land's immigration bureaucracy, Baden-Württemberg's minister of the interior.

In the aftermath of German unification in the early 1990s, when the newly created eastern Land of Brandenburg was faced with the task of setting up its own immigration authorities, its interior ministry decided, after a brief experiment with regional centralization modeled after Baden-Württemberg, to devolve deportation tasks to the county and municipal levels instead. This process of decentralization unraveled in the course of a massive wave of administrative reform, which was driven by a tug-of-war between local and regional authorities, and from which the former emerged as the winner. As was the case in Baden-Württemberg prior to centralization, these municipal authorities are directly accountable to elected mayors to whom the Land interior minister has delegated the task of implementation.

This difference in vertical structures of oversight has turned out to have far-reaching implications for the relationship between street-level bureaucrats and local politicians. In Brandenburg, where deportation orders are issued and implemented at the municipal level, immigration officers are routinely approached by local politicians to refrain from implementation. Because county and city mayors are elected officials, and their constituencies are small, they are particularly receptive to the lobbying efforts of immigrant advocates. In a comment representative of bureaucratic accounts at the local level, a deportation officer in Brandenburg described the political pressure bearing on municipal bureaucrats:

The city councilors decided to form a working group to consult with us on questions pertaining to deportation. ... We now get summoned to their meetings where we discuss individual cases. Afterwards the press reports on the meeting and creates further moral pressure.
(Personal interview, deportation officer, local immigration authority, Brandenburg a.d. Havel/Brandenburg, November 21, 2001)

The Lutheran refugee chaplain of the city of Potsdam in Brandenburg, a prominent immigrant advocate, confirmed the vulnerability of municipal authorities to case mobilization:

In Potsdam ... there are clear channels of communication between us, local politicians and the immigration authority. We usually manage to find a compromise and can avert deportation. ... Councilors cannot afford to ignore us because we have both legal expertise and political power.
(Personal interview, Lutheran refugee chaplain, Potsdam/Brandenburg, December 12, 2001)

Because media coverage of mobilization efforts largely takes place in local and regional publications, news analyses do not allow us to quantify success rates of case mobilization across a large number of cases.[5] Instead, process-tracing across particular cases can provide us with both an important check on, and an illustration of, the arguments advanced by bureaucrats and immigrant advocates. For this purpose, we will compare two prominent cases of mobilization in Brandenburg and Baden-Württemberg. Interestingly, although advocates succeeded in both instances, process-tracing reveals significant differences in executive capacity.

In 2001, Vietnamese national Ba Tan Nguyen, his wife, and two sons were issued a deportation order from the Brandenburg town of Guben. An economically depressed town close to the Polish border, Guben had made the national headlines in 1999 when a neo-Nazi attack resulted in the death of Algerian asylum-seeker Omar Ben Noui. In the aftermath, the town's police and judiciary had come under intense criticism for not acting decisively enough, and the Land government named Guben as one of four hotbeds of right-wing extremism in Brandenburg (*Frankfurter Rundschau*, November 2, 2000).

Mr. Nguyen had been legally residing in Germany for 22 years: after pursuing his undergraduate and doctoral degrees in engineering, he had spent several years working under temporary work visas before the last expired in 1998. However, because Vietnamese officials refused to issue the necessary repatriation papers, the family were able to continue to work and reside in Guben. This situation changed abruptly in early 2001 after Vietnamese officials reversed course and provided travel documents, which in turn enabled Guben's immigration authority to issue an expulsion order.

As the family started to prepare for their departure, friends and neighbors launched an antideportation campaign that spread like wildfire through the town. The mobilization drive not only involved immigrant advocacy groups and church representatives but also included the children's soccer club and schools, the city's Social Democratic mayor, a group of Christian Democratic city councilors – even the local tourism bureau joined the campaign. In many ways, the family were ideally suited to a grassroots campaign that could span the partisan divide: the Nguyens were long-term and well-liked residents of their local community, gainfully employed, without a criminal record, and with two children who were fully integrated in their schools and neighborhood. In a pattern characteristic of case mobilization, demands for lifting the deportation order were

---

[5] Most local and regional newspaper archives are not indexed and archived in any central location, either physically or electronically.

framed in terms of the moral deservingness of the family, as illustrated by the following local newspaper excerpts:

"The family is a poster-child for [immigrant] integration. The father has a job, the children are good pupils and for years have been popular and successful soccer play-ers... The [oldest] son has not yet finished high school and his German is better than his Vietnamese. What will become of him?" asked [city councilor] Fuhrmann.

(*Lausitzer Rundschau*, August 11, 2001)

Dr. Ba Tan Nguyen is a law-abiding person. "More German than the Germans," said a friend, a member of the Christian Democratic party. ... Mr. Nguyen is a man who pays his taxes punctually and does not jaywalk.

(*Berliner Morgenpost*, August 11, 2001)

These popular understandings of what constitutes integration and com-munity membership clearly consider immigration status as secondary to what Wells calls "grounded experience of community life" (Wells, 2004, p. 1314). The tension arising from the disconnect between these two bench-marks of integration is precisely articulated by an immigration bureaucrat in a neighboring Brandenburg county.

The problem is relatively simple – the disconnect between legal integration and actual integration. The standard for legal integration is the law, the standard for actual integration is set at the emotional level. And these two standards are in conflict with each other. Many people simply don't understand this. And then we have to tell politicians [contesting the deportation of particular individuals] over and over again: all we do here is implement their laws.

(Personal interview, director, local immigration authority, Beeskow/Brandenburg,
November 2, 2001)

The first phase of case mobilization, which spanned several months, involved a signature drive organized by a Christian Democratic city counci-lor, a letter-writing campaign to local and Land politicians, and an (unsuc-cessful) submission to the Land's parliamentary Committee of Petitions. Nonetheless, senior immigration bureaucrats remained firm in their resolve that, regardless of its individual merits, the case was legally too clear-cut to allow for the exercise of bureaucratic discretion in favor of the family. Both the county mayor – as the head of the local immigration authority – and Brandenburg's hardliner minister of the interior, Jörg Schönbohm, who took charge once the case had attracted sustained media attention, refused to retract the expulsion order.

However, administrative resolve quickly crumbled after Guben's Lutheran congregation offered church sanctuary to the family. This is one of the most powerful of weapons wielded by immigrant advocates. It is usually employed as a measure of last resort: not only is it politically and theologically contested – after all, harboring individuals pursued by the state constitutes an act of civil disobedience – but it also requires substantial financial and human resources. In the Nguyen case, the publicity engendered by the family's sanctuary was further fueled by media reports on the upcoming visit to the town by Federal Chancellor Gerhard Schröder. In consequence, as soon as the church sanctuary had been made public, the county mayor declared that he would refrain from issuing the police with an apprehension order. Most strikingly, just four days into the sanctuary, Social Democratic Land governor Manfred Stolpe announced that the family were to be granted permanent residency in Germany.

The case of Ba Tan Nguyen serves to illustrate several key dynamics that underlie the politics of case mobilization. First, case mobilization is not limited to liberal political environments – no one would consider Guben a liberal hotbed. Because such campaigns do not deal with policy issues but instead focus on the question of the moral deservingness of particular individuals – measured in terms of the benchmark of the law-abiding, good community member – they easily span the partisan divide. Second, the mobilization from its beginnings targeted elected officials who in turn were quick to join the campaign. In fact, among the most vocal advocates for the family were the city's Social Democratic mayor and a group of Christian Democratic city councilors. Third, as soon as the campaign had gathered steam, conflict moved up from the local level – and from the jurisdiction of the county mayor – to the Land's Christian Democratic interior minister. Although this official was renowned as an immigration hardliner, once the case had reached a critical publicity threshold, the Social Democratic Land governor initiated a change of course and intervened on behalf of the family. We will return to the significance of partisanship later in the chapter.

Moving to the case of Baden-Württemberg, the data show that the Land's regional deportation officers enjoy a far greater degree of political insulation than their municipal and county colleagues in Brandenburg. In a critical difference, the leaders of Baden-Württemberg's regional immigration bureaucracies are appointed by the Land's interior minister and are therefore not subject to oversight by low-level municipal and county mayors. Not only are these regional bureaucracies beyond the reach of local mayors, they also do not have to fear any political interference for the simple reason that there are no elected offices at this level of government. As a regional deportation officer explained:

It is no longer possible to exert political influence at the county level. Local umbrella organizations [opposed to deportation] of course continue to make statements and try to influence the outcome of decisions. But these efforts fail ... A municipal mayor can no longer use his opposition to a particular deportation decision in order to win the next election.

> (Personal interview, deportation officer "A," regional immigration authority,
> Karlsruhe/Baden-Württemberg, January 25, 2002)

Thus, in contrast to the politically exposed local bureaucrats in Brandenburg, Baden-Württemberg's regional officials operate in relative insulation from the vicissitudes of electoral politics.

The change from a municipal to a regional system of administering deportations in the late 1980s in Baden-Württemberg provides us with an additional, temporal dimension of comparison. Bureaucrats who have worked in both settings consistently commented on the impact of centralization in curtailing the political power of immigrant advocates. In the words of one officer:

When I used to work for the municipal immigration authority, we had to deal with a whole group of individuals who constantly tried to exert influence over our decisions: the principal of the local school, the pastor, and, in the end, even the municipal mayor.... Every time when a municipal authority is charged with implementing a federal law, there are countless opportunity points for local political influence.

> (Personal interview, deportation officer "A," regional immigration authority,
> Karlsruhe/Baden-Württemberg, January 25, 2002)

Significantly, this assessment of policy implementation prior to centralization – which closely mirrors the current situation in Brandenburg – is also shared by immigrant advocates. The Lutheran refugee chaplain in Baden-Württemberg points to the insulation of regional bureaucracies from the political influence of "gentlemen's agreements" between advocates and the heads of municipal authorities:

The establishment of the regional immigration authorities marked a clear turning-point. The shift of responsibility away from municipal authorities added a new element of anonymity.... Before we were able to strike deals with municipal authorities ... now these authorities have little power to influence decisions.

> (Personal interview, Lutheran refugee chaplain, Stuttgart/Baden-Württemberg,
> February 18, 2002)

It is striking that, as providers of constituency services, Land parliamentarians feature much less prominently in the politics of implementation than do elected officials at municipal levels. The near-omission of politicians at this level in interviewees' accounts of case mobilization reflects their relative lack of power over the executive: at the Land level, elected officials do not constitute a significant threat to the decision-making autonomy of administrative officials. Like the central state, the German Länder can be described in Wilson's words as "executive-centered regimes" that, by definition, "are dominated by their bureaucracies" (Wilson, 1989, p. 311). As in most parliamentary regimes, members of the majority party group face strong electoral incentives and strong disciplinary pressures to support executive decision-making. In addition, the constitutions of both Baden-Württemberg and Brandenburg further weaken legislative leverage by setting strict requirements and high thresholds for no-confidence votes.

For this reason, even in their most formalized role as overseer of the executive – the legislative Committee of Petitions, which serves as an ombudsman for the public – parliamentarians interviewed in both Länder considered the likelihood of a successful petition on immigration matters very small. Because their passage requires a majority vote, most petitions die in committee as majority-party parliamentarians collectively support government policies. Consequently, the percentage of immigration-related petitions that result in administrative action is extremely low, a pattern evident in our earlier discussion of the Nguyen case in Brandenburg. A former member of Baden-Württemberg's Committee of Petitions reflects:

> I'd say that about 3 to 5 percent of immigration-related petitions are successful, even though in committee 29 percent of all petitions are immigration-related! We spend over half of our time just dealing with immigration cases.
> (Personal interview, former CDU/CSU Land parliamentarian, Stuttgart/Baden-Württemberg, January 11, 2002)

This is not to say that executives in Baden-Württemberg are categorically immune to the moral pressures generated by case mobilization. Although it is difficult for organized advocates to get the attention of Land-level ministers, they can sometimes provoke ministerial intervention when a grassroots campaign crosses a particular threshold of political salience – often aided by liberal municipal politics – such as sustained case coverage in the regional, in addition to the municipal, media. In these instances, such as the Nguyen case, bureaucratic decision-making shifts upwards from the regional level to the interior minister as the Land's senior immigration executive. Like municipal and county bureaucrats, and unlike regional civil servants, Land executives are highly visible politicians, and are directly answerable to governors who hold prominent electoral mandates.

The following case of a Kurdish family, the Gülers, illustrates the enormity of the challenges facing immigrant advocates in Baden-Württemberg. As was true for the Nguyens in Brandenburg, the Güler case constituted one of Baden-Württemberg's most prominent instances of grassroots resistance to deportation. The Gülers had filed for political asylum in 1990 and 1991, and, although one son was granted asylum in 1995, Mr. and Mrs. Güler and their two daughters were not – a decision that was affirmed in the late 1990s following a judicial appeal. Faced with expulsion, local activists for the family started a letter-writing campaign to Land parliamentarians and approached the Christian Democratic interior minister to retract the expulsion order. Unlike the case in Brandenburg, where the political battle surrounding the fate of the Nguyens was initially fought at the local level, Baden-Württemberg's centralized system of immigration administration forced advocates to target Land-level officials. However, these efforts did not succeed in influencing administrative decision-making. Knowing that the family were about to be deported, a local parish priest approached a larger church congregation in the liberal university town of Tübingen to offer sanctuary to the family.

The family were granted sanctuary in Tübingen by a broad ecumenical coalition of eight church and university congregations. The coalition's strategic mission statement clearly considered public pressure to be the linchpin of its mobilization efforts:

Church sanctuary depends upon publicity. Only through the 'moral rampart' of broadest possible public support for the Güler family can we prevent.... their deportation.
(*Kirch am Eck Online*, May 25, 2001)

In subsequent months, advocates embarked upon a massive publicity campaign, which included countless press statements, flyers, radio and television appearances, school visits and public lectures, letter-writing campaigns to Land and federal politicians, a petition drive to the Land minister of the interior, and even direct action tactics such as public demonstrations and the release of hundreds of balloons demanding a stop to the deportation of Kurdish refugees more generally. It was not long before these efforts succeeded in mobilizing a large segment of the public in support of the family.

Yet the actual pressures bearing upon Land level ministers in situations such as this are not the particularistic requests of parliamentarians engaging in constituency service. Although legislators face strong electoral incentives to engage in constituency case work, ministers instead depend on broad support within their parties. As a result, their decisions are largely influenced by party programmatic ideology on issues, like immigration, that are subject to partisan conflict. In consequence, where ministers' political parties hold restrictionist positions on immigration – as is the case in conservative Baden-Württemberg – advocates are less likely to succeed in obstructing implementation.

Although the case of the Gülers did end in a victory for the family and their advocates, the campaign only succeeded two-and-a half years into one of the highest-profile church sanctuaries ever staged in Germany. Once we compare the sanctuary's impressive length and scope – spanning eight separate congregations – to the case of the Nguyens, the contrast is striking. Whereas the Brandenburg government acceded to advocates' demands after only four days, Baden-Württemberg officials managed to dig in their heels for two-and-a-half years. Clearly, tracing the progress of case mobilization in Baden-Württemberg speaks of the difficulty of advocacy work in this conservative *Land*. One of the Lutheran ministers involved with the case reflects on the experience:

> If it hadn't been for church sanctuary, the Güler family would have been deported long ago.... But dealing with the authorities was unspeakably difficult. ... Even Christian Democratic parliamentarians who supported our cause had difficulty getting access. It took us one year to gain access to the interior ministry.
> (Personal interview, Lutheran clergy, Working Group Ecumenical Church Sanctuary, Tübingen/Baden-Württemberg, February 5, 2002)

This view is confirmed by accounts of immigration bureaucrats who consistently expressed satisfaction with the level of political backing provided by Baden-Württemberg's right-of-center government. Their colleagues in Brandenburg, by contrast, regularly complained that that they could not categorically rely on support from the interior ministry. Compare the following comments by two senior bureaucrats in Brandenburg and Baden-Württemberg, respectively:

> Political back-up is important. ... Here in Brandenburg I get summoned to the governor just because we refuse to grant a residence permit. In [Christian Social] Bavaria, no head of administration has to subject himself to such treatment.
> (Personal interview, director, county immigration authority, Beeskow/ Brandenburg, November 2, 2001)

> The Land government does enforce immigration laws. This is the reason why petitions are unsuccessful. In Baden-Württemberg, political support [for deportations] is strong. As a consequence, the success of immigrant advocates is limited. Very limited.
> (Personal interview, deportation officer "A," regional immigration authority, Karlsruhe/Baden-Württemberg, January 25, 2002)

The importance of partisanship is evident not only when we compare across *Länder*, but also when we trace the impact of partisan changes in government over time. Brandenburg, a Social Democratic stronghold for most of the 1990s, has, since 1999, been governed by a Grand Coalition of SPD and CDU, with the prominent Christian Democratic hardliner Jörg

Schönbohm taking up the post of interior minister. Although deportation policy has become a deeply divisive issue for the government – at times even threatening its survival (*Die Welt*, November 27, 2000) – the coalition has moved its position toward restrictionism, as reflected in the comments of one enforcement officer:

> In Brandenburg we now have more political backup because of the Christian Democrats. More so than under the previous [Social Democratic] interior minister.
>
> (Personal interview, deportation officer, municipal immigration authority, Luckenwalde/Brandenburg, November 22, 2001)

And yet, as the Nguyen case illustrated, even with a conservative interior minister, the fact that the SPD is the senior partner in the Land's Grand Coalition makes it highly unlikely that immigration officers will experience the same political support for implementation as exists in Baden-Württemberg.

To conclude this discussion, once advocates succeed in politicizing a deportation case sufficiently to draw the Land interior ministry into the conflict, partisanship will become a decisive factor in accounting for enforcement outcomes. In the German case,[6] then, variation in the degree of ministerial support across the Länder is largely a function of the ideology of the governing party. By contrast, variation in bureaucratic insulation across the Länder can be attributed to divergent administrative arrangements: where immigration policy is implemented by regional, rather than local, agencies, officials are much more insulated from interference by elected politicians. These dynamics can account for the finding that executive capacity in Baden-Württemberg – with its regional administrative structures and its conservative government – is consistently strong. We will now turn to the United States and examine the conditions under which immigration bureaucrats in Miami and San Diego pursue the implementation of contested deportation decisions.

Two U.S. Cases: Decentralized Implementation Within a Federal Agency

Unlike Germany, deportations in the United States are overseen and conducted by a federal agency. From 1940 until the creation of the Department of Homeland Security in March 2003, immigration law was administered by the Justice Department's Immigration and Naturalization Service (INS). The

---

[6] Additional interviews were conducted for two shadow cases, Bavaria and North Rhine-Westphalia. Bavaria, Germany's most conservative Land, has decentralized implementation structures. Politically liberal North Rhine-Westphalia has emulated Baden-Württemberg's regional structures. The interview findings lend further support to the argument presented in this chapter and strongly suggest that the findings are generalizable beyond the two in-depth case studies.

INS operated through thirty-three district offices, which were overseen by the agency's headquarters in Washington, D.C. In contrast to Germany's Land-level implementation, this federal structure serves as a check on any significant institutional variation between the various street-level bureaucracies. At the same time, the thirty-three districts operate in divergent environments as far as their geographical location, patterns of immigrant settlement, and local politics are concerned.

In Miami, bureaucrats operate in an environment in which the highly visible and often dramatic arrival of economic and political refugees from the Caribbean combines with the activism of well-organized advocacy groups and tightly knit immigrant communities to create sustained grassroots opposition to deportation. Because of the publicity work of a well-established network of antiregulatory organizations, supported by the extensive and proimmigrant news coverage of *The Miami Herald*, deportation officers in Miami carry out their work under the constant scrutiny of the organized public and the press:

Then there is the community, issues get politicized. . . . Protest can be violent, especially as far as Cubans is concerned. All Latin countries, Haiti, and Bahamas have a strong voice. . . . Advocacy groups here will take anyone's case.
(Personal interview, deportation officer "N," INS Miami, May 28, 2002)

INS officers in Miami who have come from elsewhere tell me that they were shocked how much press there is here, how everything gets scrutinized.
(Personal interview, staff writer, *The Miami Herald*, June 6, 2002)

The San Diego district in southern California provides us with a strong test case for our institutional argument. Operating under the same institutional conditions as the Miami INS, its bureaucrats implement policies in a political environment marked by disproportionately low levels of case mobilization. Even though San Diego is home to a sizeable immigrant population, the district is marked by a weak degree of immigrant organization – a peculiarity that can be attributed to the relatively recent, and more transient, nature of San Diego's Hispanic population. The city's conservative politics provide little in the way of infrastructure for advocacy groups, with existing immigrant rights groups operating largely outside the political mainstream. The following statements, which stand in striking contrast to earlier accounts from Miami, paint a picture of San Diego as a locale much less hostile to stringent immigration enforcement:

Controversial cases are not a problem [in San Diego]; I don't know why. But we've been lucky like this.
(Personal interview, deportation officer "F," INS San Diego, July 9, 2002)

The INS has an easier job [in San Diego] than in many places. There isn't much public scrutiny.

(Personal interview, Wayne Cornelius, Director, Center for Comparative Immigration Studies, University of California, San Diego, August 6, 2002)

This contrasting assessment of the external challenges to implementation in the two districts is a consistent finding in the interviews conducted. The relative low visibility of the San Diego immigrant community is even reflected in the national news media: *New York Times* coverage of the INS district office in San Diego is less than one-eighth that of the Miami district.[7] Yet as the analysis in this chapter will demonstrate, the San Diego district's capacity to implement deportations when faced with organized opposition is hampered by the same institutional constraints that thwart implementation in Miami.

Let us take a closer look at the nature of case mobilization in the United States. Miami's well-organized immigrant communities – characteristic of metropolitan areas with large, well-established immigrant populations – provide a clear demonstration of the importance of constituency service in U.S. advocates' efforts to disrupt implementation. In interviews, both campaigners and bureaucrats argued that case mobilization was most likely to succeed when it could draw upon the support of members of Congress. A prominent Miami advocate reflected on her organization's strategy:

We need to involve Congressmen. We often first approach the House, then the Senate, sometimes both. Once we have their commitment, there is a 60% chance of success. It depends on how busy they are.

(Personal interview, Director, Haitian Women of Miami, June 22, 2002)

An INS public affairs officer concurs:

For advocacy groups, the key to success is to understand the system. Mere protesting in front of the building doesn't get them anywhere. Congressional representatives are the most promising avenue. The main factor is to really understand the system.

(Personal interview, Public Affairs Specialist, INS Miami, June 17, 2002)

Significantly, in contrast to Germany, partisanship does not appear to be a significant factor in the provision of constituency service. Even Republican Congressman Lamar Smith (TX), a renowned immigration hardliner and key sponsor of the punitive 1996 immigration reform package, is said to engage in casework for constituents under deportation orders.[8] The logic of

---

[7] For the period 1993–2003, 904 articles were published on Miami (743 excluding Elián González), 109 articles on San Diego.

[8] Personal interview, Public Affairs Specialist, INS Miami, June 17, 2002.

electoral credit-claiming clearly gives rise to divergent substantive positions across different stages in the policy process. As I have argued, although representatives stand to gain from voting in favor of immigration control bills, in the arena of implementation they face strong incentives to pursue individual exemptions from the same laws.

At the same time, the impact of constituency service varies vertically within the bureaucracy. Whether political contestation remains confined to the district level or rises up to the agency's headquarters is important for the purpose of implementation because exposure to political pressure varies across the two levels of administration. As federal employees, District Directors – unlike the heads of municipal agencies in Germany – are not accountable to politicians at the local and state levels and are only indirectly accountable to elected officials at the federal level. In contrast to senior executives, district officials are career civil servants who, in the words of one district officer, "are not so susceptible to political pressure."[9] Moreover, as heads of large decentralized units, District Directors have historically enjoyed a considerable degree of autonomy from the agency's headquarters – a fact reflected in the common practice of referring to the districts as "fiefdoms."

What determines the level at which conflict is resolved is the degree of congressional involvement. Once cases have attracted such attention, attempts by district officers to retain autonomy over case decisions run counter to the preferences of executive officials at headquarters to exert control over administrative decision-making. As a political appointee, the INS Commissioner is acutely sensitive to the need to consider the political ramifications of bureaucratic decisions. During the period under investigation, communication structures between field offices and headquarters were marked by detailed reporting requirements and a high degree of centralization. Communication took place on a daily basis and included an important mechanism of political damage control known as "significant incident reports," filed for cases that had attracted press attention at the district level. The use of these reports allowed senior agency officials to stay informed about potentially explosive decisions in the field and to anticipate congressional inquiries into contested cases.

Because the central level of decision-making is strongly exposed to congressional influence, the most promising avenue for case mobilization is the national, rather than the local district level. Unlike Germany, it is at the

[9] Personal interview, District Counsel, INS Miami, May 29, 2002.

center that the agency is least politically insulated and that advocates stand the greatest chance of success. As one advocate explained:

> The action is in D.C. Miami INS has discretion, but it only uses it to make things harder, never to make things easier. ... We have access in D.C. through congressional representatives and personal contacts.
>
> (Personal interview, advocate, Haitian-American Grassroots Coalition, Miami,
> May 30, 2002)

A senior career civil servant in Washington confirmed the exposure of the agency's headquarters to political meddling:

> Things here blow with the wind. ... We try to enforce the law, place aggravated felons in mandatory detention, and then, this is very common, a congressman calls us up and tells us about this letter from his constituent.
>
> (Personal interview, senior official, INS headquarters, Washington, D.C.,
> August 22, 2002)

The immigration agency's vulnerability to external influence becomes evident when we examine politicized cases that draw attention beyond district boundaries. Even in jurisdictions such as San Diego, where street-level bureaucrats conduct deportations relatively unobstructed by organized opposition interests, those cases that do attract attention in Washington are frequently decided in favor of immigrants. For instance, of the three most high-profile deportation cases in the year 2000 – concerning a Hungarian family, a gay Briton, and a Bahraini princess[10] – the district was only able to deport the British national Charles Lago, a gay Briton and an alternative theatre producer.

It is instructive to take a closer look at Mr. Lago's case because it reveals the conditions under which case mobilization is likely to fail, despite the immigration agency's lack of political insulation. What distinguished Charles Lago from the two other high-profile cases was the fact that it intersected with the divisive issue of gay rights, and, as a result, elicited highly divisive responses. The removal proceedings unfolded at the same time as opponents of same-sex marriage mobilized in support of Proposition 22, which sought to outlaw the recognition of same-sex marriages in California. The gay community, in turn, used the case – specifically his inability to marry his same-sex partner – to demand equal rights under immigration law and held a protest

---

[10] (1) Denis and Joy Fulop, parents of six children, had illegally immigrated from Hungary seventeen years ago. (2) British national Charles Lago was not eligible for permanent residence because he could not legally marry his partner. (3) Meriam (Al-Khalifa) Johnson had eloped from Bahrain with a U.S. marine. Although these cases are not necessarily representative of deportation cases, the arguments advanced here (focusing on humanitarian considerations) can be (and are) applied to large numbers of deportation cases.

rally in front of the city's INS building (*San Diego Union Tribune*, February 15, 2000). After the *San Diego Union Tribune* published a front-page article detailing the particulars of the case, it published eight letters to the editor, five of which were highly unsympathetic. In a representative comment, one reader complained that the story presented a "thinly veiled attempt to stir up support for those who are opposed to Proposition 22" (*San Diego Union Tribune*, February 12, 2000). Although Mr. Lago's case would likely have elicited strong public support in a location such as Los Angeles or San Francisco, the issue of his sexual orientation quickly became a stumbling block in San Diego's socially conservative environment. Thus, the case presented more of a political liability than an opportunity for credit-claiming for representatives from the city. It is not surprising that the member of Congress most outspoken in favor of Mr. Lago, Representative Jerrold Nadler, was a Democrat from New York. It is also instructive that, only months after Lago lost his battle against deportation, Proposition 22 received the support of 63 percent of voters in San Diego County.[11]

At the same time, the two other high-profile deportation cases of 2000 fared significantly better. In both cases, U.S. Senators and Representatives actively lobbied the immigration agency to allow those concerned to stay. In the case of the Fulop family from Hungary, Senator Feinstein (D-CA) and Representative Tom Lantos (D-CA) introduced private legislation to place the family on a path to citizenship.[12] Private legislation – a stage of case mobilization that only a handful of cases reach every year – forces the agency to concede while at the same time allowing for some administrative face-saving. From the point of view of the agency, private legislation is a form of legislative interference that carries the advantage of minimizing the risk of administrative precedent-setting:

> With a private bill, the INS usually signs off on the decision before, but we still go ahead with the private bill – the INS prefers this, because it will not set a precedent. A similar case would have to be resolved through another private bill, which would be an extremely arduous process.
>
> (Personal interview, Legislative Director, Congressman George W. Gekas (R-PA), Washington, D.C., August 19, 2002)

From the point of view of elected officials, private bills in support of sympathetic individuals send strong signals to their constituencies that they

---

[11] Vote2000 California Primary Election, State Ballot Measures, http://primary2000.ss.ca. gov/returns/prop/37.htm

[12] Feinstein's bill was referred to the Senate's Committee on the Judiciary in January 2007, and remains pending at the time of writing. Representative Lantos passed away in January 2008.

take their roles as representatives seriously. The arguments used to justify this step are strikingly similar to those used in the course of case mobilization in Germany. The following excerpt from a letter by Senator Feinstein to Homeland Security Undersecretary Hutchinson clearly emphasizes the moral deservingness of individuals subject to private legislation:

Since I began my term as Senator, I have introduced 11 private bills, seven of which have passed. In the 108th Congress, I already have five private bills pending and I expect to file three more in the near future. Although I consider only the most extraordinary cases for private relief legislation, there are many more cases with similar circumstances to those I described earlier. These individuals and their families have settled in this country and are law-abiding and productive members in their communities. Removing them from the United States may not be the best use of the Department of Homeland Security's resources.

(Feinstein, June 4, 2004)

U.S. senior executives, I have argued, are particularly exposed to the constituency-servicing activities of members of Congress. As leaders of a large immigration bureaucracy, the INS Commissioner and her immediate subordinates lack the institutional autonomy to provide leadership to street-level bureaucrats in support of politically contested decisions. Consequently, at the district level there is a pervasive feeling that bureaucrats cannot rely upon executive support for enforcement activities. Neither Commissioner Doris Meissner under the Clinton Administration nor Commissioner James Ziglar under George W. Bush were perceived as having provided sufficient political back-up for the implementation of immigration laws. As two San Diego deportation officers commented:

Why are we not arresting people? It's a lack of will from higher up! You could get into trouble. . . . The "Meissner doctrine" has been: if you get past the border patrol, you're safe. The upper level never stood up, with the exception of Elián [González].
(Personal interview, deportation officer "L", INS San Diego, July 10, 2002)

There is a problem with senior management – Ziglar's deputy is an open borders guy. . . . So I'm asking you: how can they put people who believe in open borders in charge of an immigration agency that is supposed to enforce immigration laws?
(Personal interview, deportation officer "C," INS San Diego, July 11, 2002)

INS Commissioners are unable to offer categorical political support to their subordinates because they themselves are vulnerable to congressional influence. As Derthick argues:

Simply to function as advocate and protector of the agency as an organization is a luxury that agency heads in the U.S. government cannot afford and some might not even enjoy. In a political environment, policy objectives override administrative considerations, and the head of an executive agency who cannot accept that fact will not remain its head for very long (1990, p. 110).

Finally, in contrast to the German case, U.S. executives cannot lean on partisanship as a reliable source of support. In the absence of a strong party organization, members of Congress rely upon organized interests for political and financial support and can rarely afford to espouse ideological positions on immigration policy that will alienate key constituencies. As a result, the bipartisan rhetorical commitment to immigration control is significantly compromised by Democrats' receptivity to the concerns of immigrant communities, on the one hand, and Republicans' endorsement of the free-market agenda of business, on the other (Gimpel & Edwards, 1999). As a result, agency leaders strive to preserve flexibility by basing case decisions on political pragmatism, rather than ideological principle.

Given these constraints, why was the INS able to enforce deportation in the most high profile case of the agency's history – that of Elián González? As the earlier statement by San Diego deportation officer "L" indicates, the return of the six-year-old Cuban boy who had been rescued off the coast of Florida on Thanksgiving Day 1999 was in fact out of the ordinary. Few immigration cases have held the American public's attention to the degree that Elián's did, and case mobilization quickly proceeded in a typical pattern, tying the hands of the immigration service:

> The big case was, of course, Elián. ... The INS could have sent Elián back right away, as soon as having located his father. But then the Cuban American National Foundation got involved.
> (Personal interview, staff writer, *The Miami Herald*, June 6, 2002)

The lobbying efforts by the Cuban American National Foundation marked just the beginning of a campaign that was to involve countless local and national advocacy groups, trigger a deluge of media reports – 161 articles in *The New York Times* alone – and result in several private congressional bills to grant the boy permanent residence in the United States.

And yet, despite the case's publicity, the INS succeeded in removing Elián. Significantly, just as was the case with Charles Lago in San Diego, public opinion regarding Elián González was polarized. Although with Mr. Lago it had been the issue of same-sex marriage that had driven a wedge into public opinion, in Elián's case it was the question of child custody. Because Elián's father was in Cuba, the question of the boy's welfare could not be simply framed in terms of the usual foreign policy arguments in this undoubtedly "deserving" case – that American democracy, not Cuban socialism, would be in the best interest of the child. This tension between political ideology and family values was reflected in public opinion polls. Accordingly, in a *Miami Herald*/NBC 6 poll, 50 percent of South Floridians thought that Elián should stay in the United States, whereas 44 percent favored his return to Cuba (*BBC News*, April 9, 2000). At the national level, support for repatriation was even more pronounced: although 56 percent of respondents favored the boy's return to this father in Cuba, only 31 percent thought he should stay with his relatives in Florida (*Gallup News Service*, April 4, 2000).

Although the INS succeeded in enforcing Elián's return, it was the case's larger repercussions that served to undercut executive capacity. For one, in this case law enforcement actions that typically occur behind closed doors became the subject of television coverage – pictures of officers pointing a machine gun at the terrified boy caused a loud public outcry. Most importantly, the publicity generated by the case ran counter to the interests of bureaucrats who strive to implement immigration laws sheltered from the vicissitudes of politics. Where executive capacity is weak, every time advocates succeed in politicizing an administrative decision, administrators stand to surrender what they cherish most – decision-making autonomy. In the aftermath of Elián, it is not surprising that the Miami district office felt particularly exposed to public scrutiny and, as a result, stayed clear of enforcement decisions that would have been likely to spark further political controversy. As an immigration lawyer in Miami comments:

The INS [in Miami] is not that active in clamping down on employment enforcement because this would be too disruptive. There was a case where the INS was clamping down on a flower business, and people were jumping on cars and everything. They stuck with that case but then tried to stay away from these type of cases. Especially since Elián, they have kept a lower profile with employer sanctions.
(Personal interview, immigration lawyer, Miami, June 10, 2002)

In an important sense, public mobilization against deportations presents a significant threat to bureaucratic capacity. Not only may such campaigns prevent bureaucrats from implementing their mandate of migration control and create unwelcome precedents of nonimplementation, but protest further serves to discredit their authority publicly. This is true in all contexts examined in this study. For instance, a deportation officer working in a small community in Brandenburg complained that he and his staff were considered "the local bogeymen" and "heartless administrators." In a typical comment, the officer argues:

In these situations [of case mobilization], immigration agencies really lose in credibility. . . . Once you get mobilization drives and there are unfair newspaper articles all over the place, then public agencies get portrayed as authoritarian machines. . . . So their reputation suffers, and civil servants feel left in the lurch. And you start forgetting that it's your first duty to uphold the law.

> (Personal interview, deportation officer, local immigration authority, Luckenwalde/Brandenburg, November 22, 2001)

This account clearly illustrates the threat that political conflict poses to bureaucratic coercive capacity. Importantly, sustained patterns of public confrontation will have implications for administrative behavior far beyond those cases that have reached the point of public contestation – a pattern reflected in the Miami district office's risk-averse implementation strategies in the aftermath of the Elián González case. To the extent that bureaucrats consistently feel powerless to defuse public opposition, they are likely to engage in anticipatory behavior and will steer clear of making unpopular decisions even before these cases attract public attention – a dynamic also identified by Janet Gilboy in her study of U.S. immigration inspectors (1992).

To summarize: the policy stage of implementation has its own story to tell. At heart, it is a story of the comparative advantage held by antiregulatory interests at this point in the cycle. Because the implementation of socially coercive policies allows the public to focus attention on the fate of regulated individuals and families, arguments by advocates that morally deserving cases be spared the costs of deportation dominate political debate time and again.

Although mobilization efforts can only target a subset of removal cases, implications for bureaucratic capacity are far-reaching indeed. Specifically, case mobilization presents a significant threat to executive capacity when it succeeds in drawing elected officials into the conflict between the state, on the one hand, and deportees and their advocates, on the other. In a policy field in which bureaucrats are charged with imposing significant costs upon individuals, politicians' postlegislative electoral incentives are biased toward nonenforcement. Thus, contrary to the expectations of standard principal–agent accounts, instances of nonimplementation in our analysis were actually the result of interference by elected officials, rather than attributable to bureaucratic shirking. Far from attempting to avoid implementation the immigration bureaucrats, in all contexts examined, demonstrated a strong commitment to the fulfillment of their legislative mandates.

Despite these common incentives and motivations, however, comparison reveals significant variation in agencies' capacity for implementation under conditions of case mobilization. I have argued that in the realm of coercive social regulation, executive capacity is a function of two key factors: first, the insulation of bureaucratic agencies from the influence of elected politicians; and, second, where agencies are insulated, the partisan ideology of ministers. It is, then, all else equal, those bureaucratic agents most shielded

from intervention by their legislative principals who are most likely to implement their statutory mandates in the face of organized opposition. Broad
programmatic ideology has a substantial effect only where agency leaders
enjoy autonomy from legislators' narrow demands; where they do not,
particularistic pressures to restrain implementation will erode agencies'
capacity to carry out contested policy measures.

5

Conclusion

> There is evidence that ordinary Americans want to change current policies, lots of evidence that judges and prosecutors at local and state levels are responding. ... Legislators and executive branch officials in the federal government and in the large, heavily populated states, however, are neither repealing nor fundamentally recasting failed policies.
>
> (Tonry, 2004, p. 4)

In the preceding chapters, we have traced the politics of deportation as it evolves over the various stages of the policy process. This final chapter will serve two distinct purposes. First, we will return to the most significant findings of this book. I will begin by summarizing the principal claims of the theory of coercive regulatory capacity developed and tested against the case of deportation. The chapter will then identify some key contributions of this research to the study of migration control: what has this analysis told us about the capacity of liberal states to control unwanted immigration?

The second purpose of this chapter is to apply the argument to two sets of larger questions. The first set of questions extends the argument across policy fields and considers how the findings of this book might be generalizable beyond the case of deportation. The second set of questions extends the argument over time. Have the immigration reforms that were passed in the aftermath of September 11, 2001, succeeded in strengthening the deportation capacity of immigration bureaucrats? And, given the pervasiveness of policy failure in this field, has there been correction by means of negative feedback effects in either of the two countries? In other words, has implementation failure served as a policy lesson for subsequent rounds of legislative reform?

THEORIZING SOCIALLY COERCIVE STATE CAPACITY

The theoretical framework presented and tested in Chapters 1 through 4 specified the basic dynamics that drive policy-making and implementation in the sphere of coercive social regulation. Let us reiterate what I have argued are the key components of a theory of coercive regulatory state capacity – components that significantly distinguish this policy field from that of economic regulation, and from the politics of distribution and redistribution.

Political Conflict across Policy Stages

Although few areas of state policy are isolated from public contestation, political conflict surrounding social regulatory policies is marked by a degree of intensity rarely encountered in other issue areas. In large part, this opposition is driven by the concentrated and severe costs of social regulation. As is the case with government regulation more generally, targeted individuals and groups face powerful incentives to ward off state intervention. However, although socially coercive policies share the concentrated costs that characterize policies of economic regulation, they distinguish themselves by their intrinsically normative nature – an attribute that both triggers and further exacerbates conflict. To return to the case of deportation, decisions on the circumstances under which an individual's residency can – and cannot – be terminated constitute de facto normative judgments on the appropriate balance between individual rights, on the one hand, and the collective welfare, on the other. In a similar vein, discussions on what should be considered as mitigating factors in cases of immigration law violation – such as family ties, past behavior, and employment history – reflect moral judgments about the "deservingness" of individuals and about their value – or threat – to the community. This normative component effectively heightens conflict: these arguments are not only highly emotive, but also fought out in the public sphere. Whereas opponents of economic regulation will strive to shelter their lobbying efforts from public view, opponents of social regulation will seek to mobilize the public in order to avert implementation.

A further defining characteristic of the politics of coercive social regulation is the systematic variation of conflict over time. The first policy stage of agenda-setting most closely resembles Wilson's characterization of "entrepreneurial politics": political entrepreneurs mobilize the unorganized public by drawing attention to the costs of nonregulation – the status quo. Because at this early stage attention is exclusively focused on the benefits of

intervention, targeted social groups are stigmatized, and efforts by antiregulatory interests to change the terms of debate rarely succeed.

Consequently, policy losers will focus their lobbying efforts on those
points of the legislative process that are relatively shielded from public view,
such as committee deliberations. Although antiregulatory interests benefit
from the relative insulation of policy-making at this post-agenda-setting
stage – insulation that carries over into subsequent executive priority-
setting – the final stage of street-level implementation offers a comparative
advantage of a quite different kind. What sets this part of the policy cycle
apart from all other stages is its confrontation of the public with the concrete, and harsh, consequences of regulatory policies. Significantly, this reality
is accompanied by a marked shift in public attention from the generalized
benefits of regulation to its individualized costs. It is thus at the point of field
implementation – and only there – that the demands of antiregulatory interests meet with substantial public support.

In sum, the policy process sets out with the agenda-setting successes of
proregulatory interests who are riding the wave of public sympathy. This is
followed by more insulated stages of legislative and executive decision-
making where antiregulatory interests are able to gain ground in the absence
of wider attention. Finally, the cycle concludes with the stage of street-level
implementation, where opponents of regulation enjoy their greatest advantage as they are finally able to capitalize on public support.

Two Types of State Capacity

This peculiar logic of political conflict has consequential implications for the
exercise of coercive regulatory state capacity. To recapitulate, at the legislative stage, the state – represented by lawmakers – confronts popular calls
for the stricter regulation of certain social groups. What I have termed
"legislative capacity" – the capacity of legislators to translate broad and
clearly identifiable public mandates into policies that reflect these demands
in their goals and choice of policy measures – depends upon the presence,
and institutional access, of public interest actors who can articulate and
defend the preferences of the unorganized citizenry against the lobbying
efforts of organized policy losers. It follows that the agenda-setting power
of voter backlash is probably a necessary, but certainly not a sufficient,
condition for regulatory reform to occur. Because policy losers will be most
likely to manipulate legislation at the more insulated points of the policy
process, lawmakers' capacity to pass public interest policies is contingent
upon the presence of institutionalized channels of public interest articulation.

These channels allow such actors to counterbalance effectively the clout of antiregulatory lobbies – or, as in the case of Germany, party ideology.

Whereas at the legislative stage, policy-makers are trapped between the competing demands of public and private lobbies, executive officials at the stage of implementation find themselves in a quite different bind. As segments of the electorate rally to obstruct enforcement and mobilize their representatives in the process, conflict takes the shape of intrastate confrontation that pits executive against legislative officials. Consequently, in fields of coercive social regulation, and contrary to conventional principal–agent models, executive state capacity is fundamentally predicated on the insulation of bureaucrats from the interference of elected officials.

By means of crossnational and within-country comparison, this analysis has shown that the primary conditions for legislative and executive capacity – institutionalized channels of public interest articulation and political insulation, respectively – are in large measure determined by the structure of political institutions. First, the availability of channels of public interest articulation – the key determinant of legislative capacity – is shaped by the vertical structure of intergovernmental relations. Because proregulatory backlash originates at the local level while policies are legislated federally, reform is ultimately contingent upon the availability of institutions that aggregate and represent these demands at the federal level. Political insulation – the primary condition underlying executive capacity – is by contrast a function of the horizontal structuring of executive-legislative relations. Because of the intrastate nature of conflict at the stage of implementation, political insulation is shaped by the relationship between enforcing bureaucrats, on the one hand, and constituency-service providing legislators, on the other. Where public servants can operate relatively autonomously, executive capacity is strong. Accordingly, the socially coercive capacity of the state in Germany – operating in an institutional environment marked by strong intergovernmental lobbies and executive dominance – is notably stronger than in the United States, where intergovernmental lobbies are weak and executive–legislative conflict high.

IMPLICATIONS FOR THE STUDY OF MIGRATION CONTROL

Can liberal states control crossborder migration? This question has inspired an extensive literature that has made great strides toward identifying the reasons why the Western world continues to receive large numbers of new arrivals, despite widespread anti-immigrant sentiment and the attendant pledges of politicians to rein in unwanted migration. Many of these contributors have posited a universal and absolute control incapacity arising from the constraints of economic globalization and an emerging human rights regime at the international level, and from the power of liberal norms, judicial protections, and the lobbying efforts of proimmigration interest coalitions domestically. The few authors who have presented evidence of an increase in state capacity, on the other hand, have tended to focus their arguments on the development of new infrastructural and technological tools, or on the use of venue-shopping in the context of European integration, without examining the realities of bureaucratic implementation.

This book differs from existing works in three important ways. First, the study adopts a highly contextualized definition of state capacity that is grounded in democratic theory. The book measures legislative state capacity in terms of the fit between the provisions of statutes, on the one hand, with broadly articulated public demands, on the other. Executive state capacity, in turn, compares concrete implementation outcomes against both the goals of agency leaders and the enforcement activities of field officers. In doing so, the study rejects the reference point of close-to-perfect migration control against which many studies have judged the policy efforts of liberal democracies. There is little doubt that in some contexts close-to-perfect control is possible – we only need to remember the successes of the Socialist Bloc in preventing both out- and unwanted in-migration. We also know, however, that the regulatory efforts of liberal states in particular fall far short of the degree of social control exercised by authoritarian and totalitarian states. It is important to realize, as Joppke reminds us, that state sovereignty in liberal democracies is indeed "self-limited" (1998). To judge the control capacity of liberal states against a reference point of internally unlimited sovereignty, then, is neither likely to yield much empirical insight (all liberal states will be found to be incapable of control) nor conducive to theory development.

By employing a definition of state capacity that rests on a number of discrete, nonideal reference points, this study has provided evidence in favor of measurable, significant, and institutionally driven variation in the capacity of two liberal democratic states to remove immigrants forcibly from their territory. In the German case, we observed additional within-case variation in executive capacity. Variation in state capacity was evident among different categories of immigrants, over time, and, most importantly, across different institutional contexts. Although liberal states will never achieve the goal of perfect control – nor has a golden age of control ever existed – we should not underestimate their ability to control migration. The finding of systematic variation in state capacity presented in this study suggests that it is not constant, but instead is contingent upon the particular arrangements of horizontal and vertical political institutions within which state and societal actors pursue their often conflicting goals.

In a second contribution, this study emphasizes a crucial policy stage neglected by the migration literature: street-level implementation. It is ironic that a literature focused on the question of state capacity has largely ignored the policy area – and the actors – arguably most critical to state capacity. By contrast, this book has made a strong case for the study of implementation as a venue of conflict in its own right. In particular, this analysis has exposed the normative controversy that is triggered by the harsh consequences of policy enforcement. As Chapter 4 illustrated, arguments that deportation imposes disproportionate costs upon defenseless individuals and violates human dignity regularly threaten to undermine the legitimacy of state coercion. Whereas existing studies have concentrated on the constraining impact of liberal judicial review, this analysis has revealed the power of liberal norms as they operate among the public. In fact, it is striking that the normative contestation of deportation decisions in Chapter 4 takes place at a point when all legal recourse has been exhausted. In other words, normative contestation occurs in situations where state coercion has been sanctioned by the judiciary. Thus, even if we exclude the courts from analysis, as this study has done,[1] we find that liberal constraints pose a significant challenge to the state in ways that previous studies have largely ignored. Finally, this book's close attention to street-level implementation has also contributed to our understanding of the state's on-the-ground capacity for migration control. As the case of Germany has shown, subject to certain institutional conditions, civil servants can weather normative conflict and pursue capacity-enhancing enforcement strategies that allow for the exercise of migration control.

In a third contribution to the immigration literature, the book traces the politics of migration control along the entire length of the policy cycle. In doing so, the study reveals systematic variation in the political logic driving regulation at various stages. Accordingly, the institutional conditions underlying state capacity in the legislative and executive realms differ from each

---

[1] In the legislative politics of migration control examined in this study, courts only enter the picture after the conclusion of immigration reform. In Germany, the Federal Constitutional Court affirmed in 1996 that the "asylum compromise" was constitutional. The U.S. Supreme Court ultimately overturned two provisions of the 1996 reforms: the retroactive nature of the criminal alien provisions and the imposition of indefinite detention for migrants who cannot be returned to their country of nationality. The Court left intact most of IIRIRA, most controversially its aggravated felon provisions, mandatory deportation and detention, and its court-stripping provisions.

other because the preferences of crucial actors change over time. Most significantly, this analysis has shown that public preferences undergo a systematic shift once policy moves from the generalizing realm of legislation to the concrete act of implementation. This shift from demonizing to humanizing frames of migration control presents an important challenge to the literature, which needs to be attended to. It is not surprising that existing research on mass attitudinal patterns has concluded that the public's immigration preferences are inherently restrictionist: opinion surveys rarely focus on issues arising at the point of implementation. Thus, this study has exposed a pressing need for public opinion research that investigates policy preferences in the context of their likely consequences.

In addition to these three sets of theoretical contributions, the study has furthered our empirical knowledge of migration control. As one of the first comparative studies on deportation, the book has offered a comprehensive account of the politics driving this increasingly prominent policy measure. In a similar vein, as one of the few analyses of implementation in the migration literature, the study has provided novel insights into the workings of immigration agencies and the ways in which these coercive bureaucracies implement – or fail to enforce – their legislative mandates. Finally, by studying immigration agencies in comparative perspective, this book has revealed both the ways in which the work routines of enforcement officials vary across jurisdictions (in terms of their degree of discretion and autonomy, for instance) and the challenges (such as case mobilization) they hold in common. We will now move beyond the case of deportation and examine the extent to which our argument is likely to hold for socially coercive policies more generally.

COERCIVE SOCIAL REGULATION BEYOND THE CASE OF DEPORTATION

Although the empirical analyses of Chapters 2 to 4 focused exclusively on the case of deportation, the theoretical propositions laid out in Chapter 1 allow us to speculate on the likelihood that the findings of this study may also hold for other social regulatory policies. We need to ask, how might any idiosyncrasies of deportation produce a politics that is different from that operating in other areas of coercive social control? Let us first revisit our definition of coercive social regulation. This type of government activity, I have argued, distinguishes itself by the substantial costs it imposes upon those subject to state intervention. Because for regulated individuals the stakes are high – they involve the loss of personal autonomy and, often, physical freedom – socially

coercive policies regularly generate intense conflict. This controversy is further intensified by the normative aspect of this policy sphere: regulatory
decisions involve moral judgments about who and what kind of behaviors
should be subject to social control and sanction, and who among the regulated might be deserving of clemency. With these characteristics in mind we
can begin to speculate on the political dynamics we might expect to observe
in other areas of migration policy such as border control, or beyond migration in social regulatory fields such as workfare, criminal justice, and homeland security. Based on my theory of socially coercive state capacity, I
propose three critical variables that will help us determine to what extent
the argument might apply to coercive policy fields more generally: the social
recognition of "deserving groups," the imposition of high costs, and, lastly,
the likelihood of advocate mobilization.

The Recognition of "Deserving" Groups

When dealing with regulated groups, the public typically distinguishes
between "deserving" and "undeserving" individuals (Hargrove & Glidewell, 1990). This vision is often obscured at the agenda-setting stage, where
punitive policy images dominate political discourse. At the stage, of implementation, however, attention becomes directed to the fate of particular
individuals and, as a result, this distinction surfaces powerfully. What determines whether or not a person is considered deserving of clemency? First,
group membership matters: some are more likely to elicit sympathy than
others, based on factors such as the level of risk they pose to a community,
their culpability for sanctioned actions, and their contributions to society.
Second, the more that individuals are integrated into the mainstream, the
greater the likelihood that they will fall into the deserving category.
This condition even applies to members of "undeserving groups" who can
nevertheless demonstrate their deservingness by establishing close commu-
nal ties.

Based on these dynamics, we would expect that list of migration regulations that conform to our theory to be limited to policies of interior control. What measures such as deportation, interior enforcement, and worksite
regulation hold in common is their targeting of migrants within the country.
Because the shift from demonizing to humanizing discourse so crucially
depends upon the public coming face to face with the human costs of policy
implementation, the theory is contingent upon personal contact between
immigrants and citizens. To return to the account of the failure of "Operation Vanguard" in Chapter 3, political contestation of socially coercive

regulation is contingent upon community integration. Once the immigration agency started to shut down some meatpacking plants,

"All hell broke loose." ... Members of Congress at first hostile to immigrants embraced 'all the same people who were so repugnant to them before, ... and they prevailed.' Congress 'came to recognize that these people . . . had become a very important part of their community, churches, schools, sports, barbecues, families – and most importantly the economy.'

(The Washington Post, June 19, 2006)

Similarly, in Jörg Alt's ethnographic study of illegal migrants in Leipzig, Germany, face-to-face interactions mattered. When asked why unionized workers rarely reported illegal coworkers to the authorities, a union representative explained:

It is one thing to use xenophobic language in the pub. It's a very different thing to betray Iwan and Wasiliy with whom you've been hauling steel beams for days. It's like being at war where you hate "the enemy" but once you meet him and put a pistol to his head then you realize that he is a human being after all.

(Alt, 1999, pp. 376–7)

It is because of the importance of personal contact that our theory is unlikely to account for the politics of immigration control at or beyond the border. The migrants who hope to cross the border undetected or who seek admission at ports of entry without valid documents are not (yet) members of local communities, nor does the public witness their confrontations with coercive bureaucracies. Most drastically, migrants who lose their lives crossing the border in remote and hostile territory usually do so terribly alone, in the absence of witnesses who could intervene on their behalf. Although it is the case that deservingness arguments can be made for migrants not yet within the territory ("every human being should have the right to live free from destitution and violence"), these arguments are likely to be articulated by immigrant advocates who are motivated by ideological conviction, rather than by personal confrontation with the human costs of migration control. To the broad public, the arrival of undocumented immigrants at the border is much more likely to trigger concerns about law and order, or cultural and economic competition.

I have argued that, among migrant groups, immigrant offenders will be least likely to be considered deserving. Moving beyond the field of migration control, then, does this finding suggest that the logic of coercive social regulation is unlikely to operate in the realm of criminal justice? Rather than comparing between regulated groups – by, for instance, contrasting the treatment of refugees with that of citizen offenders in the criminal justice system – the theory's logic rests on a distinction that operates *within* a given group, bounded by distinct legislative statutes and advocacy organizations. Accordingly, in the field of criminal justice, we would expect the public to distinguish between nonviolent ("deserving") and violent ("undeserving") offenders. For instance, we could understand recent public support for the repeal of California's draconian "Three Strikes and You're Out" law – which has resulted in long prison sentences for nonviolent offenders – as arising from this distinction. Although we should expect deservingness arguments to be more muted in the area of criminal justice than in the field of migration control – the public after all does distinguish between violations of criminal versus civil law – we nevertheless might see certain deservingness claims extended to nonviolent offenders.

Moving on to the area of social welfare, would we expect the political discourse to single out some workfare[2] recipients as deserving? Although workfare clients – like recipients of means-tested benefits more generally – are socially stigmatized, the public nonetheless may make within-group distinctions between deserving and undeserving individuals. For instance, those who are perceived as being on social assistance owing to a poor work ethic will likely be labeled as unworthy of sympathy, whereas a mother who struggles to combine paid employment with the care for young children or a disabled parent is more likely to be considered worthy. In their study of homelessness in Ottawa, Canada, Fran Klodawsky et al. found that, although the discourse generated by media coverage generally neglected the complex life histories of homeless individuals, "when hints of such complexities are mentioned, they come with subtle messages about the deserving individuals who might be redeemed ..." (Klodawsky, Farrell, & D'Aubry, 2002, p. 140). Similarly, we might expect that the public will be more sympathetic toward individuals on welfare if they are confronted with the realities of life on workfare. Just as community ties increase the likelihood that undocumented immigrants are perceived as deserving, so would we expect deservingness arguments to feature more prominently in contexts marked by social integration.

Finally, in the case of homeland security, is the public likely to distinguish between "deserving" and "undeserving" terrorist suspects? This is unlikely. I speculate that the logic of coercive social regulation is least likely to hold in the case of homeland security. The problem is not that deservingness

---

[2] Under workfare, the receipt of welfare benefits is contingent upon certain behavioral requirements such as participation in training, engaging in unpaid or underpaid work, and cooperation with efforts to establish paternity.

arguments cannot be made against individuals suspected or convicted of terrorist activities. The looseness of terms such as "terrorist activities" and "terrorist groups" can lead to criminal convictions for individuals engaged in financial transactions with charities of many kinds, for instance, individuals whose actual threat to society may be negligible at best. Similarly, the heavy-handed nature of many terrorist investigations – most famously the detention camp in Guantánamo Bay – frequently results in the arrest of innocent suspects. What distinguishes homeland security from other areas of coercive social regulation, however, is its lack of transparency. Confronted with the possibility of terrorism, the public is unlikely to throw support behind a potentially high-risk individual whom they have never met and whose circumstances are shrouded in secrecy. Similarly, because the media's access to classified information is haphazard at best, it is vulnerable to government manipulation. Although the media played a pivotal role in most of the instances of case mobilization examined in this book, journalists will be more likely to treat terrorist suspects with suspicion, as the Canadian case of Maher Arar[3] has illustrated. In fact, what is most striking about Maher Arar is how exceptional the case is. No other exonerated terrorist suspect has received the kind of public recognition that has been awarded to Arar. I therefore conclude that the first condition of the theory of socially coercive state capacity – the recognition of deservingness – is least likely to be met in the case of homeland security.

The Imposition of High Costs

Coercive social regulation is a costly enterprise for individuals at the receiving end of state intervention. These costs matter for the politics of this policy cluster because they propel resistance. Although not all socially coercive regulation imposes costs of the same magnitude as those incurred by deportation, among the three conditions examined here – deservingness, costs, advocacy – the second is the one most easily satisfied. Undocumented migrants who are apprehended at the border will often have undertaken a

---

[3] Arar, a Canadian resident with dual Canadian and Syrian citizenship, was detained by U.S. officials in 2002 while in transit when returning home from a vacation. Based on false information by Canadian authorities who labeled Arar an Islamic fundamentalist, U.S. authorities interrogated Arar about alleged links to al-Qaeda and later flew him to Syria where he was imprisoned and tortured for over ten months. After his return to Canada, under pressure from Canadian human rights organizations and increasing public mobilization, the Canadian Government instituted a Commission of Inquiry into the Actions of Canadian Officials in Relation to Maher Arar. Arar was cleared of all terrorism allegations.

hazardous journey that left them deeply financially indebted to smugglers. After being released from detention, they return empty-handed to their impoverished families and communities, having failed at the challenge of providing for a better life. Likewise, in the areas of criminal justice and homeland security, many individuals are incarcerated for long periods of time, often with disastrous consequences for their income levels and future employment opportunities, not to mention the psychological scars of having spent months or years in a violent, confined space with little connection to the outside world. Furthermore, imprisonment poses a particularly grave threat for family stability. In the United States, where prisoners are regularly housed at great distances from their families,[4] for instance, Christopher Mumola (2000) found that nearly half of all incarcerated parents never received a visit from their children.

Although the costs incurred by individuals through policies of migration control, criminal justice, and homeland security are not difficult to demonstrate, we need to ask whether the logic of coercive social regulation may also hold in fields marked by less severe hardship. Among the range of socially coercive policies, workfare arguably imposes the lowest costs upon regulated groups. Unlike the fields of migration control, criminal justice, or homeland security where individuals, once apprehended, have no choice but to remain within the control of the state, welfare recipients after all are free to leave the rolls rather than comply with workfare requirements. At the same time, however, for those receiving benefits, exit options are severely constrained by the lack of financial alternatives. For individuals whose livelihood is dependent upon the receipt of state assistance, the costs imposed through financial sanctions that follow the violation of behavioral conditions can be harsh indeed. As Mead reminds us, "the problem of consent" that plagues workfare – as it does socially coercive policies more generally – continues to be the source of ongoing political conflict:

> [A] major challenge faced by welfare reform is ongoing dissent from the very idea of conditioning aid on good behavior. That principle is popular with voters, and recent work-based welfare programs have unquestionably succeeded. Yet many leaders . . . continue to question the enforcement of work as a condition of aid. . . . Like a bad conscience, the resistance may deny the new policies full acceptance and thus undermine their achievements (2004, p. 272).

Given the costs incurred in even comparatively "low coercion" policy areas such as workfare, then, it appears that across policies of coercive social

---

[4] Male prisoners in state prisons are housed an average distance of 100 miles from their families, female prisoners 160 miles (Travis, McBride, & Solomon, 2005).

regulation, the impact of regulation is sufficiently high to satisfy the theory's condition of cost imposition.

Advocate Mobilization

Case mobilization seeks to rally public support for individuals targeted by the interventions of coercive bureaucracies. In contrast to policy mobilization, which aims at statutory change and takes place in the legislative arena, case mobilization does not depend upon the availability of abundant organizational resources. Rather, it relies upon the rallying of public support on behalf of "deserving" individuals by calling attention to the disproportionate costs that policy enforcement would impose. Although in some cases, public mobilization may be spearheaded by well-established advocacy groups, in other cases, a mere handful of concerned individuals – a neighbor, teacher, or soccer coach – may take the lead. In the case of Maher Arar, for instance, it was his wife, Monia Mazigh, who was instrumental in organizing a campaign that ultimately succeeded not only in securing Arar's return to Canada, but also in his exoneration by the Canadian government. By holding candlelight vigils, seeking the attention of the news media, and organizing demonstrations and letter-writing drives to members of parliament, Mazigh set off a grassroots campaign that was soon joined by human rights groups.

Because the organizational bar to case mobilization is low, the relative absence of advocacy groups in fields such as criminal justice or homeland security – compared to the abundance of immigrant rights and antipoverty groups – should not necessarily be considered an obstacle. Whereas *policy* mobilization often requires behind-the-door access to policy-makers, case mobilization thrives on publicity. As long as advocates can garner the support of a group of devoted volunteers and gain access to the media, they stand a chance at politicizing the fate of particular individuals. What matters more than financial and organizational resources is for campaigners to have access to the undocumented migrants, criminal offenders, and terrorist suspects they seek to defend – a condition that is more easily satisfied in areas of interior migration control, workfare, and criminal justice, than in the fields of border control and homeland security. Further, case mobilization is contingent upon a modicum of public receptiveness to deservingness claims. Thus, it is least likely to succeed at times of moral panic such as the immediate aftermath of the attacks of September 11, 2001.

These propositions regarding the generalizability of the logic of coercive social regulation will require systematic empirical testing before we can assert them with any certainty. Given these theoretical assumptions, among the policies examined above we would expect this study's explanatory leverage to be strongest in the case of interior migration control and workfare, and weakest in the area of border control and homeland security, with criminal justice occupying a space somewhere in the middle.

We will now turn our attention to the ramifications of the terrorist attacks of September 2001. The attacks constituted an exceptional "focusing event" (Kingdon, 1995) in the politics of immigration, providing state officials with a rare window of opportunity for fundamental reform of the system. Although the policy and institutional consequences of 9/11 are still unfolding, I will offer a tentative assessment of whether this focusing event might have served to increase state capacity, particularly in the United States.

MIGRATION CONTROL AND STATE CAPACITY AFTER SEPTEMBER 11, 2001

The terrorist attacks of 9/11 – masterminded and perpetrated by foreign nationals living, some of them illegally, in the United States and Germany – gave renewed impetus to a reform agenda of resolute border control. In what follows, I will examine subsequent immigration-related developments and offer some tentative assessments on whether these policy and institutional changes have served to strengthen the executive capacity of immigration officials. Our analysis for the most part will focus on the United States, where the ramifications of 9/11 have been the greatest. We will first examine developments in the immediate wake of the attacks before investigating the dynamics of migration control in the mid-2000s.

Developments in U.S. Migration Control, 2001–4

In a first development, for some time after the attacks, migration control became largely subsumed under the mantle of national security. Congress passed a catalogue of antiterror provisions that intersected with immigration controls and included measures that facilitated the detention and deportation of noncitizen terrorist suspects, tightened visa procedures, and increased the gathering and sharing of information about noncitizens. Arab and Muslim immigrants were subject to extensive and, as it turned out ineffectual, profiling, including the mandatory registration of male immigrants from thirteen countries with the INS. Immigration enforcement was frequently used as a proxy for antiterror enforcement as authorities sought to circumvent the constitutional safeguards of criminal law and charged noncitizen terrorist suspects with immigration violations instead, deporting many as a result (Chishti, Meissner, Papademetriou et al. 2003). Overall, the number of immigrants affected by the War on Terror far exceeded the small number of militant noncitizen extremists. By conflating immigration enforcement and national security, U.S. authorities implicated many permanent residents, undocumented migrants, and asylum seekers in antiterror enforcement solely on the basis of their national and religious backgrounds.

In a second, historic, development, 9/11 gave new momentum to long-standing plans to restructure the immigration bureaucracy. In March 2003, the INS was dissolved and incorporated into the newly created Department of Homeland Security. As discussed above, until 2005, the enforcement activities of Immigration and Customs Enforcement (ICE) – the agency now comprising the interior enforcement side of the former INS – were principally driven by national security concerns. Accordingly, ICE's work-site activities exclusively focused on "critical infrastructures" such as airports ("Operation Tarmac") and nuclear power plants ("Operation Glowworm"). By concentrating its resources on antiterrorism initiatives, ICE effectively abandoned all nonterrorism interior enforcement activities. As a result, the number of undocumented workers arrested during worksite enforcement operations declined about 84 percent from an already minuscule 2,849 in 1999 to 445 in 2003 (U.S. Government Accountability Office, 2005, p. 35). Similarly, in the early 2000s, we observe a steep decline in the number of employer investigations, warnings issued to audited employers, and employer fines (Brownell, September 1, 2005). Most drastically, the number of criminal cases brought against employers fell from 182 in 1999 to a paltry four in 2003 (*The Washington Post*, December 25, 2007).

Did this new focus on antiterror enforcement have any significant impact on the immigration bureaucracy's executive capacity? In the early 2000s, the public was clearly grappling to come to terms with the events of 9/11 and, as a result, antiterror enforcement was relatively uncontroversial and generated little in the way of public countermobilization. It follows that, because the targeting of immigrants in "critical infrastructures" requires little political capacity in the first place, it does not allow us easily to gauge its impact on state capacity.

In a third development, there is evidence that when immigration officials did pursue noncritical interior enforcement, they encountered less public resistance than before. As immigrant advocates across the country struggled with the national security legacy of 9/11 (*The New York Times*, April 22, 2006; September 20, 2004), deportation officers in Miami – a jurisdiction marked by weak capacity (see Chapter 4) – reported they have benefited from stronger political support for the expulsion of undocumented immigrants. In mid-2002, interviewed officers commented on the palpable impact of the attacks on the city's political climate:

9/11 has changed a lot. Things have become less liberal. We can finally do our job. Before we couldn't pick up illegals.

(INS deportation officer "O," INS Miami, May 28, 2002)

After 9/11, the focus of the nation became enforcement-minded. People didn't want to see people protesting, people didn't care about people in detention. . . . This had made things hard for advocacy groups. Public opinion is necessary for advocacy groups to be successful.

(Public Affairs Specialist, INS Miami, June 17, 2002)

These statements suggest that in the months after 9/11, the public was anxious for law enforcement authorities to "get their job done" and less likely to tolerate case mobilization. The policy and rhetorical linkages between national security and illegal immigration during this period appear to have raised the political costs of lax enforcement, thereby providing Miami deportation officers with some reprieve from case mobilization.

Although these interview accounts indicate that public support for stringent immigration enforcement was consistently high in the attacks' immediate aftermath, it is improbable that this change will persist in the long term. Opinion data suggest that the impact of 9/11 is likely to weaken with the passage of time. In Gallup polls, the percentage of respondents who wanted to see levels of immigration decreased shot up by 20 points immediately after the attacks, from 38 to 58 percent. After remaining nearly constant for a year (54 percent in 2002), by 2005, support had dropped to 46 percent. Thus, four years after the attacks public opinion on immigrant admissions was closer to pre- than to post-9/11 (Gallup & Newport, 2006, p. 451).

There is some evidence that whatever immunity from public contestation 9/11 had provided to field officers, after 2003, immigration bureaucrats were once again dealing with a political powder keg when pursuing interior enforcement measures unrelated to terrorism. When in June 2004 a border patrol team arrested 450 undocumented immigrants in interior parts of Southern California, for instance, a coalition of congressional delegates and local Latino groups quickly pressured the new agency to refrain from future arrests (*The Financial Times*, July 10/11, 2004). The apprehensions were stopped momentarily and Undersecretary for Border and Transportation Security Asa Hutchinson assured Congress that "in the future,

Homeland Security would enforce immigration laws 'in a reasonable manner' and would consider the 'sensitivities' surrounding the enforcement of those laws in its interior-enforcement program" (*The Washington Times*, August 17, 2004). Thus, three years after 9/11, nonterrorism-related interior enforcement appeared to have resurfaced once again as a "sensitive" enterprise for a politically vulnerable immigration bureaucracy.

Developments in U.S. Migration Control After 2004

Whereas public support for the heavy-handed implementation of migration control measures may be a short-lived phenomenon – limited to the immediate aftermath of focusing events such as 9/11 – the dissolution of the INS and its incorporation into the Department of Homeland Security has generated institutional changes that promise to shape enforcement in the long term. In a first change, as the immigration bureaucracy's coercive functions have become organizationally separated from its service mandate – a structure long demanded by control-minded reformers – policy priorities in ICE now unambiguously reflect an ethos of law enforcement. As a second consequence of restructuring, bureaucratic decision-making has become more centralized.

What impact should we expect these institutional reforms to have on the political capacity of U.S. immigration officials? Although the immigration bureaucracy's newly independent enforcement arm is no longer constrained by competing demands of service provision, its location in the national-security oriented Department of Homeland Security initially created competing pressures of a different kind. As we saw, in the early 2000s, ICE's activities were dominated by antiterror rather than migration control concerns. However, by the mid-2000s, we observe a shift in enforcement focus as ICE set off two migration control programs that were unrelated to terrorism: the National Fugitive Operations Program and the commencement of systematic "noncritical" worksite enforcement.

The National Fugitive Operations Program was set up in 2002 to reduce the backlog of an estimated 314,000 "fugitive aliens" by apprehending individuals with unexecuted removal orders. Although deportation officers had previously pursued immigrant absconders on an ad hoc basis, attempts to establish specialized teams for this task had failed in the past. In 1996, an initiative to establish Absconder Removal Teams was abandoned after earmarked congressional funding was absorbed into the INS' day-to-day deportation operations. Two years later, similar efforts to establish Fugitive Operations Teams did not outlast the initial training period. It was during this time that local experimentation with absconder teams in San Diego was stopped after meeting with public resistance (see Chapter 3). The terrorist attacks of September 2001 put a spotlight on immigrant absconders and led to the establishment of the National Fugitive Operations Program with a budget of $10 million in FY 2003. By 2006, this amount had increased more than tenfold to over $110 million at the same time as the number of Fugitive Operations Teams had grown from 8 to 52 (U.S. Department of Homel and Security Office of Inspector General, 2007). By 2008, 75 teams were operating nationwide (*The Washington Times*, June 3, 2008). According to ICE data, the number of apprehended absconders had risen from approximately 1,200 in 2003 to nearly 12,000 in 2006 before more than doubling to about 30,000 in 2007 (U.S. Department of Homeland Security Office of Inspector General, 2007; *The Washington Times*, June 3, 2008).

Given both the checkered history of previous absconder teams and the political sensitivity of apprehending and deporting immigrants from local communities, these figures suggest that a qualitative change in interior enforcement may be under way. However, in the absence of more qualitative data, we cannot reach any firm conclusions. Most problematically, evaluation research by the Department of Homeland Security's Office of the Inspector General (OIG) has cast doubt upon the validity of some of these data: in addition to apprehensions by Fugitive Operations Teams, ICE included apprehensions by deportation officers outside the teams as well as by officers of other federal, state, and local law enforcement agencies. As a result, OIG concluded, the data did not allow for an assessment of the teams' performance (U.S. Department of Homeland Security Office of Inspector General, 2007).

In a second development of the mid-2000s, ICE committed itself to stricter worksite enforcement. Although initially this new focus was nearly exclusively confined to sites of national security, in 2005 the agency shifted its strategy and began targeting workplaces that had long been associated with the employment of illegal immigrants (Wright, 2008). In 2006, ICE conducted a series of highly orchestrated raids in the manufacturing, meatpacking, and construction sectors, which resulted in a tripling of immigrant arrests within just one year. For instance, in April 2006 ICE simultaneously raided over forty pallet plant facilities owned by IFCO Systems North America, arresting close to 1,200 undocumented workers in addition to several senior managers. Because of their grand scale, many of these raids attracted nationwide media coverage and generated significant political controversy. Faced with criticism and lawsuits, by 2007, ICE had shifted its enforcement strategy once again to steer away from high-profile and multisite raids and instead target a higher number of small- and medium-sized businesses. These localized raids typically resulted in the apprehension of between half a dozen to a few dozen workers and received relatively little media attention (Wright, 2008). As a result, the agency made a record high of 4,000 worksite arrests in 2007, a tenfold increase over 2003 (U.S. Immigration and Customs Enforcement, 2008).

Aside from driving a consistent enforcement campaign, what is striking about ICE's worksite initiatives is the agency's new strategy of criminalizing illegal employment. Whereas in the 1990s, the INS pursued administrative proceedings against both employers and immigrants, in the mid-2000s, ICE started to team up with other law enforcement agencies to seek criminal indictments. Not only has ICE started to prosecute employers for federal felonies such as the harboring of illegal aliens, the agency has also started to tag on criminal charges – such as identity theft or document fraud – to immigration violations by illegal workers. For instance, in May 2008, ICE conducted a raid against Agriprocessors Inc., a meatpacking plant near Postville, Iowa, which resulted in convictions for document fraud and the sentencing to five months in prison (and subsequent deportation) of 270 illegal immigrants (*The New York Times*, May 24, 2008). Similarly, prosecutors are increasingly filing criminal charges against undocumented migrants under a previously little-used provision that renders illegal reentry after deportation a federal felony.

These developments pose the pressing question of whether the reorganization of the immigration bureaucracy in the aftermath of 9/11 has augmented its executive capacity. In order to answer this question, further research is necessary to examine the extent to which ICE's interior enforcement strategies have met with political opposition. If the agency was confronted with significant grassroots mobilization and congressional meddling, why did it not abandon its enforcement drives like the INS had done in the past? Did ICE strategically manage to preempt or assuage its opponents by, for instance, focusing worksite raids onto smaller employers with less political clout, or onto employers with transient workforces[5] and weak community ties, or by contesting the deservingness of undocumented workers by criminalizing illegality? If it turned out to be the case that ICE only rarely encountered opposition to its enforcement activities in the first place, is there

---

[5] In 2007, temporary labor and staffing agencies were one of the primary targets of the ICE's worksite enforcement activities.

something about post-9/11 public opinion that has fundamentally altered the implementation dynamics of interior enforcement?

Finally, we need to consider whether the reorganization of the immigration bureaucracy, which also entailed a centralization of administrative decision-making, has had any impact on its relationship with Congress. My argument implies that, in the U.S. context, centralization is likely to weaken executive capacity because Washington officials are more politically exposed than the decentralized field offices. It is interesting to note that ICE headquarters appear to have imposed particularly tight central controls upon worksite enforcement:

> [I]n 2003, ICE headquarters issued a memo inquiring field offices to request approval from ICE headquarters prior to opening any worksite enforcement investigation not related to the protection of critical infrastructure sites, such as investigation of farms and restaurants. ICE officials told us that the purpose of this memo was to help ensure that field offices focused worksite enforcement efforts on critical infrastructure protection operations. Field office representatives told us that noncritical infrastructure worksite enforcement was one of the few investigative areas for which offices had to request approval from ICE headquarters to open an investigation.
>
> (U.S. Government Accountability Office, 2005, p. 31)

If the centralization of the most sensitive of interior enforcement activities has been motivated by political damage control, and if I am correct in arguing that the INS was most vulnerable at the central level, we need to ask whether there is something systematically different about ICE that has allowed the agency to centralize decision-making while at the same time continuing to implement contested policies. Although we are left with many unanswered questions, these early tentative findings cannot rule out the possibility that the immigration bureaucracy's executive capacity is stronger today than it was in the 1980s and 1990s.

Migration Control in Germany Post 9/11

After the shock events of 9/11, German legislators approved a slate of policy measures many of which paralleled those passed by the U.S. Congress. Reforms to Germany's national security and antiterrorism laws tightened up visa procedures, facilitated the gathering and sharing of data on asylum applicants and other immigrant groups, and proscribed entry to noncitizens who support terrorism. As in the United States, Arab and Muslim immigrants were subject to widespread – and equally futile – profiling (*Rasterfahndung*) (Goldston, 2006). The reforms also had important implications for the legal framework of deportation. The new laws provided for the removal of third country nationals if they had knowingly provided false information to prolong their stay; they further introduced terrorism-related mandatory grounds for deportation and legislated new exceptions to the prohibition of expulsion.[6]

Turning to the administration of deportation, in a direct response to the attacks German bureaucrats started to target religious fundamentalists who were considered a potential threat to the public. In 2005, a new immigration law streamlined provisions that provide for the expulsion of terror suspects, religious demagogues (*Hassprediger*), and members of terrorist organizations. In particular, a deportation scandal involving Metin Kaplan, a prominent Cologne imam who had declared a Muslim state in the Rhineland, served to bring the issue to broad public attention (*Der Stern*, October 12, 2004). In the fall of 2004, when after years of judicial battles officers were given the go-ahead for removal, Kaplan went into hiding and frustrated bureaucratic attempts to expel him. Although he was eventually deported, the incident served to elicit broad criticism for what was perceived to be a lack of concern by the German state to assure the expulsion of "enemies of democracy."

Have these policy developments served to further augment the capacity of German immigration bureaucrats? Although the post-9/11 reforms have lowered the legal hurdles to deporting religious extremists, they are unlikely to strengthen capacity in a policy area historically marked by the absence of political challenge. In Germany and the United States alike, immigration bureaucrats have rarely faced sustained political opposition to the expulsion of terrorist suspects and Islamic fundamentalists, just as the removal of criminal offenders has rarely posed a serious threat to their political capacity. Whereas in the United States the post-9/11 reorganization of the immigration bureaucracy has had important implications for the implementation of migration controls beyond the area of antiterrorism, this has been less the case for Germany.[7] As a result, post-9/11 policy reforms in Germany, rather than strengthening executive capacity across the entire policy cluster, have allowed the German state to cast its net wider and to firmly draw religious fundamentalists and supporters of terrorism into its enforcement efforts.

---

[6] For persons who have committed an offense against peace, a war crime, or a crime against humanity, persons who have committed a serious non-political crime outside Germany, and persons who committed acts in contravention of the principles of the United Nations. However, the non-refoulement principle still applies.

[7] It could be argued that, in Germany, the most important consequences outside the realm of antiterrorism have been in the area of immigrant integration instead.

THE MISSING LINK: IMPLEMENTATION FAILURE AND
POLICY FEEDBACK

The evidence suggests that some of the enormous challenges facing enforcement officers in deportation bureaucracies derive from the severity of legislative mandates, which have been shaped by demonizing arguments. As
Chapter 4 demonstrated, immigration officials in both Germany and the
United States regularly confront humanitarian-motivated grassroots opposition to the implementation of deportation orders – conflict that reflects
shifts in public attention from the benefits, to the costs, of migration control.
As citizens are faced with the individualized costs of forcible removal, the
punitive, generalizing frames so successfully employed at the legislative stage
give way to the alternative frames of case mobilization that emphasize the
disproportionate costs of deportation for the many people whose characteristics do not conform to the earlier images of threat and calculated oppor-
tunism. The greater the extent to which legislative mandates are driven by
populist appeal – the more they represent knee-jerk reactions rather than
careful deliberation – the greater the degree of incongruence between the
two sets of frames.

Importantly, the implementation gaps arising from this conflict pose the
question of whether countermobilization can serve to lessen this contradic-
tion by providing the impetus for reform. Policy studies have shown that
controversy can serve an important role as a catalyst for self-correction. As
interventions encounter obstacles, and as administrative behaviors reap
diminishing returns over time, negative feedback effects can set in to allow
for policy adaptation, establishing a new equilibrium (Baumgartner &
Jones, 1993). Given the pervasiveness of enforcement failure in the area
of deportation, has there been policy correction by means of such negative
feedback effects? In other words, has implementation failure served as a
lesson for subsequent rounds of legislative reform?

While a systematic analysis of this specific question is beyond the empirical scope of this study, preliminary data for the United States suggest that
this is unlikely. Rather, the populist dynamic at work at the agenda-setting
stage presents enormously high hurdles to negative policy feedback. Since
the passage of IIRIRA in 1996, several attempts have been made to soften
what have been generally perceived as unduly harsh deportation provisions
pertaining to nonviolent criminal offenders – each has met with failure. It
appears that the political logic of coercive social regulation is so deeply
entrenched that policy feedback is not nearly as frequent as we should
expect, given the prevalence of implementation problems. Once reform

proposals informed by enforcement problems reach the legislative stage, criminalizing policy images dominate once again and thwart the emergence of a more compassionate reform agenda. As Michael Tonry has argued in the context of criminal justice reform: "Leaving things as they are poses no electoral risks. ... No one loses elections for failing to lead or support a campaign for repeal of laws that are tough on drugs or crime" (2004, p. 15).

Because of the field's susceptibility to populism, then, incremental policy change is most likely to occur behind closed doors. As a staffer for Representative Barney Frank (D-MA), one of the main driving forces behind the revision of the 1996 act, argued:

> The Administration may sign Barney's bill if there is not much controversy surrounding it. ... It depends on how politicized the criminal alien issue gets.
> (Staffer to Barney Frank (D-MA), U.S. House of Representatives,
> Washington, D.C., August 21, 2002)

Alternatively, we would expect to observe reform with the emergence of ideational change sufficiently strong to disrupt the dominance of punitive policy images – a condition unlikely to arise at a time of cultural and fiscal conservatism. Given these constraints for legislative reform, it should thus come as no surprise that the only changes to the 1996 immigration act – the removal of retroactivity and the prohibition of indefinite detention – were the result of Supreme Court decisions, rather than congressional reform efforts.

Given these constraints, are there conditions under which policy feedback is possible? To answer this question it is fruitful to turn to the German case, where we observe several instances of this phenomenon since the asylum compromise. In 1996, 1999, 2001[8] and, most recently, 2006, the Federal Conference of Interior Ministers passed special ordinances (*Altfallregelungen*, "regulation of old cases") that allowed rejected asylum seekers to remain in Germany, subject to certain preconditions such as long-term residence, self-sufficiency, a clean criminal record and basic language proficiency. In each instance, the ordinance was passed after months of protracted conflict about the fate of failed asylum applicants who had been living in Germany for years without being able to secure residence rights. Demands for an amnesty were spearheaded by the churches and immigrant rights groups and fell on receptive ears within those Land governments whose coalition partners included the SPD, the Liberals, or the Greens. These arguments closely resembled those that dominate the politics of case

---

[8] Pertaining to refugees from Bosnia-Herzegovina and the former Yugoslavia.

mobilization, as illustrated in the following newspaper excerpt from a 2005 interview with the spokesperson for North-Rhine Westphalia's interior minister Ingo Wolf (FDP) regarding the minister's amnesty proposal:

Spokesperson Harmeier explained that the reasons for the proposal were the increasingly pressing responses by "politicians across parties, organizations, and citizen initiatives" to deportations which the public considers unjust. He mentioned the example of a Kosovar family in Freudenberg ... whose deportation could be averted ten days ago by protests from neighbors and friends. "We want to give those a right to stay who are economically and socially integrated and whose children likely were born here" Wolf's spokesperson stated. ... It is not right, Harmeier added, to deport people to countries they hardly know when they have built for themselves a life and social networks [in Germany] and are needed by their employers. Problematically, he argued, so far there had been "no legal possibilities" to exempt these individuals from deportation.

(die tageszeitung, November 8, 2005)

What allowed these instances of policy feedback to take their course? First and foremost, although these measures were driven by popular pressure, they were ultimately decided upon in bureaucratic settings far removed from electoral politics. Because the Länder ministries hold jurisdiction over policy regulation and implementation, the interior ministers in liberal jurisdictions were able to respond to constituent concerns and introduce amnesty proposals in the Federal Conference of Interior Ministers. Once on the Conference's agenda, the proposals were debated largely along the fault lines of partisanship. Had these discussions played out in the legislative arena, their fate would probably have been short-lived once public debate had triggered a rhetorical shift from humanizing to demonizing arguments. Because the amnesty discussion took place behind closed doors, disagreement did not result in the demonizing of asylum seekers but instead was managed with a certain degree of pragmatism and political compromise. Those ministers in favor of amnesty could secure the support of their opponents by agreeing to handle eligibility criteria such as self-sufficiency in a restrictive manner.

It is important to point out that these administrative amnesties provided one-off regulatory exemptions – they did not leave behind a legacy of statutory reform. Because of the Conference of Interior Ministers' limited jurisdiction, policy feedback only amounted to partial, short-term solutions, leaving intact the larger framework of immigration law. The ordinances were constrained not only in terms of their often stringent conditions but, more fundamentally, in terms of their time-limited nature. Their tightly controlled reach meant that many migrants did not qualify, thereby sowing the seeds for the need for future rounds of policy feedback. Nevertheless, these instances compare favorably with the absence of feedback effects in the United States where different institutional configurations precluded similar developments. Because in the United States the possibility of self-correction is limited to legislative rather than regulatory reform, initiatives are unlikely to succeed. Although policy change is not impossible – as reflected in IRCA's amnesty provisions in 1986 – the failure of immigration reform in 2007, whose most controversial feature was a new legalization program, speaks to the enormous hurdles blocking the way of feedback in the realm of migration control.

With the path to substantive legislative reform blocked by the populist tendencies that mark the policies of coercive social regulation, are there alternative corrective mechanisms that could lessen the political challenges of implementation? Considering these constraints, reform-minded interests might be best served by procedural changes that would return more decision-making authority to bureaucrats and immigration judges. The case for professional discretion has long been established by the public administration literature; legislative statutes simply cannot be written at the level of detail necessary to take into account the ins and outs of individual cases. In addition, the bureaucrats charged with enforcing socially coercive regulations are particularly likely to confront complex circumstances that call for the exercise of bureaucratic and judicial discretion. For instance, the widely acknowledged injustices arising from the 1996 aggravated felon provisions – mandatory detention and deportation of legal permanent residents convicted of even nonviolent offenses – are in large part the result of the act's court-stripping provisions, which removed all discretion from the immigration judges adjudicating these cases.

There are a number of compelling arguments in favor of increasing bureaucratic discretion over deportation cases. From the point of view of the politically enfeebled U.S. officials, greater discretion would provide more scope for case decisions to take into account hardship and other humanitarian grounds. Consequently, bureaucrats in many instances will be able to preempt case mobilization, thereby avoiding the interference of elected officials and the subsequent undermining of agency morale. Although the outcome of both scenarios may be the same, nonimplementation resulting from the judicious use of administrative discretion is a function of bureaucratic agency, whereas nonenforcement arising from case mobilization is the product of bureaucratic incapacity.

Case mobilization, it could be argued, provides an important service to immigrants because it alerts the public to problems of disproportionality in agency decision-making. However, it is doubtful whether such campaigns serve the interests of the immigrant community as a whole. Rather, in many instances case mobilization reflects the comparative advantage of individuals with connections to those with the requisite resources. For each politicized case, there are countless individuals in comparable circumstances whose fate goes unpublicized. Case mobilization will thus always entail an element of arbitrariness. Although there have been some attempts to formalize decision-making in hardship cases – in Germany some Länder have set up so-called Hardship Commissions (*Härtefallkommissionen*), staffed by immigrant advocates and bureaucrats who advise the interior ministry on contested cases – the process by which cases are brought to the Commissions' attention continue to rely on public mobilization. Procedural fairness, it could be argued, would probably be better served if case decisions remained the prerogative of law enforcement officers, contingent upon good training, proper line supervision, and judicial review.

Clearly, these conclusions rest on a conception of bureaucratic behavior as motivated by "working," rather than "shirking." To the extent that political principals do not trust their administrative agents to implement their mandates faithfully – a presumption fundamental to most principal–agent models of legislative–executive relations – they will continue to shun delegation and instead seek to curb official discretion. Judged by the policy implications, the quest for ever greater legislative oversight is a rather ironic one, as the empirical findings of this book have shown. In the case of deportation, the imposition of stricter constraints on bureaucratic decision-making has not served to improve implementation by reducing executive shirking. Instead, in many cases of nonenforcement, it is the very exercise of legislative oversight that is the culprit. Wherever elected officials stand to gain from providing constituency services to those subject to regulation, they are likely to try to interfere with implementation. It is only where bureaucrats and their agency leaders possess the political capacity to resist these interventions without having to fear lasting negative consequences that we should expect to observe the systematic enforcement of their statutory mandates.

Appendices

APPENDIX I. *Deportation-Related Questions for Question Hour in the Bundestag*

	13th Bundestag (1994–1998)	14th Bundestag (1998–2002)
Governing coalition	Christian Democrats (CDU/CSU), Liberals (FDP)	Social Democrats (SPD), Greens (Bündnis 90/DIE GRÜNEN)
Opposition parties	Social Democrats, Greens, Socialists (PDS)	Christian Democrats, Liberals, Socialists
Number of questions by party	Christian Democrats: 7 Liberals: 2 *Total government: 9 (21%)* Social Democrats: 13 Greens: 17 Socialists: 3 *Total opposition: 33 (79%)*	Social Democrats: 1 Greens: 0 *Total government: 1 (5%)* Christian Democrats: 14 Liberals: 4 Socialists: 1 *Total opposition: 19 (95%)*
Question topics	*Rights/protection of deportees: (74%)* Social Democrats: 10 Greens: 16 Socialists: 3 Liberals: 2	*Rights/protection of deportees: (30%)* Liberals: 2 Socialists: 2 Christian Democrats: 1 Social Democrats: 1

(continued)

APPENDIX I *(continued)*

	13th Bundestag (1994–1998)	14th Bundestag (1998–2002)
	Implementation problems: (11%) Christian Democrats: 4 Social Democrats: 1	*Implementation problems: (30%)* Christian Democrats: 6 Liberals: 1
	National security and public safety: (4%) Christian Democrats: 2 *Other:* (11%) Social Democrats: 2 Greens: 1 Christian Democrats: 1	*National security and public safety: (25%)* Christian Democrats: 5 *Other:* (10%) Liberals: 1 Christian Democrats: 1
Category of Noncitizens	*Asylum seekers/refugees:* 57% of total questions (86% of questions specifying a category) *Criminals:* 10% (14% of questions specifying a category) *Illegals:* 0%	*Asylum seekers/refugees:* 45% of total questions (64% of questions specifying a category) *Criminals:* 20% (29% of questions specifying a category) *Illegals:* 5% (7% of questions specifying a category)
Type of Government Response	No response (A): 7% No information (B): 17% Deflecting criticism (C): 14% Passing the buck (D): 17% *Total responses A-D:* 55%	No response (A): 5% No information (B): 15% Deflecting criticism (C): 5% Passing the buck (D): 25% *Total responses A-D:* 50%

APPENDIX 2. *Interviews** With Deportation Officers in Brandenburg, Baden-Württemberg, San Diego, and Miami*

	Brandenburg	Baden-Württemberg	San Diego	Miami
Deportation agencies interviewed	8 local (out of 21)	2 regional (out of 4)	1 (out of 1)	1 (out of 1)
Managers interviewed	6	4	3	3
Street-level bureaucrats interviewed	14	4	12	3
Bureaucrats who raised case mobilization as a problem for decision-making	14 (70%)	0	3 (20%)("somewhat of a problem")	6 (100%)
Bureaucrats who didn't consider case mobilization a problem for decision-making	1 (5%)	8 (100%)	6 (40%)	0
Bureaucrats who didn't raise the issue of case mobilization	5	0	6 (40%)	0

** *In the majority of cases, several interviews were conducted with each officer.*

References

Aberbach, Joel D. (1990). *Keeping a Watchful Eye: The Politics of Congressional Oversight*. Washington, D.C.: Brookings.

Aberbach, Joel D., Derlien, Hans-Ulrich, Mayntz, Renate, & Rockman, Bert A. (1990). "American and German Federal Executives - Technocratic and Political Attitudes." *International Social Science Journal*, 123: 3–18.

Aberbach, Joel D., Derlien, Hans-Ulrich, & Rockman, Bert A. (1994). "Unity and Fragmentation - Themes in German and American Public Administration." In Hans-Ulrich Derlien, Uta Gerhardt, & Fritz W. Scharpf (Eds.), *Systemrationalität und Partialinteresse*, Baden-Baden: Nomos, 271–289.

Aberbach, Joel D., Putnam, Robert D., & Rockman, Bert A. (1981). *Bureaucrats and Politicians in Western Democracies*. Cambridge, MA: Harvard University Press.

Alt, Jörg. (1999). *Illegal in Deutschland*. Karlsruhe: von Loeper Literaturverlag.

Andreas, Peter. (1998–99). "The Escalation of U.S. Immigration Control in the Post-NAFTA Era." *Political Science Quarterly*, 113(4): 591–625.

Andreas, Peter. (2000). *Border Games: Policing the U.S. Mexico Divide*. Ithaca, NY: Cornell University Press.

Andreas, Peter, & Snyder, Timothy. (Eds.). (2000). *The Wall around the West: State Borders and Immigration Controls in North America and Europe*. New York, NY: Rowman & Littlefield.

Anter, Andreas. (1995). *Theorie des Modernen Staates: Herkunft, Struktur und Bedeutung*. Berlin: Duncker & Humblot.

Arbeitsgemeinschaft der Innenministerien der Bundesländer. (March 9, 1964). *Protokoll über die Sitzung des Arbeitskreises I "Staatsrecht, Verwaltung und Verwaltungsgerichtsbrarkeit" und des Arbeitskreises II "Öffentliche Sicherheit und Ordnung."* Bonn, BArch B106/39960.

Arnold, R. Douglas. (1990). *The Logic of Congressional Action*. New Haven, CT: Yale University Press.

Ausländerreferenten des Bundes und der Länder. (February 13–15, 1968). *Ausländerreferentenbesprechung*. Bonn, BArch B106/39992.

Ausländerreferenten des Bundes und der Länder. (October 15–17, 1970). *Niederschrift über die Besprechung der Ausländerreferenten des Bundes und der Länder.* Bonn, BArch B106/39994.

Barrios, Sharon A. (1999). *Inside the Immigration and Naturalization Service: The Organizational Dynamics of a Problem Agency.* Unpublished Dissertation. Princeton, NJ: Princeton University.

Baumgartner, Frank R., & Jones, Bryan D. (1993). *Agendas and Instability in American Politics.* Chicago, IL: Chicago University Press.

Bayerisches Staatsministerium des Innern. (1963). *Ministerialrat Kanein des Bayerischen Staatsministeriums des Innern to Bundesminister des Innern, Innenminister/ Senatoren der Länder, Senator für öffentliche Sicherheit und Ordnung,* Betreff: Fremdenrecht – Massnahmen gegen unerwünschte Ausländer. Berlin.

BBC News (April 9, 2000). "Miami Divided Over Elian."

Berliner Morgenpost (August 11, 2001). "Nach 22 Jahren Kam die Ausweisung."

Berry, Jerry. (1977). *Lobbying for the People.* New Haven, CT: Princeton University Press.

Brehm, John, & Gates, Scott. (1997). *Working, Shirking, and Sabotage: Bureaucratic Response to a Democratic Public.* Ann Arbor, MI: University of Michigan.

Brochmann, Grete, & Hammar, Thomas. (Eds.). (1999). *Mechanisms of Immigration Control: A Comparative Analysis of European Regulation Policies.* New York, NY: Berg.

Brownell, Peter. (September 1, 2005). "The Declining Enforcement of Employer Sanctions." *Migration Information Source,* Washington, D.C.: Migration Policy Institute.

Brubaker, Rogers. (1994). "Are Immigration Controls Really Failing?" In Wayne A. Cornelius, David A. Martin, & James F. Hollifield (Eds.), *Controlling Immigration: A Global Perspective,* Stanford, CA: Stanford University Press, 227–231.

Bundesministerium des Innern. (1999). *Bericht an den Innenausschuss des Deutschen Bundestages über den Tod des sudanesischen Staatsangehörigen Aamir Omer Mohamed Ahmed AGEEB bei dessen Rückführung am 28. Mai 1999.* Berlin: Bundesministerium des Innern.

Bundesministerium des Innern. (2003). *Bundesgrenzschutz Jahresbericht, 2002.* Berlin.

Bundesministerium des Innern. (April 11, 1967). *Bundesminister des Innern zu Stadtverordnetem Eugen Huth, Wuppertal-Vohwinkel, Betreff: Ausweisung von straffällig gewordenen Ausländern.* Bonn, BArch B106/39976.

Busch, Eckart, & Berger, Frithjof. (Eds.). (1989). *Die Parlamentarische Kontrolle: Institutionen und Funktionen des Deutschen Bundestages.* Berglen: Wirtemberg Verlag.

Cain, Bruce, Ferejohn, John, & Fiorina, Morris P (1987). *The Personal Vote: Constituency Service and Electoral Independence.* Cambridge, MA: Harvard University Press.

Calavita, Kitty. (1992). *Inside the State: The Bracero Program, Immigration, and the I.N.S.* New York, NY: Routledge.

Cammisa, Anne Marie. (1995). *Governments as Interest Groups: Intergovernmental Lobbying and the Federal System.* Westport, CT: Praeger.

Campbell, Andrea Louise, & Morgan, Kimberly J. (2005). "Federalism and the Politics of Old-Age Care in Germany and the United States." *Comparative Political Studies*, 38(8): 887–914.

Carpenter, Daniel P. (2001). *The Forging of Bureaucratic Autonomy: Reputations, Networks, and Policy Innovation in Executive Agencies, 1862–1928*. Princeton, NJ: Princeton University Press.

Chicago Sun-Times (January 31, 1994). "U.S. Asked to Pick Up Tab for Illegals; Edgar Joins Plea Citing States' Burden."

Chishti, Muzaffar A., Meissner, Doris, Papademetriou, Demetrios G., Peterzell, Jay, Wishnie, Michael J., & Yale-Loehr, Stephen W. (2003). *America's Challenge: Domestic Security, Civil Liberties, and National Unity After September 11*. Washington, D.C.: Migration Policy Institute, http://www.migrationpolicy.org/pubs/Americas_Challenges.pdf.

Christian Science Monitor (February 1, 1994). "Governors Call for More Leeway to Launch Reform."

Christian Science Monitor (May 16, 2006). "Illegal Immigrants in the U.S.: How Many Are There?"

Christian Science Monitor (November 14, 1994). "California Seen as Key to Clinton Hopes in '96."

Cornelius, Wayne A. (1998). "The Structural Embeddedness of Demand for Mexican Immigrant Labor: New Evidence from California." In Marcelo M. Suarez-Orozco (Ed.), *Crossings: Mexican Immigration in Interdisciplinary Perspectives*, Cambridge, MA: Harvard University Press, 114–144.

Cornelius, Wayne A., Martin, Philip L., & Hollifield, James F. (Eds.). (1994). *Controlling Immigration: A Global Perspective*. Stanford, CA: Stanford University Press.

Der Stern (October 12, 2004). "Kaplan in die Türkei Abgeschoben."

Derlien, Hans-Ulrich. (1988). "Repercussion of Government Change on the Career Civil Service in West Germany: The Cases of 1969 and 1982." *Governance*, 1(1): 50–78.

Derthick, Martha. (1990). *Agency Under Stress: The Social Security Administration in American Government*. Washington, D.C.: Brookings Institution.

Derthick, Martha A. (1980). *Policy-making for Social Security*. Washington, D.C.: Brookings Institution.

Deutscher Bundestag. (December 30, 1999). *Abschiebungen auf dem Luftweg*. Antwort der Bundesregierung auf die Kleine Anfrage der Abgeordneten Ulla Jelpke und der Fraktion der PDS. Berlin, Drucksache 14/2462.

Deutscher Bundestag. (February 7, 1996). *Fesselung bzw. Knebelung abzuschiebender Ausländer, u.a. des Nigerianers Kola Bankole, durch Grenzschutzbeamte. Schriftliche Antwort Dr. Horst Waffenschmidt*, Parlamentarischer Staatssekretär Bundesministerium des Innern zur Mündlichen Anfrage Manfred Such, Bündnis 90/Die Grünen. Berlin, Drucksache 13/3666.

Deutscher Bundestag. (March 30, 2001). *Abschiebungen auf dem Luftweg im Jahr 2000*. Antwort der Bundesregierung auf die Kleine Anfrage der Abgeordneten Ulla Jelpke und der Fraktion der PDS. Berlin, Drucksache 14/5734.

die tageszeitung (November 8, 2005). "Wolf: Wer Schafft, Darf Bleiben."

die tageszeitung (October 8, 1991). "CDU Plante die Antiasyldebatte."

Die Welt (November 27, 2000). "SPD setzt Schönbohm unter Druck."

Downs, Anthony. (1997). *An Economic Theory of Democracy*. Upper Saddle River, NJ: Pearson Education.

Ellermann, Antje. (2008). "The Limits of Unilateral Migration Control: Deportation and Interstate Cooperation." *Government and Opposition*, 43(2): 168–189.

Etter, Barbara. (1993). "The Police Culture: Overcoming Barriers." *Criminology Australia*, 3(2): 8–12.

European Monitoring Centre on Racism and Xenophobia. (2001). *Attitudes Towards Minority Groups in the European Union*. Vienna: SORA.

Evans, Peter B. (1995). *Embedded Autonomy: States and Industrial Transformation*. Princeton, NJ: Princeton University Press.

Evans, Peter, Rueschemeyer, Dietrich, & Skocpol, Theda. (Eds.). (1985). *Bringing the State Back In*. New York, NY: Cambridge University Press.

Feinstein, Dianne. (June 4, 2004). *Senator Feinstein Questions Deportation of Long-Term, Law-Abiding Undocumented Immigrants*. http://feinstein.senate. gov/04Releases/r-hutchinson-ltr-removal.htm.

Fekete, Liz. (2003). "Analysis: Deaths During Forced Deportation." *Independent Race and Refugee News Network*: www.irr.org.uk/2003/january/ak000003.html.

Feldman, Martha S. (1989). *Order Without Design: Information Production and Policy Making*. Stanford, CA: Stanford University Press.

Fetzer, Joel S. (2000). *Public Attitudes toward Immigration in the United States, France, and Germany*. New York, NY: Cambridge University Press.

Financial Times (July 10/11, 2004). "'Shock-jock' Radio Host Calls the Tune in U.S. Debate over Policies on Illegal Immigration."

Forschungsgruppe Wahlen Mannheim. (1992). *Landtagswahl in Baden-Württemberg 1992*. Köln: Zentralarchiv für Empirische Sozialforschung, http://www.za. uni-koeln.de/data/election-studies/ltw/codebuch/s2301.pdf.

Frankfurter Rundschau (November 2, 2000). "Ein Leidiges Thema in einer 'Leidenden Stadt'."

Freeman, Gary P. (1995). "Modes of Immigration Politics in Liberal Democratic States." *International Migration Review*, xxix(4): 881–913.

Freeman, Gary P. (2002). "Winners and Losers: Politics and the Costs and Benefits of Migration." In Anthony M. Messina (Ed.), *West European Immigration and Immigrant Policy in the New Century*, Westport, CT: Praeger, 77–95.

Gallup, Alex, & Newport, Frank. (2006). *The Gallup Poll: Public Opinion 2005*. New York, NY: Rowman & Littlefield.

Gallup News Service (April 4, 2000). "Americans Continue to Favor the Return of Elian Gonzalez to Cuba."

Garcia, Juan Ramon. (1980). *Operation Wetback: The Mass Deportation of Mexican Undocumented Workers in 1954*. Westport, CT: Greenwood Press.

Gibney, Matthew J. (2004). *The Ethics and Politics of Asylum: Liberal Democracy and the Response to Refugees*. Cambridge, UK: Cambridge University Press.

Gibney, Matthew J. (2008). "Asylum and the Expansion of Deportation in the United Kingdom." *Government and Opposition*, 43(2): 146–167.

Gibney, Matthew J., & Hansen, Randall. (2003). "Deportation and the Liberal State: The Involuntary Return of Asylum Seekers and Unlawful Migrants in Canada, the UK, and Germany." *New Issues in Refugee Research*, Working Paper 77.

Gilboy, Janet A. (1992). "Penetrability of Administrative Systems: Political 'Casework' and Immigration Inspectors." *Law & Society Review*, 26(2): 273–314.

Gimpel, James G., & Edwards, James R. (1999). *The Congressional Politics of Immigration Reform*. Boston, MA: Allyn and Bacon.

Goldston, James. (2006). *Ethnic Profiling and Counter-Terrorism: Trends, Dangers and Alternatives*. Brussels: Anti-Racism and Diversity Intergroup, European Parliament, http://snap.archivum.ws/dspace/bitstream/10039/6584/1/Ethnic_Profiling.pdf.

Goodsell, Charles. (1981). *The Public Encounter*. Bloomington, IN: Indiana University Press.

Guiraudon, Virginie. (1997). *Policy Change Behind Gilded Doors: Explaining the Evolution of Aliens' Rights in Contemporary Western Europe, 1974–1994*. Cambridge, MA: Unpublished Dissertation.

Hagan, Jacqueline, Eschbach, Karl, & Rodriguez, Nestor. (2008). "U.S. Deportation Policy, Family Separation, and Circular Migration." *International Migration Review*, 42(1): 64–88.

Haider-Markel, Donald P. (1998). "The Politics of Social Regulatory Policy: State and Federal Hate Crime Policy and Implementation Effort." *Political Research Quarterly*, 51(1): 69–88.

Hargrove, Erwin C., & Glidewell, John C. (1990). *Impossible Jobs in Public Management*. Lawrence, KS: University Press of Kansas.

Heclo, Hugh. (1974). *Modern Social Politics in Britain and Sweden: From Relief to Income Maintenance*. Princeton, NJ: Princeton University Press.

Heclo, Hugh. (1977). *A Government of Strangers: Executive Politics in Washington*. Washington, D.C.: Brookings.

Höfling-Semnar, Bettina. (1995). *Flucht und Deutsche Asylpolitik: Von der Krise des Asylrechts zur Perfektionierung der Zugangsverhinderung*. Münster: Westfälisches Dampfboot.

Hollifield, James F. (1992). *Immigrants, Markets, and States*. Cambridge, MA: Harvard University Press.

Huber, John D. (2000). "Delegation to Civil Servants in Parliamentary Bureaucracies." *European Journal of Political Research*, 37: 397–413.

Huber, John D., & McCarty, Nolan. (2004). "Bureaucratic Capacity, Delegation, and Political Reform." *American Political Science Review*, 98(3): 481–494.

Idelson, Holly. (March 23, 1996). "House Votes to Crack Down on Illegal Immigrants." *Congressional Quarterly Weekly Report*, 54(12): 794–797.

Idelson, Holly. (May 4, 1996). "Bill Heads to Conference After Senate Passage." *Congressional Quarterly Weekly Report*, 54(18): 1221–1225.

Innenministerium Baden-Württemberg. (2001). *Verwaltungsvorschrift des Innenministeriums über die stärkere Berücksichtigung arbeitsmarktpolitischer Interessen des Mittelstandes bei der Anwendung von §8 AAV*. Stuttgart: Innenministerium Baden-Württemberg.

Ismayr, Wolfgang. (1992). *Der Deutsche Bundestag: Funktionen, Willensbildung, Reformansätze*. Opladen: Leske & Budrich.

Jacobson, David. (1996). *Rights Across Borders: Immigration and the Decline of Citizenship*. Baltimore, MD: John Hopkins University Press.

Johnson, Nevil. (1979). "Committees in the West German Bundestag." In John D. Lees, & Malcolm Shaw (Eds.), *Committees in Legislatures: A Comparative Analysis*, Oxford, UK: Martin Robinson.

Johnson, Nevil. (1982). *State and Government in the Federal Republic of Germany: The Executive at Work*. New York, NY: Pergamon Press.

Joppke, Christian. (1998). "Why Liberal States Accept Unwanted Immigration." *World Politics*, 50: 266–293.

Kaufman, Herbert. (1967). *The Forest Ranger: A Study in Administrative Behavior.* Washington, D.C.: Resources for the Future.

Kaufman, Herbert. (1981). *The Administrative Behavior of Federal Bureau Chiefs.* Washington, D.C.: Brookings.

Kingdon, John W. (1995). *Agendas, Alternatives, and Public Policies.* New York, NY: Logman.

Kirch am Eck Online (May 25, 2001). "Das Ökumenische Kirchenasyl in Tübingen."

Klodawsky, Fran, Farrell, Susan, & D'Aubry, Tim. (2002). "Images of Homelessness in Ottawa: Implications for Local Politics." *The Canadian Geographer*, 46(2): 126–143.

König, Jürgen. (2000). *Rückkehr und Verbleib von Asylbewerbern und Flüchtlingen in Deutschland.* Bonn: Geographische Institute der Rheinischen Friedrich-Wilhelms-Universität Bonn, Unpublished Dissertation.

Krasner, Stephen D. (1978). *Defending the National Interest: Raw Materials, Investments and U.S. Foreign Policy.* Princeton, NJ: Princeton University Press.

Lahav, Gallya, & Guiraudon, Virginie. (2000). "Comparative Perspectives on Border Control: Away from the Border and Outside the State." In Peter Andreas, & Timothy Snyder (Eds.), *The Wall Around the West: State Borders and Immigration Controls in North American and Europe*, New York, NY: Rowman & Littlefield, 55–77.

Landtag Baden-Württemberg. (1996). *Verlängerung der Duldung für Bosnische Flüchtlinge.* Stuttgart: Landtag Baden-Württemberg, Drucksache 12/296.

Landtag Baden-Württemberg. (1997). *Befristetes Bleiberecht für Bosnische Auszubildende.* Stuttgart: Landtag Baden-Württemberg, Drucksache 12/1582.

Landtag Baden-Württemberg. (1998). *Abschiebestopp für Flüchtlinge aus Kosovo-Albanien.* Stuttgart: Landtag Baden-Württemberg, Drucksache 12/2637.

Lausitzer Rundschau (August 11, 2001). "Unfreiwillige Ausreise nach 22 Jahren Deutschland."

Lee, Kenneth K. (1998). *Huddled Masses, Muddled Laws: Why Contemporary Immigration Policy Fails to Reflect Public Opinion.* Westport, CT: Praeger Publishers.

Lichtenberg, Peter. (1986). *Die Aktuelle Stunde im Deutschen Bundestag, 1965–1985.* Bad Honnef: Bock + Herchen.

Lijphart, Arend. (1999). *Patterns of Democracy: Government Forms and Performancein Thirty-Six Countries.* New Haven, CT: Yale University Press.

Lipsky, Michael. (1983). *Street Level Bureaucracy.* New York, NY: Russell Sage.

Lupia, Arthur. (2003). "Delegation and Its Perils." In Kaare Strøm, Wolfgang C. Müller, & Torbjörn Bergman (Eds.), *Delegation and Accountability in Parliamentary Democracies*, New York, NY: Oxford University Press, 33–55.

Magaña, Lisa. (2003). *Straddling the Border: Immigration Policy and the INS.* Austin, TX: University of Texas Press.

Mann, Michael. (1993). *The Sources of Social Power: The Rise of Classes and Nation-States, 1760–1914.* New York, NY: Cambridge University Press.

Manning, Peter K. (1977). *Police Work: The Social Organization of Policing.* Cambridge, MA: MIT Press.

Manning, Peter K., & Van Maanen, J. (1978). *Policing: A View from the Street.* Santa Monica, CA: Goodyear.

Marshall, Barbara. (2000). *The New Germany and Migration in Europe.* New York, NY: St. Martin's Press.

Masci, David. (March 16, 1996). "Odds for Curb on Legal Immigrants Grow Longer as Senate Panel Splits Bill." *Congressional Quarterly Weekly Report,* 54(11): 698–700.

May, Diane. (1992). "The Bremen Land Election of September 1991." *German Politics,* 1(1): 119–123.

Mayntz, Renate. (1984). "German Federal Bureaucrats: A Functional Elite Between Politics and Administration." In Ezra N. Suleiman (Ed.), *Bureaucrats and Policy-making: A Comparative Overview,* New York, NY: Holmes & Meier, 174–205.

Mayntz, Renate, & Scharpf, Fritz W. (1975). *Policy-making in the German Federal Bureaucracy.* New York, NY: Elsevier.

McCubbins, Mathew D., & Kiewiet, D. Roderick. (1991). *Logic of Delegation: Congressional Parties and the Appropriations Process.* Chicago, IL: Chicago University Press.

McCubbins, Mathew D., Noll, Roger G., & Weingast, Barry R. (1987). "Administrative Procedures as Instruments of Political Control." *Journal of Law, Economics, and Organization,* 3(2): 243–277.

McCubbins, Mathew D., & Schwartz, Thomas. (1984). " Congressional Oversight Overlooked: Police Patrols Versus Fire Alarms." *Journal of Political Science,* 2(1): 165–179.

Mead, Lawrence M. (2004). *Government Matters: Welfare Reform in Wisconsin.* Princeton, NJ: Princeton University Press.

Meier, Kenneth. (1979). *Politics and the Bureaucracy: Policy-making in the Fourth Branch of Government.* Belmont, CA: Wadsworth Publishing Company.

Melnick, R. Shep. (1994). *Between the Lines: Interpreting Welfare Rights.* Washington, D.C.: Brookings Institution.

Migdal, Joel S. (2001). *State In Society: Studying How States and Societies Transform and Constitute One Another.* New York, NY: Cambridge University Press.

Mitchell, Timothy. (1991). "The Limits of the State: Beyond Statist Approaches and Their Critics." *The American Political Science Review,* 85(1): 77–96.

Money, Jeannette. (1997). "No Vacancy: The Political Geography of Immigration Control in Advanced Industrial Countries." *International Organization,* 51(4): 685–720.

Money, Jeannette. (1999). *Fences and Neighbors: The Political Geography of Immigration Control.* Ithaca, NY: Cornell University Press.

Morris, Milton D. (1985). *Immigration the Beleaguered Bureaucracy*. Washington, D.C.: Brookings.

Mumola, Christopher. (2000). *Incarcerated Parents and Their Children*. Special Report. NCJ 182335. Washington, D.C.: Department of Justice, Bureau of Justice Statistics.

Münch, Ursula. (1993). *Asylpolitik in der Bundesrepublik Deutschland: Entwicklungen und Alternativen*. Opladen: Leske & Budrich.

Naím, Moisés. (2002). "On the Fence: Former INS Commissioner Doris Meissner on the Contradictions of Migration Policy in a Globalizing World." *Foreign Policy*, 129: 22–35.

Neue Zürcher Zeitung (May 27, 1993). "Marathondebatte unter Massivem Polizeischutz: Verabschiedung der Asylrechtsreform in Bonn."

News Herald (January 2, 2008). "County Prepared to Enforce Employer Sanctions Law."

New York Times (October 1, 1991). "A Wave of Attacks On Foreigners Stirs Shock in Germany."

New York Times (October 26, 1994). "California Governor Suggests Requiring Citizenship Cards."

New York Times (December 4, 1994). "Anti-Alien Sentiment Spreading in Wake of California's Measure."

New York Times (September 20, 2004). "Immigrants Lost in the Din: Security vs. the Dream."

New York Times (April 22, 2006). "Illegal Workers Divided over Federal Crackdown."

New York Times (August 6, 2007). "Surge in Immigration Laws Around U.S."

New York Times (May 24, 2008). "270 Illegal Immigrants Sent to Prison in Federal Push."

Niskanen, William A. (1971). *Bureaucracy and Representative Government*. Chicago, IL: Aldine Publishing.

Nordlinger, Eric. (1981). *On the Autonomy of the Democratic State*. Cambridge, MA: Harvard University Press.

Norris, Pippa. (2003). *Electoral Engineering: Voting Rules and Political Behavior*. New York, NY: Cambridge University Press.

Nuscheler, Franz. (1995). *Internationale Migration. Flucht und Asyl*. Opladen: Leske & Budrich.

Odum Institute. (August 1993). http://cgi.irss.unc.edu/cgi-bin/POLL/search.poll.cgi, accessed December 20, 2004, page now discontinued.

Odum Institute. (July 1994). http://cgi.irss.unc.edu/cgi-bin/POLL/search.poll.cgi, accessed December 20, 2004, page now discontinued.

Panunzio, Constantine M. (1921). *The Deportation Cases of 1919–1920*. New York, NY: Commission on the Church and Social Service.

Patashnik, Eric. (2003). "After the Public Interest Prevails: The Political Sustainability of Policy Reform." *Governance*, 16(2): 203–234.

Peabody, Robert. (1964). *Organizational Authority*. New York, NY: Atherton Press.

Persson, Torsten, Roland, Gerard, & Tabellini, Guido. (1997). "Separation of Powers and Political Accountability." *Quarterly Journal of Economics*, 112: 310–327.

Phoenix Business Journal (February 8, 2008). "Federal Judge Upholds Employer Sanctions Law."

pro asyl. (1992). *Pressemitteilung vom 28. September 1991.* Frankfurt/Main: pro asyl.

Progressive Punch (October 28, 2003). "H.R. 2359. Employment Verification Program/ Vote to Extend and Expand a 1996 Employment Verification Pilot Program Through 2008."

Reimers, David. (1999). *Unwelcome Strangers: American Identity and the Turn Against Immigration.* New York, NY: Columbia University Press.

Reiner, Robert. (1992). *The Politics of Police.* Toronto, ON: University of Toronto Press.

Rheinische Post (February 17, 1960). "15,000 Ausländer in Düsseldorf: Ausländeramt Hat Viel zu Tun."

Rheinische Post (July 20, 1968). "Auf Staatskosten: Gratisflug in die Heimat: Wenn Gastarbeiter Ausgewiesen Werden."

Roberts, Julian V., Stalans, Loretta J.,Indermaur, David, & Hough, Mike. (2003). *Penal Populism and Public Opinion: Lessons from Five Countries.* New York, NY: Oxford University Press.

Rocky Mountain News (December 10, 1995). "Law Undercut by Law Enforcement of Hiring Illegals."

Rose, Richard. (1969). "The Variability of Party Government: A Theoretical and Empirical Critique." *Political Studies,* 17(4): 413–445.

Saalfeld, Thomas. (2003). "Germany: Multiple Veto Points, Informal Coordination, and Problems of Hidden Action." In Kaare Strøm, Wolfgang C. Müller, & Torbjörn Bergman (Eds.), *Delegation and Accountability in Parliamentary Democracies,* New York, NY: Oxford University Press, 347–376.

San Diego Union Tribune (February 12, 2000). "Letters to the Editor."

San Diego Union Tribune (February 15, 2000). "Gays, Lesbians Rally in San Diego, Seeking Equal Immigration Rights."

San Francisco Chronicle (February 1, 1994). "Governors Threaten to Sue U.S.: Wilson, Others, Say Federal Funds Must Pay Illegal Immigrants' Costs."

San Francisco Chronicle (October 15, 1994). "Brown Blasts Wilson on Crime Issue: They Meet in Only Scheduled TV Debate."

San Francisco Chronicle (March 18, 1996). "Border Guarded, Workplace Ignored: A Major Flaw in the Crackdown on Immigration."

Sassen, Saskia. (1988). *The Mobility of Labor and Capital.* Cambridge, UK: Cambridge University Press.

Schattschneider, Elmer E. (1975). *The Semi-sovereign People: A Realist View of Democracy in America.* Hindsdale, IL: Dryden Press.

Schrecker, Ellen. (1997). "Immigration and Internal Security: Political Deportations During the McCarthy Era." *Science and Society,* 60(4): 393–426.

Schwarze, Susan (2000). *The Arena Negotiation Model – German Asylum Policy in the European Context between 1989 and 1993.* Unpublished Dissertation. Berlin: Freie Universität Berlin.

Shepsle, Kenneth A. (1992). "Bureaucratic Drift, Coalitional Drift, and Time Consistency: A Comment on Macey." *Journal of Law, Economics, and Organization,* 8(1): 111–118.

Simon, Rita, & Alexander, Susan. (1993). *The Ambivalent Welcome: Print Media, Public Opinion and Immigration.* Westport, CT: Praeger.

Skocpol, Theda. (1985). "Bringing the State Back In: Strategies of Analysis in Current Research." In Peter Evans, Dietrich Rueschemeyer, & Theda Skocpol (Eds.), *Bringing the State Back In,* New York, NY: Cambridge University Press.

Skocpol, Theda, & Finegold, Kenneth. (1982). "State Capacity and Economic Intervention in the Early New Deal." *Political Science Quarterly,* 97(2): 255–278.

Skolnick, Jerome H. (1966). *Justice Without Trial.* New York, NY: John Wiley and Sons.

Skolnick, Jerome H., & Fyfe, James. (1993). *Above the Law: Police and the Excessive Use of Force.* New York, NY: The Free Press.

Soroka, Stuart N., & Wlezien, Christopher. (2004). "Opinion Representation and Policy Feedback: Canada in Comparative Perspective." *Canadian Journal of Political Science,* 37(3): 531–559.

Soysal, Yasemin Nuhoglu. (1994). *Limits of Citizenship: Migrants and Postnational Membership in Europe.* Chicago, IL: University of Chicago.

Sozialdemokratische Partei Deutschlands. (1992). *Protokoll vom Ausserordentlichen Parteitag der SPD vom 16–17 November 1992.* Bonn.

St. Petersburg Times (November 20, 1994). "Clinton Agenda to Make Move Toward the Right."

Steiner, Niklaus. (2000). *Arguing about Asylum: The Complexity of Refugee Debates in Europe.* New York, NY: St. Martin's Press.

Strøm, Kaare, Müller, Wolfgang C., & Bergman, Torbjörn. (Eds.). (2003). *Delegation and Accountability in Parliamentary Democracies.* New York, NY: Oxford University Press.

Stuttgarter Zeitung (September 15, 1965). "Ausländer mit Rechten und Pflichten."

Süddeutsche Zeitung (April 6, 1992). "15 Sitze für Republikaner, CDU Büsst 9.4 Prozent Ein."

Süddeutsche Zeitung (April 13, 1992). "Asylbewerber in München: "Ein Problem, das Objektiv Gar Keines Ist."

Süddeutsche Zeitung (December 2, 1992). "In der Asylpolitik zum Erfolg Verdammt: Kronawitter Feuert die Bonner Politiker An."

Süddeutsche Zeitung (March 5, 1992). "Armutswanderung Zentrales Thema am Politischen Aschermittwoch."

Süddeutsche Zeitung (May 29, 1993). "Das Neue Asylrecht Kann am 1. Juli in Kraft Treten."

Süddeutsche Zeitung (October 1, 1991a). "Bremen Nach der Wahl: Ursachenforschung und Schuldzuweisungen."

Süddeutsche Zeitung (October 1, 1991b). "Die Deutschen Zeitungen Kommentieren das Ergebnis der Landtagswahl."

Süddeutsche Zeitung (October 5, 1992). "Fragen an Kardinal Friedrich Wetter zur Asylproblematik: 'Es Sind Immer Menschen, Die Zu Uns Kommen.' "

Süddeutsche Zeitung (September 7, 1992). "Bundespräsident; Asylverfahren Weizäcker/ Aufmacher; Europäische Lösung der Flüchtlingsfrage Gerster und Kronawitter."

Süddeutsche Zeitung (September 21, 1992). "Herbstvollversammlung der Deutschen Bischöfe zum Jubliläum: Ringen ums Asylrecht."

Tampa Tribune (July 13, 1995). "Chiles Says He Supports ID Cards: The Governor Said the Measure Would Deter the Hiring of Illegal Immigrants."

Tampa Tribune (September 24, 1995). "Citizen Identification Card Attacked by Several Camps: House and Senate Proposals are Rapped as Costly by Business and an Invasion of Privacy Rights."

Tatalovich, Raymond, & Daynes, Byron W. (Eds.). (1988). *Social Regulatory Policy: Moral Controversies in American Politics.* Boulder, CO: Westview Press.

Tichenor, Daniel J. (2002). *Dividing Lines: The Politics of Immigration Control in America.* Princeton, NJ: Princeton University Press.

Tonry, Michael. (2004). *Thinking about Crime: Sense and Sensibility in American Penal Culture.* New York, NY: Oxford University Press.

Torpey, John. (2000). *The Invention of the Passport: Surveillance, Citizenship and the State.* Cambridge, UK: Cambridge University Press.

Travis, Jeremy, McBride Elizabeth Cincotta, & Solomon, Amy L. (2005). *Families Left Behind: The Hidden Costs of Incarceration and Reentry.* Washington, D.C.: The Urban Institute, http://www.urban.org/uploadedPDF/310882_families_left_behind. pdf.

U.S. Commission on Immigration Reform. (1994). *U.S. Immigration Policy: Restoring Credibility.* Washington, D.C.

U.S. Department of Homeland Security Office of Inspector General. (2007). *An Assessment of United States Immigration and Customs Enforcement's Fugitive Operations Teams.* Washington, D.C.

U.S. Department of Justice Office of the Inspector General. (1996a). *Alleged Deception of Congress: The Congressional Task Force on Immigration Reform's Fact-Finding Visit to the Miami District of INS in June 1995.* Washington, D.C.

U.S. Department of Justice Office of the Inspector General. (1996b). *Immigration and Naturalization Service Efforts to Combat Harboring and Employing Illegal Aliens in Sweatshops.* Washington, D.C.

U.S. Department of Justice Office of the Inspector General. (1997). *Immigration and Naturalization Service Monitoring of Nonimmigrant Overstays.* Washington, D.C.

U.S. Department of Justice Office of the Inspector General. (2001). *Criminal Aliens: The INS Escort of Criminal Aliens.* Washington, D.C.

U.S. Department of Justice Office of the Inspector General. (2002). *Follow-Up Report On INS Efforts To Improve The Control Of Nonimmigrant Overstays.* Washington, D.C.

U.S. General Accounting Office. (1998). *Illegal Aliens: Changes in the Process of Denying Aliens Entry Into the United States.* Washington, D.C.

U.S. General Accounting Office. (1999a). *Criminal Aliens: INS' Efforts to Identify and Remove Imprisoned Aliens Need to Be Improved.* Washington, D.C.

U.S. General Accounting Office. (1999b). *Illegal Aliens: Significant Obstacles to Reducing Unauthorized Alien Employment Exist.* Washington, D.C.

U.S. General Accounting Office. (2000). *Illegal Aliens: Opportunities Exist to Improve the Expedited Removal Process.* Washington, D.C.

U.S. Government Accountability Office. (2005). *Immigration Enforcement: Weaknesses Hinder Employment and Worksite Enforcement Efforts.* Washington, D.C.

U.S. House of Representatives. (February 11, 1997). *Implementation of Title III of the Illegal Immigration Reform and Immigrant Responsibility Act of 1996.* Oversight Hearing before the Subcommittee on Immigration and Claims. Washington, D.C.

U.S. House of Representatives. (February 25, 1999). *Immigration and Naturalization Service Decisions Impacting the Agency's Ability to Control Criminal and Illegal Aliens.* Oversight Hearing before the Subcommittee on Immigration and Claims. Washington, D.C.

U.S. House of Representatives. (July 1, 1999). *Immigration and Naturalization Service's Interior Enforcement Strategy.* Oversight Hearing before the Subcommittee on Immigration and Claims. Washington, D.C.

U.S. House of Representatives. (July 15, 1997). *Institutional Hearing Program.* Oversight Hearing before the Subcommittee on Immigration and Claims. Washington, D.C.

U.S. House of Representatives. (July 27, 1998). *Problems Related to Criminal Aliens in the State of Utah.* Oversight Hearing before the Subcommittee on Immigration and Claims. Washington, D.C.

U.S. House of Representatives. (June 10, 1999). *Illegal Immigration Issues.* Oversight Hearing before the Subcommittee on Immigration and Claims. Washington, D.C.

U.S. House of Representatives. (June 19, 2002). *Immigration and Naturalization Service's (INS) Interior Enforcement Strategy.* Hearing before the Subcommittee on Immigration, Border Security, and Claims. Washington, D.C.

U.S. House of Representatives. (March 18, 1999). *Illegal Aliens in the United States.* Oversight Hearing before the Subcommittee on Immigration and Claims. Washington, D.C.

U.S. Immigration and Customs Enforcement. (2008). *ICE Fiscal Year 2007 Annual Report.* Washington, D.C.

U.S. Immigration and Naturalization Service. (2003a). *2001 Statistical Yearbook of the Immigration and Naturalization Service.* Washington, D.C.

U.S. Immigration and Naturalization Service. (2003b). *Estimates of the Unauthorized Immigrant Population Residing in the United States: 1990 to 2000.* Washington, D.C.

Unabhängige Kommission Zuwanderung. (2001). *Zuwanderung gestalten – Integration fördern.* Berlin: Bundesministerium des Innern.

Vogel, Dita. (2000). "Migration Control in Germany and the United States." *International Migration Review*, 34(2): 390–422.

Washington Post (May 5, 1994). "Stopping Illegal Immigrants: New Tactic Has Weak Points; Border-Crossers Find Paths of Less Resistance."

Washington Post (November 22, 1994). "Kemp Says Battle over Immigration May Rend Republicans."

Washington Post (February 2, 1995). "INS 'Enforcement Deficit' Tied to Law; Voluntary Compliance Provision Fails to Deter Hiring of Illegals."

Washington Post (March 3, 1996). "Immigration: Rhetoric and Reform."

Washington Post (June 19, 2006). "Illegal Hiring Is Rarely Penalized: Politics, 9/11 Cited in Lax Enforcement."

Washington Post (December 25, 2007). "Immigrant Crackdown Falls Short: Despite Tough Rhetoric, Few Employers of Illegal Workers Face Criminal Charges."

Washington Times (August 17, 2004). "Limits Sought on Border Patrol."

Washington Times (June 3, 2008). "ICE Effort Snares 1,808 in Six States; Most Being Quickly Deported."

Weatherly, Richard, Byrum Kottwitz, Claudia, Lishner, Denise, Reid, Kelley, Roset, Grant, & Wong, Karen. (1980). "Accountability of Social Service Workers at the Front Line." *Social Service Review*, 54(4): 556–571.

Weaver, R. Kent. (2000). *Ending Welfare As We Know It*. Washington, D.C.: Brookings Institution.

Weaver, R. Kent, & Rockman, Bert A. (Eds.). (1993). *Do Institutions Matter? Government Capabilities in the United States and Abroad*. Washington, D.C.: Brookings Institution.

Weber, Max. (1979). *Economy and Society: An Outline of Interpretative Sociology*. Berkeley, CA: University of California Press.

Weingast, Barry R., & Moran, Mark J. (1983). "Bureaucratic Discretion or Congressional Control? Regulatory Policymaking by the Federal Trade Commission." *Journal of Political Economy*, 91(5): 765–800.

Weissinger, George. (1996). *Law Enforcement and the INS: A Participant Observation Study of Control Agents*. New York, NY: University Press of America.

Welch, Michael. (2002). *Detained: Immigration and the Expanding I.N.S. Jail Complex*. Philadelphia, PA: Temple University Press.

Wells, Miriam J. (2004). "The Grassroots Reconfiguration of U.S. Immigration Policy." *International Migration Review*, 38(4): 1308–1347.

Wessels, Bernhard. (1999). "Whom to Represent? The Role Orientations of Legislators in Europe." In Hermann Schmitt, & Jacques Thomassen (Eds.), *Political Representation and Legitimacy in the European Union, Oxford: Oxford University Press*, Oxford, UK: Oxford University Press, pp. 211–236.

Wilson, James Q. (1973). *Political Organizations*. New York, NY: Basic Books.

Wilson, James Q. (1978). *The Investigators: Managing FBI and Narcotics Agents*. New York, NY: Basic Books.

Wilson, James Q. (1980). "The Politics of Regulation." In James Q. Wilson (Ed.), *The Politics of Regulation*, New York, NY: Basic Books.

Wilson, James Q. (1989). *Bureaucracy: What Government Agencies Do And Why They Do It*. New York, NY: Basic Books.

Wright, Scott W. (2008). *Worksite Enforcement of U.S. Immigration Law: A Comprehensive Review of the Federal Government's 2007 Worksite Enforcement Actions and a Forecast for 2008*. Minneapolis, MN: Faegre & Benson LLP.

Index